Intimate Terrorism

Intimate Terrorism

*The Crisis of Love in
an Age of Disillusion*

Michael Vincent Miller

W. W. Norton & Company / New York / London

Copyright © 1995 by Michael Vincent Miller

All rights reserved
Printed in the United States of America
First published as a Norton paperback 1996

"Jamesian" by Thom Gunn is reprinted from *The Man with Night Sweats*
Copyright © 1992 by Thom Gunn by permission of Farrar, Straus &
Giroux, and Faber & Faber, Ltd.

Lines from "The Munich Mannequins" by Sylvia Plath are reprinted
from *Ariel* by Sylvia Plath (HarperCollins, New York, 1981; Faber &
Faber Ltd., London, 1965) by permission of HarperCollins Publishers,
Inc. and Faber & Faber Ltd.

Lines from *Collected Poems* by Wallace Stevens, Copyright © 1954 by
Wallace Stevens, are reprinted by permission of Alfred A. Knopf Inc.

Lines from "Souls Belated" in *Roman Fever and Other Stories* by Edith
Wharton (Collier Books, New York, 1993) are reprinted by permission
of Scribners, an imprint of Simon & Schuster.

The text of this book is composed in Bembo with the display set in Trio
Composition and Manufacturing by the Haddon Craftsmen, Inc.
Book design by Chris Welch

Library of Congress Cataloging-in-Publication Data
Miller, Michael Vincent.
Intimate terrorism : the deterioration of erotic life / Michael Vincent
Miller.
p.   cm.
Includes bibliographical references and index.
1. Love.   2. Control (Psychology)   3. Intimacy (Psychology)
I. Title.
BF575.L8M48   1995
306.7—dc20   94-41704

ISBN 0-393-31532-0 pbk.

W.W. Norton & Company, Inc.
500 Fifth Avenue, New York, N.Y. 10110
W.W. Norton & Company Ltd.
10 Coptic Street, London WC1A1PU

1   2   3   4   5   6   7   8   9   0

For my family. And for C.W., A.B., and I.F.
who, if they had been able to stay around, would
have, like my family, been pleased.

Contents

Preface

It began to dawn on me gradually as I saw more and more members of married and other intimate couples together in psychotherapy that the very nature of our culture helped prevent these relationships from flourishing. In a sense, then, this book has spent a long time in gestation. A short, considerably different version of Chapter 1 was published many years ago in *Psychology Today*. That article represented my first attempt to understand the role that anxiety plays in causing love to become vexed by too much concern with power, but it was still mostly confined to a psychodynamic mode of thinking. I am indebted to Morris Schwartz, Rosabeth Kanter, Gordon Fellman, and David Kantor, all of whom in different ways stretched my growing awareness that no interpretation of intimacy that ignores its social setting can possibly be adequate.

A small portion of the Epilogue appeared much later in the *Gestalt Journal* as part of an essay where I tried, among other things, to apply the literary categories of the tragic, the comic, and the ironical to the kind of change that occurs in therapy. My thanks to the editor, Joe

Wysong, who allowed me a free hand in exploring such fanciful notions. I have also plundered a couple of my reviews for the *New York Times Book Review* for some of the paragraphs that make up a section of Chapter 7. Various editors at the *Times Book Review* have been unusually alert to my peculiar combination of interests; they have sent me books to grapple with that stimulated the further development of my chief concerns.

A number of friends and colleagues have looked in to offer suggestions and encouragement at various points during the solitary labor of writing. I am grateful to them. I am also thankful for invitations that enabled me to give lectures and workshops on some of this material in the United States as well as in Italy, Spain, France, Belgium, and Finland. For a very special kind of gratitude, I want to mention the late Anatole Broyard, who was constantly my good friend, my partner in flights of conversation, and my literary conscience; and the late Isadore From, who, both as my supervisor for several years and my friend for many more, kept me on my toes and taught me much about integrating intellect with intuition.

I have benefited greatly from the support—and, I might add, the patience—of Henning Gutmann and Gerald Howard, two gifted editors at Norton, who were more than willing to accompany me as I wandered across disciplines. They did so with broad intellectual sympathy, sensitivity to the implications of an argument, and valuable critical commentary in general. In a very real way, they were collaborators in making this book possible. And, of course, I will be forever indebted to Gwindale, Jared, and Cassie for their forbearance during a period when my preoccupation with thinking about intimacy left something to be desired in my practice of it.

Introduction

"What are they saying, what are these violent,
frightened people discussing?"
                    —*John Updike,* Too Far to Go

W e have lost our innocence about love and marriage—they
     certainly no longer go together like a horse and carriage. It's
as though some darker force has intervened, causing the horse to
bolt and rush headlong into the woods. One can imagine a panicked
couple holding on for dear life inside their careening carriage, waiting for the wheels to give way. It's not surprising that many of us
now view the ride as too dangerous—men afraid of responsibility,
women afraid of being enslaved. We have become so thoroughly
disillusioned with love that we are on the verge of becoming a culture of cynics about one of our most cherished traditional values—
the ideal of romantic love.

But then cynicism is often the fate of betrayed romantics. Ask
anyone these days whether they know of any good marriages, and
the reply is apt to be an ironic roll of the eyes or shrug of the shoulders. In his memoir about Greenwich Village just after World War
II, the late literary critic Anatole Broyard describes living with a
woman, an avant-garde painter, who compared making love to

"one drowned person resuscitating the other."[1] I'm not sure that this insight would be considered out of the ordinary in our present mood.

That darker force could be called power. The point is not that this is new: An unequal distribution of power has always operated between people in close relationships, but in the past it has been a kind of nameless secret, hidden from view. Nowadays, power looms so large that it has almost overtaken the foreground. It is almost impossible in our times to think about love, sex, intimacy, or marriage without thinking about power. The old sentimental image of Cupid has changed. He is no longer a mischievous, unpredictable tyke with a bow, a kind of sexual Dennis the Menace, but a fiercer god who all too often seems to exercise power with brutal or demonic intent.

Considering the continual outpouring of stories in the news about caretakers of all sorts—including parents, stepparents, doctors, therapists, priests, ministers, daycare workers, and teachers—sexually violating those under their guidance or protection; the recent senate hearings and court trials involving celebrities charged with rape, sexual harassment, or child abuse; and the alarming increase in domestic violence—everything appears to be conspiring to persuade us that our erotic impulses and intimate attachments create not happy couples or couplings but victims and oppressors. And once that perception is in place, we have left the world of romance for that of politics, which is the attempt to grapple strategically with power. Modern intimacy, whatever else it might be, has become political.

Our new emphasis on power, however, tends to leave out an important age-old theme: Love makes us anxious. Except perhaps in the lives of saints and other enlightened souls, there is no love without anxiety. One has to lean a good ways out of the self in order to love another, and that always feels dangerous, especially if one has had any experience of abandonment, betrayal, or predatory behavior at the hands of those to whom one has become attached. We are creatures who, in the course of growing up, learn to fear what we most desire.

This book is about love and power, but it is also about the anxiety of loving, which it takes to be a major cause of our intimacies becoming overly contaminated with a concern for power. The part that anxiety plays in shaping intimate relations has not received sufficient attention in recent times, because anxiety no longer inhabits a central place in our thinking about the human condition. In part this is because modern psychiatry concerns itself more and more with eliminating anxiety through pills, as though it were a kind of infection. Contemporary theorists of intimate and family behavior, including social scientists, feminists, and family therapists, are so concerned with sexual politics at present that on the whole they ignore the fact that love makes both men and women anxious.

What has been lost is an older literary and philosophical understanding that anxiety attends virtually every human gathering, an uninvited but inevitable guest who brings unease to our relations with ourselves, nature, and each other. Anxiety is related to knowledge of our limited powers, to our consciousness of mortality, to the doubts that plague us precisely because, unlike the other animals, we can reflect on the roads not taken as well as on facing the unknown when we try to anticipate what will happen next. This is how writers from Kierkegaard to Heidegger and Sartre have treated anxiety, also social scientists like Durkheim and Freud. For that matter, the poet W. H. Auden, in naming a book-length poem about life during the World War II era *The Age of Anxiety,* was not referring to something that could be cured by a pill.

Perhaps no one has looked upon anxiety with more awe than Freud. It played as dramatic a role in his interpretation of human development as original sin did in Christian doctrine. Individual character was largely determined, Freud argued, by how a person reacted to anxiety during the first phase of childhood. Precisely because anxiety flourished in the humid weather of the family, the original site of love, it tended to blossom again, like a perennial shrub, in later intimate relations. Although this is also one of my points of departure in my search for the roots of our current difficulties, I find myself diverging from psychoanalytic thought in several important respects. To my thinking, psychoanalysis has never really built a strong enough bridge from the anxious individual soul to what goes on *between* people. Not that it doesn't strive to, but even the most elaborate theories in contemporary psychoanalytic thought, such as object-relations and self-psychology, end up batting their wings against the cage of the lone self.

My own preoccupation with the difficulties that turn dreams of love into nightmarish power struggles has evolved over a period of twenty years during which I have been treating couples in psychotherapy. Husbands and wives, as well as lovers, both straight and gay, have come in together to fill a considerable portion, probably a third to a half, of my private-practice hours. This is due partly to my particular interests, but it would not have come about without the development of a widespread tendency for intimate partners to seek help in pairs from therapists. Some of these couples have been referred to me by other therapists who were seeing one or the other partner. Just as often, though, they refer themselves. Rarely have people been so self-consciously aware as they are at present of where their troubles reside.

Although psychotherapy has always concerned itself with love and sex, treating intimate partners in the same therapy session represents a radical new departure. Seeing husbands and wives or lovers together in therapy would have been almost unthinkable during the first half of this century, when psychoanalysis still reigned supreme in the treatment of mental disorders. Psychoanalysts explored the damage that repressed sexual impulses produced in the individual personality. The task of therapy was viewed as a slow burrowing with a minute probe into the primitive depths of the self to uncover what lay buried there.

The recurring problems that are brought before the psychotherapist, however, reflect those areas where a society has failed to ease tensions between social institutions, cultural values, and individual needs. A large percentage of early psychoanalytic patients were so-called hysterics, suffering from the contradiction between the pull of a sexually repressive official reality and the internal push of forbidden impulses and desires which they could not acknowledge even to themselves. These nineteenth-century character types needed a spokesman like Freud to bring their hidden sexual conflicts into the open. The psychoanalytic method of interpreting the unconscious is in part an act of publicity, a form of healthy gossip about closely guarded family and state secrets. Freud and his followers used it so effectively—at least with this kind of patient, as well as in their writings—that they helped shift public opinion toward favoring more openness about sex. As a result, the classical "conversion hysteria" with its odd array of physical symptoms—paralyzed limbs, fainting spells, chronic vomiting, and so on—has nearly disappeared from the clinics and psychotherapists' consulting rooms.

As the symptoms change, so do the remedies. Many therapists have concluded that people's present intimate relationships, not just their early childhood experiences, participate in the creation of their mental suffering. On these grounds, they have introduced mates, lovers, and even children directly into the therapeutic process. Psychotherapy with couples and families represents a significant step toward recognizing the *social* character of psychological pain. For that matter, a great many of the patients I see individually entered therapy because their marriages or other intimacies—their most deeply important social ties—are in various stages of collapse.

The wreckage of relationships that these patients strew around my office has led me to wonder whether as a society we might be witnessing a general deterioration of erotic life in America. Obviously a psychotherapist spends more time with misery than well-being, at least at work, and he or she might be prone to develop a jaundiced point of view. But I long ago gave up thinking that the anguish in my patients' intimate relationships is merely a symptomatic consequence of individual sickness. The couples I see are mostly successful, educated, middle-class people, accomplished in their professional lives, surrounded by nourishing friendships, absorbed in enjoyable recreational activities. In their marriages and other couplings, however, they are among the casualties of a widening cultural crisis.

Couples don't exist in a vacuum, though this is how most psychotherapists have generally treated them. How we love and make love are shaped by history: The most tender, private, and passionate or the most overwhelming and disturbing erotic feelings are embedded in a social milieu made up of beliefs and expectations, myths and values that shape intimate conduct in fundamental ways. For example, in the Victorian period, romantic love was embedded in the belief that close emotional relations, such as those inside the family, represented a "haven in a heartless world." Love was considered an oasis to which one retreated for relief and emotional refreshment after being battered in a punishing outside world of work and public affairs. But modern history has swept us to a shore from which Matthew Arnold's famous sigh in "Dover Beach," "Ah, love, let us be true / To one another! for . . . we are here as on a darkling plain . . . Where ignorant armies clash by night," seems quaint and nostalgic. By now the clash of armies has permeated everything from the kitchen to the bedroom.

Intimate relations can't flourish unless the surrounding culture supports their flourishing. At this point in our history, our basic cultural myth about love—the ideal of romantic love—supports the developmental tasks of adolescence better than it does the requirements of marriage. The phenomenon that I describe as "intimate terrorism" is the frequent outcome when two adults try to make a life together equipped with little more than a vision of intimacy suitable for adolescent first love. Romantic love is under siege, both from within marriage and from outside it, but neither have we yet come up with a new ideal to replace it.

There now exists a voluminous technical literature on couples therapy, in addition to all the self-help manuals intended to teach couples how to get more sexual excitement, fight fairly, put an end to jealousy and possessiveness, or divorce "creatively." In other words, we have developed a lot of technology for improving individual situations but very little insight that helps us understand how the causes of marital pain are deeply woven into our social fabric.

This book casts a wider net in an effort to address the need for a more embracing explanation. Psychotherapy in our day must reach beyond the customary boundaries of psychology and psychiatry—into history, literature, and the neighboring social sciences—if it is to cope effectively with the radical transformations that have thrown love, sex, and marriage into turmoil in the modern world. Psychotherapists who address their patients' failures at intimacy need to be not only social psychologists but students of society and culture at large as well.

I use several kinds of "case histories" to illuminate my speculations. There are portraits of actual couples and individuals (or composite portraits based on them), slightly fictionalized to protect their privacy, most of whom are shown in various states of crisis. I have plucked them from my clinical notes, changing their names, backgrounds, and other details that might have enabled someone to identify who they are. I hope that their mingled voices, often heard in these pages raised in cries of pain or rage or bewilderment, will prove to be sufficiently recognizable to make it clear that they speak the language of our common modern anguish.

In addition, I draw on movies, television, and newspapers because it seems to me clear that the media not only inform and entertain us but also present us with a collective case history—the dreams, free associations, and even the obsessions—which we can use to grasp the direction of our culture. I also introduce material from quite a few works of literature, novels especially, which I proceed to examine as though they, too, are case histories in social and cultural dilemmas. Beyond its exemplary illustrative power, literature serves another purpose here as well—expressed in Matthew Arnold's idea that literature is a "criticism of life." This does not mean that literature is above or apart from life, but that important writers, like good therapists, lay bare for our scrutiny the underlying forces—beliefs, impulses, habits of conduct, longings—of social life (including and perhaps particularly erotic life), thus broadening our understanding of the interplay between culture and individual relationships.

I have a special motive in giving this study a strong literary flavor. The psychological theories that psychotherapists use to inform their work with patients have, for the most part, been woefully inadequate and narrow. This is largely due to the aspiration of psychology, after it was severed from philosophy and became a specialized discipline in the nineteenth century, to gain a place among the sciences. As a result, most psychology provides a minimal sense of how the social and cultural environment gives form to the direction of individual lives. The human figures depicted in psychological theories lead curiously melancholy, impoverished lives, as though they are stranded on a windswept heath. And their relations to one another have the stark, discontinuous quality of a modern dance performance.

In my view, therapists are not to be considered scientists or artists, but something less grandiose: They should function as critics of individual character, analogous to literary or art critics, whose task is to help patients live more graceful, vital, and economical lives, lives with a more satisfying shape, by freeing themselves from those elements that produce stereotyped, repetitive, rigid, or otherwise deformed behavior. On all these counts, I think that therapists have a great deal to learn from literature—at least as much as from their psychology texts.

If I have some things to say along the way about the current direction of psychotherapy, it is not only because that is my profession, but because in our times the therapist's consulting room is an important observation post for a close-up of the culture. Therapists have privileged access to our private lives; they are invited as third parties, as bystanders or helpful voyeurs, into the boudoirs and other intimate places usually reserved only for two people. Psychotherapy has also developed some powerful conceptual means for making sense of what it discovers.

I intend this book to reach out to anyone who wonders why love in the modern era becomes so perilous an undertaking. Each of my chapters concentrates on points of crisis or potential crisis that seriously affect how things go in marriages and other long-term intimate relationships. In part my emphasis is clinical, particularly when I look very closely at the way people treat each other in matters of love, but more often it is cultural, since I believe that our culture is the ultimate source of the trouble—not that I think these two facets of social experience operate independently of each other.

When I speak of crisis, I mean several different kinds. Some are chronic (anxiety, for example, is always a crisis and can become

chronic). Some are developmental (every stage of human development involves its special crises; adolescence, for instance, is a crisis in
the individual personality as it struggles to become at once distinc
tive and socially acceptable). Others are acute (disappointment in
the transition from courtship to married life; adultery and other betrayals; violent quarrels; the birth of a child; separation and divorce).
Love itself can become a recurrent state of crisis. In no other arena
are people so vividly confronted as they are in their erotic life with
the central dilemma of human relationships—how to be, in the
words of the poet Wallace Stevens, "Supremely true each to its
separate self," yet flourish "In the pale light that each upon the other
throws." Marriage and other adult intimacies resurrect earlier periods of crisis in the relations between self and other, from the infant's
first intimations of separateness from its parents to the adolescent's
efforts to consolidate a secure identity, yet remain closely connected
with others.

Crises may be painful, but they can also be highly useful. The
ideogram used as the written word for *crisis* in the Chinese language,
like many Chinese words, is made up of two smaller image-words.
One is the word for *emergency,* the other the word for *opportunity.*
This perspective yields a valuable insight into the crises that arise in
making an intimate relationship successful. Being intimate is a fluctuating activity, not a continuous state one is in, and it inevitably
passes through periods of emergency. But emergencies can mobilize
one's best responses and thus create an opportunity, through coping
with obstacles, to grow wiser about loving others.

A final word about the point of view from which I write. In this
day and age, in which we are so sharply sensitive, perhaps too sensitive at times, to sex roles and sexual preferences, as well as social class
and ethnic background, it is important to remind ourselves that
there are no omniscient narrators in nonfiction, that no one has a
monopoly on reality. This does not invalidate what one has to say; it
simply limits it. For example, I suspect that it will turn out that my
observations about the passions and characters of men are keener
than what I say about women. That ought to be the case, at any rate,
given that I am a man and therefore know something firsthand

about male desire. A similar stipulation holds for my concentrating in these pages on heterosexual love. Although I am a straight, white, middle-class male, I like to believe that twenty-four years of practicing psychotherapy has given me a sympathetic grasp of female and gay passion. I hope that women in general, as well as both gay men and women, as they read this book, will add whatever fine-tuning is required to adapt my conception of intimate terrorism to their particular points of view.

I don't offer these thoughts in the hope of warding off attack. I would be surprised if some of my discussion does not earn me enemies from both cultural radicals and cultural conservatives. So be it. As I tell those among my patients who are too intent on pleasing everyone, a person without enemies has no real position in life.

Part I

Intimate
Terrorism

All Love is lost Terror succeeds . . .
—*William Blake*, The Four Zoas

1

The Politics of
Anxiety

We have always taken it for granted, as the old saying goes,
that politics makes strange bedfellows. It's a typical American idea: one of those expressions of our disenchantment with public life that throughout much of our history has accompanied our
retreat into privacy, perhaps with a family and a few friends. But
although American culture has increasingly turned inward, the disenchantment has spread as well, till even romantic love is no longer
exempt.

Like worried parents raiding a teenage party, we find ourselves
nowadays compelled to rush in and turn up the lights in rooms
where couples lie tangled in each other's arms, and the sudden glare
confirms our growing suspicions: Those caresses and murmured
promises are as much about jockeying for power as they are about
exploring the possibilities of love. It's as though the battle of the
sexes never lets up; it just disguises itself sometimes as tenderness.
This may be too harsh a verdict, one that consigns centuries of
Western idealism to the flames. But by now, who can any longer

distinguish love from power? The modern era has discovered that bedfellows make strange politics.

The women's movement alerted us that it was time to crash the party when it announced some twenty years ago that sex, courtship, and marriage are stages in a class war between a male ruling elite and a female proletariat. Even before that we were given an inkling that something was going wrong in the very place where people are trained for intimacy. A new trend in psychotherapy took whole families for its patients and tried to persuade us that the depressed wife, the schizophrenic son, the anorexic daughter, and the alcoholic father are among the casualties of territorial disputes, and that sabotage, secret coalitions, and cruel tyrannies are among the tactics for wielding power in that tight-knit, supposedly harmonious little community.

Nowadays it is a widely popular idea to believe that the nuclear family lies in ruins of its own making. Our latest high-tech euphemism for this disaster is "dysfunctional." But that term, applied to families and marriages, only succeeds in once again burying the perception that power plays as important a role as love when people get close. Until recently, Americans have tended to shy away from openly acknowledging the exercise of power. From our foreign policy to the bedroom, and from our welfare programs to our child-rearing procedures, power often masquerades as love in our culture. We are always proclaiming, in one way or another, "I'm doing this in your best interests." Sometimes what is being done may be in the recipient's best interests, and sometimes not; the question is, who has the right to decide?

Whatever the case, in general it is best for everyone when the label describes accurately what is in the package. Otherwise, the confusion of love and power can be damaging to both relationships and individuals. Being able to distinguish the relative proportions of love and power in any relationship and act accordingly seems to me essential to the health of the relationship. Of course, the confusion can extend in both directions: Too much sentimentality about love without taking into account the inevitable workings of power tends to make people emotionally gullible and dependent; but overemphasizing power to the point of losing track of love leaves them feeling paranoid and isolated.

I'm a psychotherapist, and my professional life is mainly devoted to shooting photographs of unhappiness through a special lens for extreme close-up portraits. But I've always been interested in how the shifting cultural panorama affects the people whom I see. For example, why during the past two decades have more and more of my new patients shown up with their spouses or lovers in tow? Does this trend toward therapy for couples have anything to do with our changing beliefs about love and power? I think that it does, though not only for the reasons that have been emerging from the debates among schools of psychotherapy or the current social conflicts over masculine and feminine roles. In order to make this clear, I need to point out some connections between certain social trends, viewed through a wide-angle lens, and what can be observed in the intimacy of the clinical setting.

Married couples usually walk into a therapist's consulting room as a next-to-last resort. It's a kind of doctor's office, after all, and they are about to place their relationship with all its culturally sanctified meanings, vanished passion, complicated loyalties, discarded dreams, and private suffering on an examining table. So they come in hesitantly from the waiting room, barely glancing at each other, their faces set in polite but embarrassed smiles. What do they hope for from this odd, solitary professional whom they phoned for an appointment in a mood of desperation, this stranger with whom they find themselves so quickly engaged in urgent conversation?

They may have come in a final bid to keep their home intact, especially if there are children, before lawyers appear on the scene to divide up the booty. A few arrive with a project of grander scope: They dream of a cure that will make it "like it used to be" before things went wrong. There are also those who hope that therapy will perform a more radical surgery—that it will free them from bondage, enabling them to make a long-delayed decision to divorce. And then it's supposed to help them through the terrible process of picking up the pieces.

Whatever their intentions, they often wind up in therapy because they have been living together in pain, able neither to get closer nor to separate. They seem to have become entangled in a web of need and resentment where they have lost their way. They may even have lost track of whether or not they ever really cared about each other. The mystery of their initial act of faith in choosing each other deepens as its emotional origins recede. Greg and Sarah are a good example:

When I first found them at opposite ends of the sofa in my waiting room, they looked like discouraged baseball players killing time in the dugout during a game they were losing. He was staring absently at the carpet, and she was frowning at pictures on the wall. In their early thirties, they were both quite attractive, despite the evident unhappiness that dimmed their features. He had the long-legged, graceful build of a cross-country runner and the high cheekbones and dreamy eyes of a part-time melancholic. Whether he was more poet or athlete, it was too soon to tell. She was more compact, energetic, and quite beautiful—the mover of this couple, I guessed. Indeed, she stood up first as I introduced myself and looked at me with gray eyes alive with inquiry and cool appraisal, the eyes of someone willing to take a chance and used to having impact on other people. If I had been a personnel manager, I would have hired her at once.

Now, as they sit in my office, her eyes seek his, but he avoids her gaze. She speaks first: "Greg, why don't you talk about how hard it is for you to say what you're feeling?" He sinks farther into his chair, his eyes narrow, and he folds his arms tightly across his chest. Two spots of color appear on his cheeks. She reaches across to touch his arm, which causes his whole body to stiffen.

"For one thing, you wouldn't be depressed so much," she says, "if you'd learn to express your feelings more openly." Her voice makes this statement sound like an accusation. "Look," he replies, "I didn't want to come here in the first place. It was your idea. So you tell the doctor what's bothering you about me. Then maybe you won't have to keep telling me all the time."

She turns to me: "He never lets me know whether he gives a

damn about me. I can't remember the last time he even hinted that he loved me. He forgets my birthday. We agreed to split the chores, since we both work, but he lets the dishes pile up until I do them. And he leaves his clothes and stuff scattered around . . . I think it's because he knows I hate disorder. If I ask him to do almost anything at all, he yells that I'm taking away his freedom."

"That's not true," he says in a flat voice. "I do the dishes probably half the time. I've been picking up around the house a lot more anyway. You don't pay any attention when I improve because with you everything's got to be perfect immediately. As long as we're here, I think we ought to talk about our sex problem. That's the sort of stuff you help people fix, isn't it, Dr. Miller? She hardly ever wants to have sex any more."

She grits her teeth. "It's not that I don't want to. You just want to stick it in. That really turns me off. You think you can lie around, leave me to take care of the house, and then pounce on me when you're horny."

At this he lunges to the edge of his seat, his voice rising in anger: "Your nagging about the dishes and the laundry and the way I make love drives me crazy. I feel like I can't do anything right. Who does the shopping? Who pays the bills? And if you don't think I'm neat enough for your designer household, that's your problem." She stares at the floor, her cheeks puffed out and her lips pursed, as though she were holding her breath under water. Her eyebrows arch with bewilderment and indignation.

The way this couple opened the therapy session pretty well summarizes their predicament. Following a long period of going together, they married about four years ago and as yet have no children. He is a software engineer with a large computer firm; she is a high-school teacher. During the past couple of years their intimacy has soured, like spoiled fruit. One can easily imagine them having been breathless lovers once upon a time. But the tension between them has drained the relationship of spontaneous sexual excitement. By now their bedroom is more a setting for pathos than pleasure. Their responses to each other mostly range from explosive anger to grim resignation. In therapy and at home, they talk of separating, but at this stage it's more a scare tactic than the expression of any real intention to part. Beneath the monotonous rhetoric of their bickering, you can hear how anxious and vulnerable they feel.

What do Sarah and Greg want from each other? They talk of housekeeping and finances, of moods and lovemaking, but all these topics have been contaminated by the power struggle that drives them both. Each feels deprived and is trying to control the other in a different way: she by pressing claims for more intimacy; he by demanding more freedom. Every intimate relationship must deal with the needs of each member for both closeness and autonomy. But how inefficiently Greg and Sarah flail away to achieve these ends. They paint each other into separate corners from which neither can escape to reach the other in a fulfilling way. He interprets her demands for more emotional communication as attempts to destroy his spontaneity and independence. She interprets his attempts to guard his freedom as a denial of love for her and of responsibility for their marriage. She feels neglected and taken for granted; he feels imprisoned and punished unjustly. Blame has replaced desire, and the role of lover has been exchanged for that of victim.

This kind of wounding quarrel becomes a way of life once a formerly happy union disintegrates into the two-person civil war that I call *intimate terrorism*. Although its apparent causes have to do with disappointments, misunderstandings, attempts to dramatize grievances, and efforts to get each other to toe the line, its ultimate root, as I will argue throughout this book, is an underlying cancerous expansion of the anxiety that plagues all erotic love. Chronic strife like that between Greg and Sarah takes over when intimate partners get trapped in a vicious cycle of complementary anxieties—fears each has of being either abandoned or engulfed by the other.

Although we usually associate terrorism with governments and warring political factions, it also describes pretty well what can happen in troubled marriages and other intimate relationships. In their quest for power, terrorists, whether in politics or love, prey on vulnerability. They make use of threats, rouse fear and doubt in order to paralyze their opponents' will. Intimate terrorism feeds on fears of being deserted or overwhelmed by parents that we all carry with us from childhood.

Intimate terrorism is a metaphor but not one remote from literal meanings. Although the violence portrayed in this book is mostly psychological, involving people who exploit each other's anxiety, it can easily turn into actual danger to life and limb when the provocation gets out of hand. Metaphors of this kind bring to light phenomena that are hidden from view or dimmed by familiarity. Freud's Oedipus complex, for example, illuminated the love and aggression, and the corresponding mixture of yearning and apprehension, that children feel toward their parents and, later, toward each other in their adult relations, by viewing them through the lens of a Greek myth. It makes sense now to reexamine these strong emotions through the lens of contemporary politics.

Like the Oedipus complex, intimate terrorism reflects a perplexing fact in human experience: What we want most from each other seems to cause us the most anxiety. Both metaphors represent the conflict between desire and anxiety and the ensuing confusion of love and power. The differences between them reflect changes our culture has undergone since the late nineteenth century. Freud's Oedipal imagery captured the mood of a social structure based on patriarchy and monarchy, as well as a private life clogged with sexual repression, and it showed how these traits shaped individual personalities. In the family, order was preserved by an authoritarian father and intimacy supplied by an idealized mother. Intimate terrorism is an image suited to our historical moment. It derives from the modern style in politics—the tendency to violate the boundaries of others and disguise it as concern for their welfare; the climate, until recently at least, of bad faith and intimidation in cold-war diplomacy; the carrying out of political conflict through guerrilla warfare and sabotage. In our private affections, we have replaced inhibition with a liberated sexuality that can readily be turned into an instrument of aggression for coercing another person.

Ours has been an age of masks, roles, and manipulativeness masquerading as openness, communication, and liberalism. If Freud's was the era of the Prussian father, who ruled through fear, ours could be characterized as the era of the Jewish mother, who rules by a suffocating love that generates guilt (as portrayed, for example, by Philip Roth and Woody Allen). These lead to different models of pathological intimacy. There can be pathologies of freedom as well as pathologies of authority. If nineteenth-century intimacy suffered from too much repression, perhaps twentieth-century intimacy suffers from too much expression. As Mia Farrow puts it to Woody Allen in the film *Husbands and Wives,* "You use sex to express everything except love."

When it comes to love and sex, anxiety, which we generally treat as a vague and shapeless emotion akin to fear, is actually better understood as a relationship. Although it is a kind of fear, it goes on *between* people and not just inside them. Nor is it shapeless: Like the devil disguised so as to better tempt souls, anxiety prefers cloaking itself in deceptive roles, taking different forms depending on the nature of the difficulties two people are having with each other. In intimate relations, anxiety might appear as a helpless victim, or it might show up as a benevolent tyrant. In other situations, it wears a mask of disapproval or the face of an obedient child who is trying hard to please. There are numerous other possibilities; what they share is a common purpose: the exercise of power, sometimes secretly, sometimes blatantly, in the name of love.

This idea is a key to understanding how intimate terrorism plays itself out. What you typically see in a relationship besieged by intimate terrorism is two people preoccupied with attacking one another's autonomy or security, giving rise to engulfment or abandonment anxiety in each other. Though neither of them is ready to give up the other—or at least not yet—each has the aim of seizing control of the relationship. Anxiety always starts from those challenges in human existence that bring one face-to-face with the limits of what one can control—the darkness of the unknown, uncertainty about who one is or how others feel about one, unpredictability about the future. In close relationships, among those limits one comes up against is the ultimate mystery of the other's motives, especially the other's radical freedom to move toward one or away as he or she wishes, even to change his or her mind altogether about the whole enterprise.

Kierkegaard, referring to the individual soul, once described anxiety as "the dizziness of freedom." That kind of vertigo often becomes especially pronounced in intimate relations. If you open yourself to another person, yet leave the other's freedom intact, you might be unpleasantly surprised. Your trust might be mistakenly placed, and you might find yourself being used as a security blanket or an ornament for someone else's ego. In many other respects, the other person may turn out not to be whom you thought, so you begin to feel clouds of disappointment moving in, you begin to worry about being betrayed, or you suspect you might be ditched without warning. When dire premonitions of this kind begin to haunt two people's exchanges, they usually begin to develop strategies of gaining control over one another in an effort to make the relationship seem more safe and predictable.

Love cannot be controlled; it has to be freely given, or it becomes little more than a coerced charade. But when one feels sufficiently anxious, one seeks control over what one cannot control. In fact, efforts in that direction follow so immediately and inevitably when anxiety is aroused that they probably ought to be part of its definition: Anxiety is the attempt to control what cannot be controlled.

Both kinds of anxiety that intimate partners stir up in one another—one person's fear of occupying a void left behind by the departure of the other; another's fear of being swallowed up or dominated by the other's constant need—are connected to acute feelings of powerlessness, of being rendered helpless to direct one's own destiny. Such feelings carry both individuals back to the painful dependencies of childhood. They create a state of emergency, like skidding on wet pavement, so each tries to grab the steering wheel and take charge of the direction of the relationship. If these power struggles rarely show up at first, it is because infatuation and courtship are so mutually satisfying, but they often surface once the relationship becomes a matter of daily living. When two people begin to fail at making each other feel powerful through appreciating and affirming one another, each may soon seek to gain power, for the sake of self-protection, at the other's expense. The ensuing conflict leads them to employ increasingly drastic means of bringing psychological pressure against one another.

Let me illustrate this with a classic scene of communication gone bad between a husband and wife. This one takes place in bed rather than in my office, but it is pieced together from what the couple described to me in therapy. The themes are not unlike those Greg and Sarah brought in, though the power tactics are more sophisticated. I remember this couple all too well: The husband, a smallish but squarely built man in his forties, a corporate lawyer, was one of those people whose self-doubt is always showing slightly, like a nylon slip hanging just below the hem of a dress. He managed to act arrogant and look defeated at the same time, which made his bluster seem like a plea for approval. I had trouble warming up to him at first, but I wasn't much drawn to his wife either. She was a slim, reticent woman, with a strict elegance in her appearance, a housewife who looked like a middle-management executive. She gave one the impression of having untapped reserves, though one sensed that this meant in particular untapped by him. His special vulnerability was his manly pride, and she knew it. The husband begins:

"You don't really want to make love, do you?" (He already knows the answer.)

"Yes I do." (This means "You're right. I don't.")

"How come you're so tense?" (It's too early in the game to tell whether he is exhibiting his sensitivity to her feelings or blaming her. Probably both.)

"What do you expect? You know what my days are like, lugging the kids everywhere, picking up after all of you. Nobody gives me any help." (He wishes she would at least dream up a new excuse.)

"You've been distant for weeks."

At this remark, both sigh and shift positions in bed. He has chosen to take a rather heavy psychological line, which could ignite an all-night discussion. She chooses to ignore it:

"Couldn't we just go to sleep tonight?"

"We haven't made love in over a month. Do you know how

frustrating that is?" (The male appeal to biology.)

"Oh all right. Let's get it over with." (Punitive martyrdom.)

"You make it sound like taking out the trash." (This ups the ante: Now he insists on romance, too.)

"Then let's wait till we feel better with each other." She kisses him on the cheek.

Her last statement panics him. Another month at least. And the kiss makes him feel five years old. The only thing left to do is to invoke, rather abjectly, the authority of history:

"I used to turn you on."

"For Christ's sake, George. We've been married for eleven years." (Fighting fire with fire.)

"There are plenty of other women who find me attractive." (This only slightly veiled threat is a particularly weak ploy at this point. He knows she has him. So he loses his cool and turns desperate.) "They're not all frigid bitches like you!"

"I'm glad you've finally said how you really feel about me."

She says this without a trace of emotion. It's a low blow, fully the equal of his invective, though much subtler and therefore able to cut all the more deeply. She is no doubt aware that he went further than he meant to out of helpless rage and a need to get a rise out of her. By taking his explosion literally, as if he had just confessed a long-hidden truth, she makes him feel he has committed an unforgivable sin. He certainly won't dare approach her again sexually for a long time. One has to admire her deft mastery, but then she does have the aid of a basic sociological principle, first enunciated in 1938 by the sociologist Willard Waller, which says that the least interested party has the most power.[1]

Long before he blows up and she ices him, you can sense the resentment and accusation in his pleas and her contemptuous assent to them or evasion of them. She treats him like one of those little dogs bursting at the seams with energy aimed at you who dashes up and tries to have congress with your shin; when you kick them away, they just come back and try again. In response, he stubbornly pursues, but his manner becomes less and less inviting, since it is soon driven, whatever his original intentions, by little besides anger and shattered self-esteem, neither of which is a notably sexy attribute.

Each tries to make it clear that the other is the problem, the one who is selfish and uncaring, depriving or too demanding, childish or neurotic. His tactics of seduction put her to a test, coerce her emotions, and end up in a tantrum. She parries by combining resentful self-sacrifice with condescension that makes him out to be first an infant and then a monster. Like Sarah, he insists on closing in, and like Greg, she is intent on putting more distance between them.

If my blow-by-blow parenthetical commentary resembles annotations to a chess match, the similarity is not accidental. Like chess, George's and Jill's tactics are efforts to acquire more territory, gain and consolidate a position least vulnerable to the other's moves, and end up with the power to have one's way over a helpless, floundering opponent.

In intimate terrorism, talk is no longer simply talk, nor is sex primarily sex. Every exchange suggests a different meaning than what lies on the surface, because virtually everything that goes on between two people in these predicaments can be pressed into service to further their battle for control of the relationship. Even the most everyday domestic materials can be turned into weapons by intimate terrorists. In his posthumously published journals, the novelist John Cheever presents an example of his parents assaulting each other at the breakfast table, an episode in which eggs are no longer eggs nor is a pot merely a pot:

> "Leave me alone, just leave me alone is all I ask," says she. "All I want," he says, "is a boiled egg. Is that too much to ask?" "Well, boil yourself an egg then," she screams; and this is the full voice of tragedy, the goat cry. "Boil yourself an egg then, but leave me alone." "But how in hell can I boil an egg," he shouts, "if you won't let me use the pot?" "I'd let you use the pot," she screams, "but you leave it so filthy. I don't know what it is, but you leave everything you touch covered with filth." "I bought the pot," he roars, "the soap, the eggs. I pay the water and the gas bills, and here I sit in my own

house unable to boil an egg. Starving." "Here," she screams, "eat my breakfast. I can't eat it. You've ruined my appetite. You've ruined my day."[2]

Such fights between mates are analogous to symptoms in an individual. As Freud showed, symptoms are a kind of indirect symbol for thwarted or repressed wishes, and nothing is really resolved by attending only to the symptoms. So not much goes forward in these symbolic battles because in an important sense, the couple is fighting the wrong fight. It's difficult to negotiate disputes about who loves whom more, whose needs are being recognized, whether one is free to be oneself, and so on when the war is waged in terms of boiled eggs, frequency of intercourse, and clothes strewn on the floor. Dirty diapers already weigh enough without taking on an additional burden of underlying meaning, as they do when a husband and wife argue over taking responsibility for changing them. And the body of one's partner or oneself, once buoyant in the delicate, spontaneous give-and-take of erotic play, when it becomes too clinging with need or stiff with reluctance now sinks like a stone.

Couples like Greg and Sarah or George and Jill could be said to be playing games, but they can't be having much fun doing it. Feeling anxious, as every psychotherapist rediscovers daily in contending with his or her patients' symptoms, is not fun, and anxiety does not characteristically lead people to be good to one another. Regarding the time they spend together, one imagines that these husbands and wives might agree with the character in one of Donald Barthelme's short stories who sums up his troubled marriage with laconic brevity: "Our evenings lacked promise."[3]

The three rather explosive vignettes I've presented thus far represent moments in terrorized relationships when the battle is openly engaged, the volume turned up almost to full blast. Some couples carry on like this nearly all the time. But many of them traverse their lives together in a mood more like the one prevalent during the cold-war years—a draining, uncommunicative standoff, perhaps with frequent regional flare-ups—as two people struggle to hold down the fight "for the sake of the kids" or to put up a front for the neighbors but, above all, to keep their marriage more or less intact. The atmosphere evoked by Barthelme's remark is more the everyday mood of intimate terrorism, an atmosphere of deadness muffling a constant underlying tension, of silent, tentative despair, punctuated by eruptions as people try to get relief from their anxiety. Why keep such a relationship together? The reasons are complicated, but one thing emerges clearly: It turns out that intimate terrorism is ultimately about coexistence, however unpeaceful.

As I noted earlier, although two mates may frequently issue threats to each other about separating or divorcing, an actual parting rarely occurs while they are still busy exploiting one another's fears. In fact, one of the main functions of intimate terrorism is to keep the relationship together, even if this can be accomplished only through suffering and coercion rather than pleasure and choice. It may be that both partners do seek a kind of peace, namely, an end to the smoke and noise of anxiety, but on whose terms? Their civil war is an attempt to settle that question.

If such couples are often found to be quite tenacious about staying together, this is not so strange or paradoxical as it may seem at first. Intimate terrorism obeys a principle that social thinkers who have studied dictatorships and revolutionary movements have known for a long time: Terror can be employed as an effective method of group organization. It can freeze people in place, stripping them of will and keeping them bound to an authority or a way of life. In his later writings, for example, Jean-Paul Sartre concerned himself with the social bonds created by terror. Within every human group, he declared, there exists a feeling of "unbridgeable distance,"[4] and its members experience this gap as a continual apprehension that they might become indifferent to one another, causing the group to dissolve. Terror, Sartre points out, can be used to oppose dissolution through "liquidating, by means of violence, the indefinite flight of the Other."[5] His implication is that human community cannot tolerate a very wide margin of freedom. When apprehension begins to overtake spontaneous affection in an intimate relationship, neither can two partners.

Since sexual attachments tend to become so possessive, intimate partners often have a particularly strong investment in preventing "the indefinite flight of the Other." When passionate attraction or a sense of common purpose has dried up in a marriage, provoking one another's anxiety can serve to keep two people thoroughly engrossed in each other. Thus the manipulation of anxiety replaces love as the chief means of social cohesion.

It works because love and anxiety are so closely allied, and when love fails to bind us to another person, anxiety can fill the same function. Kierkegaard must have recognized this when he compared erotic passion to anxiety and concluded that "anxiety has another element in it that makes it cling even more strongly to its object, for it both loves and fears it."[6] That is a very modern idea, hailing from the nineteenth century, and Elaine Walster, a contemporary social psychologist, has taken it further. She performed a series of experiments which show that almost any sufficiently stirring emotion, including fear or frustration, can serve as the basis for becoming attached to, even thinking oneself in love with, someone of the opposite sex.[7] You could say that intimate terrorism is the dark underside of love, a form of negative love. It consists of two people clinging to one another in an atmosphere of mutual intimidation.

People who fall in love speak of not being able to help themselves. Intimate terrorism often involves a similar suspension of will. In many cases, intimate partners who are actively promoting each other's misery no longer feel certain whether they are choosing to stick together, but feel they are stuck. Each claims to be a prisoner. The notion that there are real options—that they can part or live together differently—seems to them an unrealistic fantasy (though a fantasy each of them may spend a great deal of time entertaining). This radical narrowing of choice is an important feature of most deeply troubled intimate relationships.

Thus, couples like Greg and Sarah stay together not in spite of but by means of the anxiety they rouse in each other. That does not mean, however, that they grow closer to each other. They do not move in any decisive way in either direction, which leaves them locked in place, though living on chronic thin ice with one another.

The hungers that united them in the first place—the desire for commitment, security, and a meaningful life with someone else—are so strong that if love fails to fulfill them, they tend to prefer the heat of intimate terrorism to the coldness of separation. Lovers touch one another in tender places, but so do intimate terrorists—lovers for the sake of pleasure, terrorists for the sake of power. The experience in both cases is stimulating and provides a sense of intense relatedness.

Perhaps a familiar even if painful intensity offers something more reassuring than the risk of the unknown. Things could be worse, such couples imagine. Their present circumstance, whatever else it accomplishes, keeps them, so to speak, off the streets where life might prove lonely and hollow. Greg and Sarah, Jill and George, John Cheever's parents remind one of shipwrecked people huddled on a small life-raft with few supplies. Out of desperation they turn against each other more than to each other, even though they know that they still need one another. But where else can they go, since there is no boat anywhere in sight?

The tactics of intimate terrorism are endlessly varied, limited only by the character, the imagination, and, some might add, the unconscious of its practitioners. There are tactics that operate with subtle effect; others go for the jugular. I have seen couples in therapy who create a regime of terror through the use of saintliness, rationality, complacency, ambivalence, emotional openness, endless explanations, lying, telling the truth, and silence. The most obvious stratagems, however, include infidelity, coldness in bed, indifference to the other's concerns, jealousy, criticism, threatened or actual physical violence, sexual coercion, and infantilizing the other person by acting like a parent (a modern variation of this is to behave like a therapist and treat the other as a patient). To be sure, not every instance of infidelity, jealousy, and so on is a terror tactic. They become so when their chief aim is to keep the relationship intact while giving one partner the reins of power.

Most of these maneuvers work in one of two ways. They deny or withdraw responses the partner has come to expect, or they invade the partner's body, will, or experience. The first approach keeps the victim uncertain and searching for love and support. The second colonizes the victim by overwhelming her and diminishing her freedom. (For the sake of simplicity in what follows, I'll use *he* or *she*, *him* or *her* interchangeably, or maybe just whimsically.)

Such tactics of withdrawal or invasion would no doubt stir up plenty of trouble without help from any other source, but they gain an added charge, and probably their most telling impact, from evoking the childhood anxieties that I mentioned earlier. Children dread separation from their parents, since they are so dependent on them physically and emotionally. At the same time, they need to feel competent and self-sufficient. Between the need to stay connected to parents and the growing desire to carve out some autonomy, every youngster is faced with maintaining a delicate balance. On either side of the road down which human development travels there are sheer drop-offs into abandonment or engulfment. As the psychologist Ernest Schachtel puts it, human development is a "conflict of emergence from embeddedness."[8] There is conflict because at both ends of the spectrum from aloneness to union with others the self feels endangered. Separation can pose threats, but so can too much connection. Both types of threat are commonly expressed in children's nightmares: the abandonment dreams of falling or being lost, and the engulfment dreams of being attacked or devoured by monsters.

Indeed, if a child's relations with his parents interfere consistently, in either direction, with keeping this balance, the anxiety of being separate or being intimate tends to become amplified and plant itself firmly in his growing personality. I have no doubt that all of us are subject to both kinds of anxiety, given the long dependence of the young human animal on adult caretakers, but it also seems clear that some people are more vulnerable to the fear of abandonment, others to the fear of engulfment.

For example, the more flamboyant, outgoing personalities who constantly surround themselves with people and prefer to be in the center of the social stage, who say yes more frequently than no, which means they are likely to make promises they don't keep, who return to the party after they have already said an effusive goodbye because they forgot their gloves, and who spend inordinate amounts of time on the telephone usually turn out to be the people especially prone to abandonment anxiety. The quieter types who keep a lid on their emotions, look noncommital but watch you with a kind of vigilance that suggests a radar scan, say no far more than yes, mutter vaguely when you try to pin them down, and drift toward the margins of every social gathering tend to be the engulfment-anxiety personalities.

So what happens when you get one of each type, broadly defined, in, say, a marriage? By the time a couple comes in for therapy or heads for the lawyers, that is usually what their interaction looks like. I don't mean to imply that a person whose anxiety is mostly due to fear of abandonment necessarily marries someone who characteristically suffers bouts of engulfment anxiety. The mysteries of human sexual attraction will never be encompassed by formulas such as "opposites attract." And I don't know, nor does anyone, how much people's differences, including their different ways of handling anxiety, are due to nature, how much to nurture, how much to culturally determined male and female roles, and how much to what's going on in a particular relationship. There exists a smorgasbord of psychological theories—psychodynamic, cognitive, behavioral, systemic, phenomenological—that one can pull in to argue any of these cases or some combination of all of them.

But one thing is certain: In marriages and similar intimate relationships, where closeness is expected, both anxieties can become constant and pressing. We spend much of our adult lives caught in the tension between the push for autonomy and the pull of intimacy. We want to be independent, self-reliant, in command of ourselves, but at the same time deeply attached to someone else. The needs for separate identity and intimate attachment often seem to be at odds and yet they are really aspects of each other. Some of our deepest thinkers about human behavior, such as John Dewey, George Herbert Mead, and Harry Stack Sullivan, have insisted that they are inextricable. The sociologist Erving Goffman, a more recent member of that undersung American psychological tradition, puts it as well as anybody: "What the individual is for himself is not something that he invented. It is what his significant others have come to see he should be, what they have come to treat him as being, and what in consequence, he must treat himself as being if he is to deal with their dealings with him."[9]

This perspective is an important corrective to our traditional celebration of the freedom to be whoever one wants to be, a deeply cherished American theme, ornamented by busts of Emerson, Thoreau, and Whitman. Even the most American of selves is partially dependent for its responses and prospects upon the social environment. Obviously a person's identity has always been influenced by race, social class, and religion. At the very least, these factors used to restrict what neighborhoods an individual could live in and let him know whether he could join the country club. Nowadays, in the age of information, you would probably have to add one's inclusion in the databases parked in the computers of direct marketers, insurance companies, and the like to the labeling of who one is. But the most telling impact on individual identity comes from how one is shaped and reshaped by the more intimate messages, which can often become tempestuous, that travel back and forth between two people who have to deal with one another face-to-face.

The trouble occurs when in such close relationships, especially ones that last and even more particularly in marriages, the need for a strong sense of one's own identity (being oneself, as it is popularly called) and a secure sense of intimate connection to the other (often called commitment) become split off from each other, as though one side of the equation were handed over to one person, the remaining side to the other. This is the kind of false split that anxiety helps create. As we saw explicitly in the case of Greg and Sarah and more implicitly with George and Jill, you get one partner calling for more intense intimacy and the other trying to diminish the intensity. The outcome is that every move that one of them makes to satisfy his or her special need steps up the anxiety of the other, who replies with countermoves that increase the first one's feeling of being deprived or overwhelmed. A marriage that functions like this is an effective perpetual-motion machine.

All the tactics of intimate terrorism grease the wheels of these constantly escalating complementary anxieties. The manipulations people use to hold on to a relationship while they attempt to escape from engulfment anxiety tend to be the more subtle and insidious ones. Consider from a tactical point of view, for example, the individual who chronically responds to an intimate partner's needs or wishes with ambivalence. Ambivalence is an intimate style popularly attributed to men, who are then often characterized as "passive-aggressive," though surely it is by no means limited to men, judging by what I have seen from my observation post. (According to traditional stereotypes of masculine and feminine, women suffer from abandonment fears, and men are the main carriers of engulfment anxiety. And in response to such cultural images, people tend to behave and feel as they are expected to.)

The ambivalent person delivers a double message in order to ward off engulfment threats from his or her mate without looking too nasty about it. Ambivalence is an indirect refusal, and it gives one the strategic advantage of depriving the other person while deflecting responsibility for the other's pained responses. A shrewdly ambivalent individual can even lay claim to a measure of victim status by conveying to the real victim, who has been consigned to a kind of limbo, "My inability to make a decision, which I have no control over, hurts me as much as it does you."

In the competition of wills that intimate terrorism sets in motion, there are no winners. When one person tries to hold on to power through ambivalence, both people are eventually undone by the ungratifying exchanges that result: The ambivalent person loses the strength and integrity that come from taking a position and standing up for it. He or she ends up looking like a wimp. The other person, whether especially vulnerable to abandonment anxiety or not, winds up psychologically drained because dealing with a partner's doubtfulness becomes a full-time job.

Take this couple, for instance, who came in for therapy because they are thinking about getting married. They were looking for some preventive medicine, so to speak, as unmarried couples sometimes do. Both of them had left behind first marriages not very long ago.

Those marriages were a mess, and so far as I can see, they are about to mess things up again, thanks in large measure to how he systematically envelops the relationship in a vague, punishing fog of indecisiveness. Her low opinion of her own worth plays a part as well, because it feeds on waiting around resentfully for the final judgment to be passed. He is like a man going through a revolving door continuously without taking the step that would lead him finally inside the lobby or out onto the street. And she responds by endlessly picking petals off mental daisies—"He loves me, he loves me not."

A handsome and energetic pair, these two—let's call them Ralph and Maureen—are still young, still reaching for love's promise despite having been through the debilitating experience of separation and divorce. When they met, they experienced that lifting of a curtain that reveals a glittering future. Ralph is a tall man, a professor with a slightly stiff and formal air when he's nervous, but he lights up with a big grin when he unbends, and his Harrison Ford–like rumpled locks and air of forgetfulness give him a boyish charm. He would never have to sleep alone, which may be unfortunate because he uses an abundance of opportunities as an escape hatch, and it eventually becomes his albatross. Maureen is equally striking in appearance; she would attract notice in any crowd. She moves with the langorous yet sure-footed grace of a born aristocrat or a professional dancer. It's easy to see why they were drawn to each other. But now Ralph keeps protesting that he doesn't know whether he ought to see other women, and Maureen is beginning to deliver ultimatums, although not yet with much conviction. What in heaven's name is he waiting for, I ask myself. And why does she put up with it?

Maureen, who works for a state agency, is a talented appreciator of others, although, sad to tell, not of herself. Her gorgeous physical presence has a life of its own, entirely at odds with her self-deprecating way of thinking about herself. At first I imagine that Ralph's line about other women might just be the natural caution of the recently divorced: "Play the field. Take your time. You don't want to make another mistake," they often tell themselves. But it quickly becomes clear that this is not the major issue, as his habitual two-sidedness becomes apparent in more and more areas. For one thing, he keeps insistently *telling* her about his doubts instead of just thinking them. He discusses them with her as though she were his therapist. Unfortunately she listens, though it wounds her and conspires with her self-criticism to further diminish her luster. As her anger and hurt accumulate, she tries to hold in unpleasant feelings, becoming tight-lipped and downcast. This causes her glow to fade in his eyes, confirming for him that he is right in hesitating.

They tell me a story that demonstrates how his ambivalence and her way of handling it affect them both. It's late summer, and they have decided to rent a beach cottage where they can vacation together on weekends away from the humidity of the city and the remaining loose ends of divorce proceedings. Since he is involved in a research project at school, he is (of course) dubious, but she is firm, so he agrees to go along with it. At one point they plan a long romantic weekend, beginning on a Thursday evening, at the beach. Maureen leaves town a day early in order to get things ready. She prepares a candlelit dinner overlooking the water, since Ralph is supposed to arrive at 5:30 that evening. At 5:00 he calls from school to say that he is just finishing writing a grant proposal but will get there by 7:30. At 8:30 he finally shows up, looking harried and preoccupied. Dinner by that time is pretty much a ruined afterthought.

Maureen was deeply disappointed, but she said little in the hope that they could make the most of the remaining time. When they got up the next morning she dressed for the beach. Ralph, however, announced that he had a few things to take care of, and he proceeded to telephone his research assistant, his secretary, and a colleague. He stayed on the telephone until lunchtime. By then Muareen's whole body was stinging with resentment. Feeling now like the overcooked dinner from the night before, she concluded that she, too, was becoming an afterthought. She thought to herself that she ought to tell him to clear out, but she didn't because she anticipated that being alone would make her feel even worse. Instead she became increasingly tense and sour, falling into a silent depression, while he periodically uttered grudging apologies, pointing out that he felt trapped between the demands of the research and her needs. Thus they proceeded through the remainder of the weekend.

That night, though she felt anything but sexy, she initiated love-making, as though it were her last resort to test his caring for her. It was angry, defensive, imploring sex on her part and little more than compensatory on his. They made love like two people backed up against a wall, each trying to hold an attacker at bay.

Characters like Ralph try to evade engulfment anxiety by making themselves invisible, drawing their ambivalence over their head like a magical cloak. Wherever they are, they are somewhere else at the same time, as when Ralph uses the phone to be simultaneously at work and on vacation. Nobody can pin them down. They remind me of those villagers from primitive tribes who refuse to be photographed because they are afraid that the camera will steal their souls.

Ambivalent individuals appear to be keeping all their options open so that they retain ample free choice, but they rarely experience any freedom resulting from their actions. Their lives become shackled to a sense of obligation that winds tighter and tighter around them because they have managed to turn all their attractions, that which they initially think they want, into distractions, that which they don't know if they want any longer.

As long as the recipients of another's ambivalent elusiveness stay in the relationship, as does Maureen, they are not really making a choice either, certainly not a self-affirming one. The more Maureen's abandonment anxiety flares up, the harder she holds on, cranking up the pressure for Ralph to make up his mind. Thus she gravitates to a passive position also, as if her well-being depends on his coming through, which will probably never happen.

A closely related tactic—it might be considered a variation on ambivalence—is employed by men and women who withdraw and in the same breath deny that this is what they are doing in order to maintain power by leaving their partners in the grip of a disorienting abandonment anxiety. In this case, the intimate terrorist is more directly engaged in perpetrating a sham. She goes through the motions of intimacy at the same time as she withdraws from it. She says one thing and at the same time transmits overtones that contradict her words. If her husband or lover asks, "Do you still love me?," she treats the question as though it were absurdly unnecessary, saying "Don't you know?" or "What do you think?" She may insist that she does love him, but states the fact too elaborately. (A simple "I love you" is much more reliable than "I *really* love you." The adverbial intensifier gives one the feeling that the lover threw it in because, not altogether meaning it, she doesn't expect to be believed.) Or she may allow an incongruity between words and action to creep in, letting her eyes drift away as she embraces him and proclaims her love.

This technique—withdrawal combined with a denial of withdrawal—unsettles the victim.[10] He feels rejected, but uncertain about just what is going on or whose fault it is. If the other person were to say clearly "It's over," he might mourn the loss and eventually move on to other concerns and other people. Instead, the relationship is stuck fast, moving neither toward more satisfying intimacy nor to dissolution.

The victim of such tactics sometimes contributes to the paralysis by trying to repossess the other person through entreaties, accusations, and heart-to-heart talks that make the first terrorist feel both guilty and trapped. So the terrorist, now terrorized herself, broadens the arena of her withdrawal. She might develop an air of perpetual preoccupation, a way of looking at her mate without seeing him, nodding in agreement without hearing what he said. As I suggested, abandonment tactics by one partner typically bring on an engulfing response by the other, and vice versa. The problem of chronic jealousy, which plagues many terrorized relationships, illustrates how these mutual threats develop.

Jealousy involves a particularly debilitating kind of abandonment anxiety. To overcome his increasing feelings of powerlessness, the jealous person strives to engulf his partner and keep her close. His compulsive interrogations and endless demands for confessions and guarantees of fidelity are attempts to control her by replacing her will with his own. To protect herself she moves still further away, while protesting her innocence and even her love, maybe because she means it or perhaps just to get him off her back. He sinks deeper into self-hatred and hatred of her, even as he pursues her, demanding love.

Since uncertainty is intolerable to a jealous person, he searches for hurtful details, sometimes to the point of spying on her. Every ambiguity must be resolved, every shadow illuminated. Yet this obsessive interest in the other's feelings and actions extends only to the point where they affect him. If they don't, he wrenches them around until they do. He finally comes to know his wife only as a reflection of himself, a silhouette drained of distinctive personality and otherness.

Intimate terror tactics turn back upon the terrorist as well as hurt the victim. Both people are damaged by them. The jealous individual diminishes his own humanity along with his self-respect. There is a shameful exposure of his inner life, as though he were caught with his psyche unbuttoned. Vulnerability and self-disclosure, always present in intimacy, are here debased into humiliation, because they are no longer a voluntary choice but a compelled demonstration. Even when he tries to cover up his feelings, he stands revealed—for the other can see right through the artificiality of his attempt to look indifferent. Georg Simmel, a shrewd late-nineteenth-century German sociologist, remarked that "absolute knowledge . . . paralyzes the vitality of relations" in marriage[11]; and indeed the jealous person is known absolutely.

The most successful intimates, Simmel also informs us, "have an inexhaustible reservoir of latent psychological possessions, and hence can no more reveal and give them away at one stroke than a tree can give away next year's fruits with those of the season."[12] The reserves of self that can keep renewing the excitement of being intimate are no longer available to the person torn by jealousy. He has already played out all his cards. But this makes him feel continually smaller and more alone, adding fuel to the abandonment anxiety his actions strive to alleviate.

Similarly, an individual who practices the tactics of disguised withdrawal slowly poisons her own reality through always having to present a version of herself that she cannot support wholeheartedly.

If she persists, she ultimately becomes a stranger to herself, as well as to the other. Since it was her engulfment anxiety—the fear of losing herself—that probably led her to resort to those tactics in the first place, she winds up amplifying it rather than getting free of it.

I trust that it is clear from all these examples that in intimate terrorism, nobody wins. The two keep ricocheting off each other's anxieties, each increasing his or her own in the process.

The foregoing are, for the most part, relatively polite terror tactics that usually keep the fight within the bounds of middle-class decorum (though not always—if a couple's frustration gets hot enough, they might start throwing things or each other.) Ambivalent people and others who can't say yes or no wholeheartedly are among the oversocialized: In growing up, they learned too well that they would be loved only if they were good boys and girls. So they maintain a facade of obedience, while they find other ways to refuse— delaying until the last minute, telling white lies, being late, protesting too much, trying to live up to two opposing commitments at once. I think of such tactics as the intimate terrorism par excellence of the 1980s, an era during which everybody was accusing everybody else of narcissistic self-involvement after taking workshops on how to deal with the problem of commitment or reading self-help books with titles like *The Dance-away Lover* and *The Pan Syndrome*.

There are, of course, more blatant, savage terror tactics that make use of direct physical and sexual coercion, which brings us square into the nineties, a period when much of our erotic life seems aimed at a headlong dive into the barbarism of the Dark Ages. This reversion to Neanderthal behavior, alas, appears to be the present cutting edge of intimate terrorism. It occurs, for example, when jealousy turns black and dangerous through a sudden volcanic eruption of abandonment anxiety that some people keep buried as long as they have control over their partners.

The individual who uses violence against his intimate partner, or even threatens to, strikes at the heart of the other person's separateness, eliminating her freedom of will by attacking it directly through her body. He treats his victim as an extension of himself, something that exists solely to meet his needs. As women who find themselves under the thumbs of husbands and boyfriends given to this sort of pathology more often walk out these days, they sometimes find that they may be taking their lives in their hands. Intimacy under so murderous a regime eats away at one of our most cherished premises—that love is in the service of life.

Terrorism, whether in a marriage or a society, emerges when at least a percentage of the participants have concluded that all other avenues of negotiation have become exhausted. It represents among those who resort to it the end of a moral order based on faith that people make contact with one another for any other purpose than self-interest, greed, or power. Terrorism is thus the last refuge of political despair. In marriages and other intimate relations, such faith comes to an end when two people, owing to their anxieties, are no longer able to experience one another as whole, if imperfect, beings who have genuine affection for one another and the capacity to change through their dealings with each other. We commonly say that love is blind, because new lovers tend to clothe one another in idealized images or projections. The anxiety that leads to intimate terrorism equally darkens people's vision. They react blindly to one another because they can no longer see each other fully or with discrimination. Whereas a person in love usually gives the beloved the benefit of the doubt by glossing over any number of defects and putting them in a positive light, intimate terrorists do the opposite. They fasten on every possibility that the other's intentions are malevolent and about to issue forth in manipulations, lies, rejections, and power plays. And then they reply in kind.

Exposed to the terrorist tactics that produce abandonment anxiety or engulfment anxiety, the victims feel that their innermost selves are being treated as objects that have life and importance only in relation to someone else. Intimate terrorism thus illustrates vividly a negative sense in which knowledge is power. Ralph Waldo Emerson wrote, "There is no terror like that of being known."[13] He was referring to a dread in society lest the artificial and arbitrary nature behind its pretense to authority be revealed. In an intimate relationship between two people, this terror springs from an impulse almost the opposite: that the truth and complexity of one's personality be reduced to a shadow when it is known through the eyes of the other's anxiety.

2

The Postmodern Battle of the Sexes

"One man's vision may be another man's hal-
lucination."
—*Hanns Sachs,* Masks of Love and Life

To what extent is intimate terrorism, with its confusion of love and power, a contemporary variant of a phenomenon that may be as old as love itself—the battle of the sexes? To what extent is it rather a battle of *sex*—the latest evidence that erotic love and its demands, in making people deeply anxious, can drive them to becoming hazardous to each other's health? These are by no means mutually exclusive questions, but neither are they identical. To see where they mingle and where they diverge in modern life involves understanding the interplay between our tumultuous culture and the often forlorn quality of individual intimacy.

Many commentators speak of our era as "postmodern," which implies that a fragmentation and unraveling of nearly everything we used to take for granted is under way. We have come to inhabit a sexual landscape in which there are multiple realities, none of which is any longer clearly dominant. The postmodern era in culture is also, importantly, post–sexual liberation, although it not only retains but has, if anything, expanded the pluralistic possibilities of sexual behavior that the free-wheeling 1960s and 1970s first opened up. Sex and love in that earlier period not only seemed safe but fun, a kind of thrilling calesthenics, a thoroughly entertaining, thoroughly American program for good mental health and aerobic fitness. Even falling in love was just frosting on the cake, a romantic high not to be taken too seriously. The anxieties that linger alongside the yearnings in all erotic contact seemed quelled. If they surfaced, they were written off as relics of our Puritan legacy, which had for so long stoked our guilt and fear in order to inhibit spontaneous animal impulses and thus prevent us from following a more gratifying road to self-realization.

But sex, whatever else it may be, is an agent of demonic forces, as our tragicomic literary tradition from Socrates to Shakespeare to D. H. Lawrence has always maintained. This is the facet of eros that we overlooked, caught up as we were in those heady excitements that reached high tide twenty-five or thirty years ago and proceeded to flood the urban coasts of America, sending tributaries streaming through the campuses and city streets across the rest of the country. With that incorrigible, innocent, and in some ways beautiful American optimism, a whole generation thought for a time that it could tame everything—wars, bureaucracies, mind-altering chemicals, racial differences—through love, and in addition tame love itself, turning it all to positive purposes. On an intimate scale, if monogamous marriage seemed confining and ended up in bitterness, we would simply revise it and create open marriages, group marriages, spouse-swapping, and communal live-in sex without marriage, all sorts of alternative arrangements. Both the anxiety of sex and the battle of the sexes were declared to be at an end.

In many respects those were wonderful decades to grow up in, combining intense hopes about making a better society with experimental adventures and sheer good times. They were the time of my own political and sexual coming of age, and I still look back on them with grateful nostalgia. But from a contemporary perspective, they have also revealed themselves to be filled with utopian hubris—and not the least where sexual intimacy is concerned. You might succeed in taming sex for a while, but if you don't treat it with respect, even humility, its darker consequences will come back to haunt you. Now it looks as if the darker side is upon us with a vengeance. Like some furious Old Testament deity punishing the revelers at the orgy, nature itself seems to have contrived the blackest conceivable comeuppance in the form of AIDS, perhaps the most fearsome sexual demon yet, invisible, insidious, and a relentless killer. It has reintroduced all of us to sexual terror—and done so with a kind of fiendish irony—by slipping in through a door that our culture had only just begun to open: homosexual sex.

To make things worse, the repressed shady side of our own natures has broken loose at the same moment and seems to be running amuck. If you go by rumors, allegations, and the news, it appears that just about every wicked impulse that traditional religion and conventional morals had tried to hold at bay has slipped its leash: rape, incest, wife-beating, pedophilia in churches and daycare centers, simulated obscenity and perversion on MTV and for real on nightclub stages, smut on the path to the Supreme Court. It is hard to tell how much of this is dire reality, how much a projection of our deepening anxieties. Either way, sexual pessimism dominates our present mood. Comparing the original Woodstock concert with its sequel in August 1994, a *New York Times* editorial claimed that "the music is darker than that of Woodstock I, the dancing rougher, but so are the times."[1]

The 1987 film *Fatal Attraction* was one marker in our popular mythology of changing currents that reflected a newfound fear, or reversion to an old one: Horrible things can occur if you engage in casual recreational sex. The movie, however much it captured the new mood, distorted the actual issues that were developing, since it presents the dilemma as a clash of obsolete stereotypes: A married man, whose lust is portrayed as merely a pleasure-seeking chink in the armor of his commitment to his family, runs up against the more devious lust of an engulfing female with ulterior motives. When he abandons her by treating their fling as a one-night stand, she turns into a modern Medea, a psychotic witch out for his blood. In the end, marriage prevails, as the briefly straying husband and his suburban wife team up, like a domestic SWAT team, to dispatch the

vindictive witch in one of the most ghoulish bathtub scenes Hollywood has yet devised. The husband, whether you regard him as a
leftover from the sixties or just a case of your typical adulterous,
fun-loving male who means no harm, is treated as though he were
the vulnerable victim of a predatory female and gets off the hook.

In fact, nobody gets off the hook so easily any longer. And what's
more, the old roles these days are just as often reversed. Through the
1950s, men graduating from college or even high school, having
sampled the available wares and at least temporarily spent their quota
of mischief, were slipping off into marriages (especially with the
women who held out) before the print on the diploma had dried, all
the while still muttering half-joking condemnations of the "tender
trap" that spelled the end of male freedom at the bachelor parties we
gave one another, like Last Suppers, a few days before the wedding.
And we imagined that the prospective bride was being told by her
chums at *her* final party as a single woman that she had made a good
catch—was she ever lucky to nail him! In other words, early marriage helped secure a woman against abandonment, though she
might have to evolve some new sexy wiles to keep her husband
from going astray, whereas it tamed the beast in men only temporarily—they were still prone to be pulled out of line by a volatile mix of
engulfment anxiety and lust. These, of course, were the persistent
stereotypes of the time: Women, the dependent sex, were especially
vulnerable to abandonment, and men, those free spirits, tended to
react, however ambivalently, like caged animals.

Over the past twenty years, these stereotypes have faded like old
postcards, only to be replaced by their mirror images. I've witnessed
this change often enough in my office. Couples used to sit down,
the wife would open with "You don't act as though you care about
me," and the husband would reply "I need more space." Now it's
just as often the husband who begins complaining about the loss of
intimacy and the wife who answers "I need more space." Women's
liberation has proved that men are frequently abandonment sheep in
engulfment lion's clothing. So which sex is the more dependent
one? The kind of "fatal attraction" that hits the newsstands daily at
present and thus gives the lie to Hollywood's version goes like this:

Women seeking a way out of stifling domestic or ornamental roles are leaving men, who sometimes respond by turning into possessive monsters all too willing to maim or slaughter their abandoning caretakers in order to hang on to a semblance of traditional male domination.

Amid so much havoc in the temples of Venus, from AIDS to confusions about roles to domestic violence, sex doesn't seem as much fun as it used to be, and the battle of the sexes at times resembles a medieval dance of death. What are the prospects for old-fashioned intimacy, two people trying to convert desire and closeness into a way of sharing a life together? The battle of the sexes used to be a subplot to courtship and marriage, an acknowledgment that there are difficulties along the path of romance. The very idea that the sexes are at war recognized that coping with male-female differences at close quarters produces friction as well as harmony, that sexual heat, however much it might move two people to try to melt into one, also gives the proceedings a hostile edge. This is not only a human foible: Observers of other species find aggressive behavior widely distributed in mating rituals all through the animal kingdom. But what is specifically human is how the pattern of friction changes. Witnessing the latest human battles of the sexes, we might be tempted to ask: What sexes, how many sexes, what is a man or a woman?

The battle of the sexes has outlasted all other wars. Ancient Greek literature and religion, for example, are filled with belligerent sexual skirmishes: The Greeks worshipped both male and female deities, who regularly practiced the arts of sabotage, ambush, and deception on one another. Thus the ancients extended the battle of the sexes to the administration of the cosmos. Perhaps that in itself was reason enough for a shift to monotheism.

But it turns out that not even monotheism is exempt from power struggle and rivalry. For many centuries of apparent calm, God, reflecting relatively secure male domination, was always referred to as "he." Since the rise of the women's movement, God in certain circles has become "she." Ideally the sex of a single deity probably ought to be indeterminate, but we do not yet have a way to express such a concept—obviously "it" won't do. Our language, like our lives, is filled with two sexes, which nowadays struggle for grammatical dominance.

Even the most archetypal human behaviors are conditioned by history. Every era updates the battle of the sexes, producing its own idiosyncratic version. As befits our heightened awareness of power in all human interaction, our version is more thoroughly politicized than ever before, as I have already suggested. What equally distinguishes today's battle is its self-conscious perplexity about sex roles, which sends it spinning around on itself, like one of those fight scenes in movies where two antagonists, locked in combat, go rolling over and over down a steep incline until you can't tell who is going to end up on top and who on the bottom. The battle of the sexes has become a battle over sexual identities, sexual meanings, and sexual politics, including the very definitions of "masculine" and "feminine." Beyond the usual power struggles, contemporary sexual warfare is full of agonizing about what portion of our erotic behavior is dictated by biology and what portion by culture, how much is masquerade or pose and how much is authentic emotion, and whether romance is an idealization of love or just a subtle form of imperialism, in which each of the sexes tries to subjugate the other.

All this leaves us in a state of extreme doubt about the very nature of sexual love, which deepens the anxieties and insecurities that fuel the battle of the sexes in the first place by adding an additional level of ambiguity. Two scenes in *Annie Hall,* probably Woody Allen's best-known film, effectively strike the typical modern note: self-doubt and paranoia, accompanied by continual scrutiny of one's own and the other's motives. In one scene, Allen and Diane Keaton are engaged in the conversation that first establishes their courtship. The talk is all awkward innuendo, since each is too shy and vulnerable to say what he or she really means, so we are provided with subtitles, as though conversation between the sexes has to be translated like a foreign language. (And now we have Deborah Tannen's best-selling books, which carry this idea out with full seriousness.)

It's a relatively innocent moment, but it also foreshadows the secretiveness, mistrust, infidelities, and breakdowns of communication to come.

The other scene depicts Diane Keaton's ghostly silhouette departing from her body, which remains lying on the bed where she is making love. The silhouette takes a seat nearby to watch the proceedings with a bemused look. This staking out of an observation post amid the throes of love is a common maneuver between contemporary intimates—it says in effect, "I may appear to be involved in this, but I'm not really all *that* involved, because I'm also evaluating what's going on." If we use sexual intercourse as a weapon in a political struggle, we also use it as a diagnostic tool with which to test both ourselves and our partners. We plumb the sexual depths of another like someone shouting from the edge of a cliff and then wondering if it's an echo or the other person's voice that returns across the distance.

Thus far I have for the most part resisted using the word "gender" in talking about the sexes, unlike virtually every recent article or book I have read that deals with the differences between men and women in love, work, or just about every other area of social life. The human condition has now been divided up according to one's "gender"; the word itself has become as ideological as "proletariat" or "bourgeois." The writer Leonard Kriegel claims that "[r]ace and ethnicity still command attention, but one senses that their appeal has begun to wane as sex and gender questions increasingly dominate cultural discourse."[2] That may be an overstatement, but it is true that the idea of gender has so thoroughly infiltrated our thinking and vocabulary that, alas, the word frequently appears now as an adjectival past participle, as in "gendered behavior," meaning that men and women sometimes conduct themselves differently. As usual, the mental-health professionals are among the worst offenders against the canons of decent prose: They now write about "gender socialization," "gendered development," and "gendered psychotherapy." Long before all this came about, H. W. Fowler, in his standard reference work *A Dictionary of Modern English Usage*, had already penned an acid commentary on the tendency to misuse the word "gender." He insisted that "**gender,** n., is a grammatical term only. To talk of *persons* or *creatures of the masculine* or *feminine g.,* meaning *of the male* or *female sex,* is either a jocularity (permissible or not according to context) or a blunder."[3]

What Fowler in 1926 could not have foreseen, however, is the extent to which all relatively stable structures by means of which people through the ages have tried to civilize their instincts and impulses, from the religious to the scientific, have been taken down or taken apart in the modern world. "Deconstructed" is the contemporary term for this relentless activity of reducing wholes to their parts, external givens to mere internal fabrications, until everything human that we assumed was "real" is treated as though it is nothing more than an arbitrary set of signs or symbols. In the same way that people can mistake a word for the thing it represents, according to the deconstructionist view, mere symbols come to feel definitive, meaningful, real to us because we have hung them on a scaffolding which has a logic akin to the grammar of a language.

Whether through ancient Greek stories of gods and goddesses or medieval ideals of romantic love, through biblical exhortations to practice sexual restraint or biological theories that support fuller sexual expression, civilization has always depended on myths of one kind or another for safe passage through the riptides of sex. But all these traditional myths are being torn to pieces in our current restless discontent and controversy about sexual love.

Perhaps it is fitting after all that the idea of the "sexes," a concept based on a belief in irreducible biological entities, has been replaced by a grammatical term, "gender." We seem to like the idea that reality boils down to linguistic conventions, that modern men and women are little more than categories or texts that we create and can uncreate. But these are notions that leave us in a considerable quandary: For in Western cultures today, we no longer know for sure what constitutes manliness or womanliness, what is permissible sexual behavior, and what it all has to do with love. Or as English sociologist Annette Lawson, in a study of adultery, quotes a young woman she interviewed as saying, "Well, I suppose I am having an affair. I just don't know what is an affair, what is a relationship, what is anything particularly."[4]

Before I trek any further through this swamp of ambiguities, let me retreat to some basic considerations. There are only two directions one can go in life—toward others or away from them. Both the reaching out and the turning away in themselves are as natural as heartbeats or breathing. Every living organism pulsates in accord with a rhythm of expansion and contraction, contact and withdrawal. All creatures have to go out to the environment for nourishment or safety in numbers or to mate and procreate; but they also must retreat for digestion, sleep, healing, and so on. Such fundamental fluctuations occur at every level of existence, not excluding human intimacy, where to an extraordinary degree, however, they can become entangled in problematic issues.

As long as things are going well in an intimate relationship, you could think of contact and withdrawal as a kind of psychological breathing between two people, as though each inhaled to take in and experience the "we," followed by exhalation to let go and recapture the "I." But as I proposed in the last chapter, it is precisely in this relation between the "we" and the "I" of intimacy that snags begin to develop. Two intimate partners' movements toward and away from each other ought to affirm by turns both the self and the other person, but they are also liable to become driven by hungers and fears that make them turbulent and destructive, such as the anxieties I discussed in the preceding chapter. In an essay on the fiction of Katherine Mansfield, the novelist Willa Cather described the disturbing side of this elemental give-and-take: "Human relationships are the tragic necessity of human life; that they can never be wholly satisfactory, that every ego is half the time greedily seeking them, and half the time pulling away from them."[5] Or as a French writer said of his mistress, "Her existence is intolerable, but her absence is unsupportable," an elegant way of saying you can't live with them and you can't live without them.

D. H. Lawrence, who wrote about such matters with penetrating insight (despite his vulnerability, in today's sexual climate, to charges of male chauvinism), remarked, "We may as well admit it: men and women need one another. . . . We are all individualists: we are all egoists: we all believe intensely in freedom, our own at all events. We all want to be absolute, and sufficient unto ourselves. And it is a great blow to our self-esteem that we simply *need* another human being." He went on to define the nature of this need more emphatically: "There is hardly a man living who can exist at all cheerfully without a relationship to some particular woman: unless, of course, he makes another man play the role of woman. And the same of woman. There is hardly a woman on earth who can live cheerfully without some intimate relationship to a man; unless she substitutes some other woman for the man."[6]

This seems to me an absolutely accurate depiction of the conflict, although, surprisingly for Lawrence, it doesn't go far enough. In his novels he certainly understood the demonic power of sex, if anyone did, so in a sense I'm being more Laurentian than the Lawrence of this passage when I claim that our acute need for intimacy is not only a blow to self-esteem, but a terrifying prospect that threatens the individual personality with disintegration. Although we may yearn to turn ourselves over to another person, the idea also seems fraught with peril, entailing the possibility of losing oneself in abject submission to the will of another. The very language of erotic experience reveals this mixture of freedom and determinism—love and power disguised in each other's clothes—that can make intimacy seem so frightening. For instance, "surrender" can describe an ecstatic loosening of the self or a capitulation to another's will. "Bonds" can refer to a freely chosen close attachment or to the bondage of slavery. "Commitment" can mean a voluntary, enduring loyalty or a miniature version of what society does to criminals or the insane.

The same sort of double meanings can underlie even the most apparently straightforward interaction between two intimates. If one of them tells the other "I love you," it might be simply intended to convey appreciation, or it might be a move aimed to obligate the other to answer the hidden question "Do you love me?" Similarly, one can pull back from a relationship out of a need for an interval of solitude, like blinking after a long gaze, or because one has the urge to flee or wall oneself off or to punish the other through deprivation.

That the battle of the sexes has been around at least as long as Western civilization is probably the inevitable external expression of this inner tug-of-war, the product of simultaneous attraction and revulsion as people try to negotiate the jagged terrain of their relationships. There is a fundamental instinctual clash between people who both need and fear one another, and thus a negative, sometimes violent form of love can result from the friction, willfulness, and self-protection that occur in all our erotic activities. Take a man and a woman, each wanting something from the other, with each also wanting to control the terms of getting it, and you have the grounds for war. But the question remains whether these grounds originate in the difference between the sexes or in the very nature of all intimacy, whether straight or gay.

Obviously both issues are involved, but I am convinced that the decline of so many modern relationships into enmity mostly has its roots in the anxieties that wind themselves around all love. The battle is not only a battle of the *sexes,* though that may well be the most vivid and elaborate shape of our battles to come to terms with the anxieties of intimacy. Because anxiety drives people to attempt control of what cannot be controlled in the hope of making things more predictable, it creates stasis, sameness, and fixation that cause a relationship to become clogged and rapidly winded. Anxiety-ridden intimacy turns into stale intimacy, life shared in a closet, and no one can any longer grow from it. The battle of the sexes, or, for that matter, any intimate battle, expresses their desperate organic need to breathe again.

Here is an example, drawn from my files of marital therapy, that illustrates the pathos in this unfortunate process. It is the history of a couple that begins with two young people coming together through the pull of romance and culminates in my office more than a decade later with a chronic situation in which every attempt they make to reach each other flares up into an ugly incident because neither of them is able any longer to respond to a very sizable portion of the other's personality. But then perhaps they never were able to, even from the beginning.

Now in their late thirties, married for a dozen years, solid citizens of their town, this husband and wife described to me in a therapy session a typically lousy evening they had just spent in a restaurant. The background to that evening is important: The husband had thought things between them were in good shape, if not exactly scintillating, and suddenly, during the past few months, here she was threatening to leave him! He explained this to me in a composed tone, but it wasn't hard to tell that he felt demolished. And she, for her part, was incensed and adamant in a way that he simply could not comprehend. Not that he had ever questioned their relationship to any great extent. They had fallen in love when they were both still in school, where he was finishing a graduate degree in business, already looking every inch the man of the world, and she, aspiring to be an artist but feeling unsure of herself and very much in love, allowed him to sweep her off to raise a family instead.

The pattern they had established was characterized by its stability. Each morning he left her, generally in front of the washing machine or the stove, while he hustled off to see his clients at the agency or, on weekends, to meet his golf partners. Now and then, once the kids were in school, she managed to get away to the partly finished attic of their stolid Georgian brick house and work on a painting, an activity he still found charming but no more significant than her long conversations on the phone with her girlfriends. At night, after dinner, there was little going on between them. He reread the *Wall Street Journal,* scouring tables of mutual funds until his eyelids grew heavy; she returned to the kitchen and then sat down with a novel or magazine. In a pinch, as for so many American couples, there was the TV crooning its lullaby of the eleven o'clock news.

One could address their burgeoning troubles on many levels, given their habitual assumptions about the division of labor in their marriage. He has a remorselessly conventional mind, and she is full of unexpressed hungers. But for the moment I want to return to the scene in the restaurant. Sitting by themselves in a dimly lit cavern, joined neither by his business associates and their wives, couples that usually bored her to death, nor by any of her artistic girlfriends whose husbands he found pretentious: This was a new kind of recreation for them, one that they had not experienced together for years.

He had recently initiated this return to dating, because he was puzzled by her growing dissatisfaction—hadn't he always provided everything for her?—and in a sense he was courting her anew. But it wasn't working very well.

On the night in question, he had sought out this pleasant underground terrain, where young lovers sat by candlelight at the other tables, in the hope once again of patching things up. She seemed to be enjoying herself, so at one point during dinner, he reached over abruptly and removed his wife's glasses. He told me that he did this so he could gaze more directly into her eyes. Her response was, "What the fuck right do you have to take my glasses off?" She insisted that he meant to put her at a disadvantage by leaving her unable to see and therefore helpless. (Is this what people mean when they say love is blind?, I thought to myself.) So much for settling anything further that night.

The husband, a burly man with thinning hair and an air of decisiveness, obviously used to having his way in the office or at home, claims that his sudden action was only an effort to make them feel closer to each other, eyes being windows to the soul and so forth. "What the hell is wrong with her?" he asks me or the world in general. Is she having an affair? Chronic PMS? He grabs at such speculations in his effort to understand what is going on. What he doesn't see is that she experiences his move in the restaurant as just another of his many manipulations to hold on to his power over her, an attempt to keep her vulnerable and dependent.

The issue here is not who is right—they are both telling the truth as each experiences it. But it is also true that he doesn't bother to negotiate his moves toward intimacy with her; he just goes ahead, whether in sex or planning a vacation. As she puts it, "Franklin manages to make me feel helpless in what look like the nicest ways." He often complains about her dependence on him, yet, half unwittingly, sabotages her bids for autonomy. On one occasion, he announced in therapy, "Vera just can't seem to cope with practical things," implying that he therefore has to take charge, an attitude that makes her justifiably furious. At his worst, he has been known to walk into the den and switch the channel on the TV, either not noticing that she is sitting there absorbed in a program or taking it as self-evident that she would rather watch what he wants to watch.

For many years, when Vera was more docile, this arrangement appeared to work relatively smoothly. But for a number of reasons, both cultural and personal, she has had a change of heart and, with the heightened perception of the recent convert, now perceives only a repetitious exercise of power in Franklin's dealings with her. This includes his present one-way attempts at closeness or to bring about reconciliation. Having caught on to the hierarchical dimension of their married life, she is now as steadfast in her opposition to him as she used to be in following his lead. A mild, rather prim woman, her eyes sometimes at sea behind her spectacles, who talks to me and probably everyone else in the reassuring tones of the practiced hostess, she has learned to harden her perimeters when Franklin approaches, even to ward him off with a curse, as she did in the restaurant, almost a hiss of menace, like someone who is taking a martial arts course.

One can understand her newly found defensive posture, but it compels her to ignore the possibility that his actions may be prompted by affection as well as domination, and that it might be worth giving some credence to the former even while resisting and trying to instruct him about the effect of the latter. Granted that it is extremely difficult, maybe impossible, to change habits and assumptions so thoroughly entrenched in Franklin's character. But as things stand, Vera also helps perpetuate the situation, because she makes him feel so totally in the wrong and so mystified about it that he is too busy defending himself to learn anything useful about what she feels.

I take Franklin's and Vera's marital woes to be deeply about the battle of the sexes. I'll go further than this: I think that their relationship was almost always about the battle of the sexes: The seeds of war were planted near the beginning when Vera gave up her art and so much of herself and when Franklin assumed executive power over their joint enterprise, analogous to that which he wields at work. Granted that there may have been little visible warfare between them for a very long time, very few of the firefights that happen all the time now; but the prospect of war was seething there nevertheless, embedded like a dormant virus in the very tissues of their marriage. One can't blame either of them for this misfortune. They were thoroughly trained to assume their hierarchical and ultimately antagonistic roles by their entire culture.

One psychological process among the many complications in Franklin's and Vera's interaction bears further discussion since it has a much wider reference, not only to the plight of individuals like them and their slide into intimate terrorism, but also because this process is replicated on a cultural level. It points to an important reason our culture keeps failing to provide such individuals with a pathway out of their suffering.

In healthy relationships the partners retain the ability to make rather fine distinctions about one another's motives, despite all the factors—projections of the past, second-guessing each other's wants or intents, social expectations, and cultural influences—that combine to create noise in virtually all human communication. Where there's love, as I have been arguing repeatedly, there's anxiety as well as attempts to regulate it through power, just as where there's smoke, there's fire. Couples who are still in love don't notice this so much as a rule. For them, appreciation of each other overwhelms issues of their control over each other. When they get anxious, they don't so regularly take it out on one another as do troubled couples like the ones I have been discussing. Instead, they give each other the benefit of the doubt and treat each other as innocent until proven guilty, a concept that our legal system is supposed to respect but which our intimacies do not for very long.

Considering the nature of the human will, including its alliance with possessiveness and a distaste for unpredictability, the issue of who is in control moves relentlessly over time toward the foreground in intimate relationships. If love thins out too much in the wear and tear of daily life, power comes to stand out all the more starkly. Of course, to be aware of the elements of power is not automatically an altogether bad thing. In Vera's case, for example, her realization of how she was being stifled by Franklin's seemingly benevolent exercise of power took her a great many years—or at least her willingness to express her recognition did. Love may make people blind, but so does anxiety, and it often paralyzes them as well. To discern Franklin's control over her life and her sense of self and be able to counter it with her own will may have been the only road toward a measure of freedom and maturation for Vera. Even if she had always felt it—and she must have—to know it and not to do anything about it is nearly tantamount to not knowing it at all. As Yeats said, "seeming that lasts a lifetime is no different than reality."

There's still a problem with Vera's new view of Franklin, however, as penetrating as it may look compared to his well-meaning thick-headedness. Much of the unchanging character of disturbed, anxiety-ridden intimacy comes from the reduced perceptions each person has of the other. At the beginning these "projections," as psychologists usually call them, tend to result in overly idealized images of the other person; later, intimate partners are likely to take a paranoid reading of the other's motives and dwell on the worst episodes in their history together, which exacerbates their freezing each other into negative snapshots. Franklin considers Vera a hysterical, nagging child, she sees him as a self-centered tyrant, and neither can get out from under these definitions, for every move one or the other makes can be bent to fit the mold.

Thus the interplay of contact and withdrawal in anxious unions gradually becomes more and more lopsided and stuck in that position. Polarizations into complementary yet adversarial stereotypes, like Franklin's and Vera's views of each other, acquire an inexorable quality. It's as if two people's personal attributes and basic needs have been put through a grinder. Then they are redistributed in a mutually exclusive fashion between them.

In therapy, for example, you often find that one spouse makes impassioned speeches to save the marriage at all costs, while the other twists and turns as though craning his or her neck to spot the exit at a boring lecture. And that is only one way in which their relationship has tilted unevenly on its foundations. The psychotherapist who works with couples spends a great deal of time helping them sift through asymmetrical patterns of behavior and communication. One loves too much; the other not enough. One wants sex;

the other doesn't. One keeps talking; the other falls silent. One is angry; the other afraid. Or both are furious, but they express it differently: One of them throws tantrums, while the other sulks. One dominates and the other submits or resists, as though the marriage is a miniature dictatorship.

Such growing oppositions, which intensify and harden over time, reflect not only how abandonment or engulfment anxiety distributes itself between intimate partners but how the partners wind up stranded in roles they cannot get beyond, at least not with each other. One of them always seems to be saying, in effect, "It's not enough. I feel neglected. We don't enjoy doing things together the way we used to. We hardly ever make love any more. You have to give more of yourself to this relationship if it's going to work." The other one inevitably replies in various ways, "It's too much. I need room to breathe. I have to find myself, and if you really cared about me, you'd let me do it. How can I feel anything positive with you on my back demanding love all the time?" Such exchanges are what you might call the dialectic of modern anxious love. An intriguing feature of this dialectic is that the two partners sometimes reverse roles and waltz the other way around; but they have an enormously difficult time getting unstuck from the poles.

Intimacy can flourish only when it recognizes that *both* individuals have fundamental needs for both autonomy and intimacy. In a troubled relationship, the mates square off like two armies, one bearing a standard on which is emblazoned the letters "we," the other, with equal militance, waving the letter "I." In the past, the source of opposition seemed clear: "We" was the badge of the feminine, and "I" of the masculine. Abandonment was essentially a female anxiety, whereas males feared engulfment. Our tradition of individualism and self-reliance was an ideology for American masculinity. Men rode off into the sunset, after conquest in episodes of sex or aggression; women were ranchers' doe-eyed daughters who tried to seduce these wandering men into domesticity. Men piloted the nation down its course of industrial and commercial progress; women baked, changed diapers, and nagged. Men were powerful; women were needy.

Not that men regarded women as simply unnecessary beyond an

overnight escapade, as cowboy versions of the myth often implied, including updated ones with heroes such as Chuck Norris, Sylvester Stallone, or Arnold Schwarzenegger dressed in inner-city costumes and bearing high-tech weapons. "There is nothing you can name / That is anything like a dame," sang the chorus of randy sailors in *South Pacific,* giving voice to an almost unsublimated depiction of how women come to be perceived as ideal objects. But however desirable, women were the "helpless sex," the keepers of the hearth or, at best, the powers behind (or, more accurately, under) the throne.

Cultural forces have been breaking up this set of myths and the values that they embody at an extraordinary rate, the consequence of a shift that represents one of the most revolutionary transformations that American society has gone through. The doorways have been widened for women to enter social life as full beings—sexually, in careers, in government. The destruction of the old myths is a necessary part of this transformation; but like any revolution, this change has also produced a great deal of floundering and perplexity in our arrangements for intimacy.

In fact, no society carries on very long without evolving myths about the nature of man and woman. Even as the traditional ones are being dismantled and fought over in our society, new ones are already beginning to take shape. What they demonstrate is that we are by no means succeeding in eliminating the tangled issues of anxiety and power in intimate relations, even though the choreography may look very different. The battle of the sexes rages on, with a tougher, more explicitly independent breed of women on the offensive and men who are scattered in postures of retreat, defense, and remobilization. Unfortunately, a growing number of these men are resorting to desperate measures, which accounts in large part for the spread of domestic violence.

If anything, the battle of the sexes is increasing in intensity, and the warriors are pitching their camps in new territory. In some circles it looks like hand-to-hand combat between Iron John and a Woman Who Runs with Wolves, two new archetypes. The trouble with archetypes is that they readily devolve into boring stereotypes

once again, which doesn't leave us a great deal better off than we
were.

On a more concrete level, the male and female troops are emerging from behind the barricades of private residences to slug it out in
the middle of our public life—in congressional hearing chambers, in
criminal and divorce courts, on TV talk shows. The quarrel between Anita Hill and Clarence Thomas, for example, elevated the
battle of the sexes onto the stage of national politics, where it may
remain for quite some time. It has already altered the ground of
American political debates in certain important respects, perhaps
forever: Having injected politics into sex, women are now turning it
around to make sexual harassment a telling issue in elections and
political appointments.

Thus an old historical pattern found at virtually every level of
human social organization is borne out in the contemporary battle
of the sexes. We don't seem to move forward through time from
war to peace so much as from less effective to more devastating
weapons of war. From the news, it appears that weapons capable of
inflicting damage on a wider scale in the battle of the sexes are
becoming standard issue: sexual abuse, sexual harassment, mostly
aimed at women by men, and their counterparts, charges of abuse or
harassment, mostly aimed at men by women. I will take up the
immense implications of this development for our society and our
intimacies in Chapter 7.

The view that anxiety creates pathological entanglements of love
and power and leads to a battle of the sexes can help us reinterpret
some ancient questions: Why is the pursuit of love so inherently
difficult and bewildering? After the wonderful prospects at the outset of a relationship, why so frequently the downward drift into a
togetherness which is at best poignant and full of loss, or at worst
malevolent and tormenting? Why do two people who once
dreamed their dreams together become intent on killing each
other's dreams, hopes, and aspirations—why, if I may put it in my
terms, the passage from romance to intimate terrorism, from the
sweet taste of a couple's original passion to a passionate negation of

each other? Short of sainthood and other enlightened states, there is no love worth anything that is free of potentially virulent anxieties—and this is what strews the path of erotic intimacy with so many dangerous obstructions.

In intimate relations between men and women, the unhappy, polarizing facets of their movements toward and away from each other often grow stronger as they build a history together. Sometimes it seems that there is almost too much at stake: Men and women approach each other with powerful residual childhood anxieties in tow; and in Western civilization, if not all civilizations, as a result, the psychological fate of the self gets bound up with sexual love.

When people fear what they need, they become angry both at themselves and at those from whom they seek to get their needs met. Such conflicting feelings, if they are not worked out, leave a deposit of rage, on the surface or buried just out of sight, between close partners. Often you see a man and a woman in an intimate relationship, especially a marriage, treat one another with cruelty that they would never consider directing toward anyone who meant less to them. Otto Rank, one of the original and most inventive shapers of psychoanalysis, wrote that "in every more intimate human relation . . . the punishing element is set up in the other spontaneously and unavoidably, and this is what makes the relationship, as a rule, so hard to understand and often impossible to bear."[7]

Rank's diagnosis—especially his parenthetical "as a rule"—seems too jaded and sinister. But weary veterans who have spent a long time waging the battle of the sexes or other intimate wars might look around at the casualties and tend to agree with Rank, even those who understand the important changes brought about by the women's movement. A good friend of mine, a former professor of history and a man with an acute historical sensibility, wondering whether he ought to marry for the third time, put his doubts succinctly: "This is the Age of the Woman," he told me one night in a Cambridge bistro. "They've been fucked over and shit on for so long . . . Now it's their turn. Fair enough! But I can't go through it again—marriage, therapy, divorce." If these are indeed the phases of modern adult life, one can sympathize with his malaise.

Part II

The Culture of
Romance:
Arrested at
Adolescence

3

"I Concentrate on You"*:
A Brief History of
Romantic Love

A s it goes in the family, so it goes in what an individual comes to expect from romantic love. A couple of generations ago, children growing up in a still relatively stable nuclear family were likely to take for granted the assumption that family ties were the primary source of emotional fulfillment. Whether or not this was their actual experience, it was supposed to be, and if you didn't get enough of it, or got the wrong kind, in your first home, you could try for it again in the second one, the one that you made yourself.

As I pointed out in the preceding chapter, young people in the 1950s and early 1960s tended to marry early, just about the time they graduated from high school or college. Once they had thereby settled the emotional question, they could go on to other things, like raising children and getting ahead in careers, presumably with the secure feeling that love and sex would remain gratifyingly in place. In those days, it was not a long journey from the backseat

*Cole Porter.

of a car, where one may have first experimented with satisfying one's burning sexual curiosity, to the altar.

Certain ideal expectations accelerated this passage from sexual longings to marital vows. To the extent that one emerged from childhood feeling disappointed and deprived, the romance of marriage held out a promise of compensation. This is wholly a modern idea, so far as I know. Perhaps people have always looked to marriage to fill their needs for reliable sex, for emotional security, and for some measure of relief from the wear and tear of survival, along with whatever social and economic benefits might accrue from the union. I doubt, however, that anyone before our own era also expected marriage to make up for the pain of history. On the most immediate personal level, this meant that finding the right intimate partner would heal the wounds left over from the struggle of growing up. Marriage would complement one, fill one out, make one whole again. And though few people might have articulated it this way, the dream of a perfect lifelong mate expressed a longing for rescue from contemporary social history—from the loneliness and strain of living in an overwhelming and impersonal technological society.

Such in brief was the shape that the romantic expectation regularly assumed three or four decades ago. It had a certain expedient charm, but in retrospect, looking back from the age of divorce and remarriage, it now seems pretty naive. A few years ago, I went to my thirtieth college reunion. A small though still athletic-looking man, an old college chum as it turned out, somehow recognized me at one of the cocktail parties and approached with a woman in tow. "I'd like you to meet my wife, Angela," he said, and then added with a shamefaced grin, "Whoops, Angela was my first wife. I'd like you to meet my second wife, Marjorie." He had also probably forgotten that Angela was a girl I had known slightly thirty years earlier, our mutual classmate. Perhaps she was also at the crowded reunion, but I decided that enough was enough and didn't inquire any further at that particular moment. Marjorie, however, was a social worker, and she handled the awkward episode with a winsome therapeutic smile that put us all at ease.

The point is that this generation's romantic experience, whatever its childhood experience, did not bear out the notion that the emotional fulfillment we had hoped to derive from married intimacy was so easily achieved as most of us had led ourselves to believe. Now in our middle age, about half of us already had divorces trailing behind us, and a large portion of those who had divorced, like my college friend, had also remarried. Some had completed this cycle more than once. Another portion made up the vanguard of that rapidly growing segment of the population who constitute, alone or with their children, households headed by singles.

Moreover, in the years between whatever one's current status might be and those wistful late spring weddings where one barely had time to shed a cap and gown before donning a tux or white veils, sexual mores had changed radically. Almost everyone had moved on from the backseat of the car parked at the drive-in movie or along the shoulder of a country road into any number of bedrooms with any number of sexual partners, sexual positions, living arrangements, and other assorted intimate choreographies. Some of these new possibilities would have been, if not quite inconceivable, little more than adolescent fantasies to most of my college generation, other than the boldest or most bohemian among us.

Hollywood announced its view of the change from the fifties to the sixties in the closing scene of Mike Nichols's 1967 film *The Graduate,* where a genteel end-of-college wedding ceremony is brutally shattered by the bride's rejected suitor. He is a disgruntled, vulnerable young man, just out of college, who finds himself in a lonely rebellion against the norms of his parents' upper-middle-class life. When his girlfriend discovers her mother had seduced him, she walks out on him and decides to marry a more conforming specimen. He becomes frantic. In his eyes, winning back her love takes on an existential aspect: It comes to constitute the entire meaning of his otherwise alienated life. As she and the nondescript groom stand before the altar, our hero bursts in and breaks up the wedding just before she says "I do." She runs to him as he physically fends off the wedding party including her furious parents, and the two of them, looking as though they had pulled off a magnificent prank, dash from the church to a bus, which carts them off to some unspecified destination and equally unspecified destiny.

Apparently his wild display in the church had persuaded her on the spot that so desperate a love is worth more than a conventional marriage. They now have each other, but what else? The bus, in effect, runs smack up against the wall of modern intimacy, where passion has become disconnected from, even opposed to, convention and community.

In *The Pursuit of Loneliness,* Philip Slater points out that the ending of this film represents the new triumph of personal feeling over social decorum and ritual, which of course was precisely what the cultural revolution during the 1960s was all about.[1] *The Graduate* by no means overturned romantic love, however; it merely weakened the ties of romance to marriage, reestablishing in a new way the ancient link between romantic love and rebellion. In earlier eras this had almost always led to tragedy; in *The Graduate* it merely becomes uncertain.

The myth of romantic love, which still held my generation spellbound and hugely influenced what we hoped to gain from marriage, had a venerable history that stretched all the way back to twelfth-century Europe. In its remote medieval origins, it had nothing whatsoever to do with an enterprise that society took so seriously as two people marrying, a crucial socioeconomic decision that entire families participated in. On the contrary, it began among the aristocracy as a kind of spiritual recreation, an idealized form of adultery, which acquired mystical overtones, evolved a highly civilized moral code called chivalry, and flowered into the production of enduring works of art and literature.

Not until much later, with the rise of a bourgeois middle class, engaged in industry, commerce, and the professions, did romantic love become a prominent basis for two people on their own to make an internal, emotional decision to marry. Here was a stroke of cultural genius on the part of the rising business-oriented middle class—this bending of a starry-eyed aristocratic ideal, in its origins hardly congruent with marital vows, into the ideological and emotional glue to hold a man and a woman in the embrace of a lifelong, officially monogamous marriage. It helped create and sustain small,

enduring family units suited to the requirements of increasingly cen-
tralized production and consumption. The historian E. P. Thompson has proposed that the aristocracy in pre-industrial times considered society a stage upon which it could carry out a theatrical display
of class dominance.[2] Intimacy, whatever else it was, was partly art
and theater. In industrial bourgeois society, however, intimacy becomes a necessity of life, a survival mechanism for the middle class as
it retreats into relatively isolated domestic units.

Since medieval courtly love was strongly encouraged—one
might go so far as to say that it was partly created—by the troubadour poets,[3] it might be worthwhile to notice how the reshaping of
romantic ideals for the bourgeois era also turns up early in poetry.
Perhaps because poets are so often occupied with celebrating or re-
gretting love, they tend to anticipate the cultural changes that influence erotic life. One of the earliest applications of chivalric conventions to marriage with which I am familiar appears toward the end of
the sixteenth century in the Elizabethan poet Edmund Spenser's
two long poems in honor of weddings—his *Epithalamion* (concerning his own courtship and marriage), and the *Prothalamion* (written
for the double wedding of the Earl of Worcester's daughters). These
poems still concern aristocratic doings, but Spenser adds a new twist
by drawing on the language of courtly love to praise upper-class
marriages rather than adulterous affairs.

Some of the comedies by Spenser's contemporary, Shakespeare,
also use imagery from the courtly tradition, although frequently
with satirical flavor, to celebrate love between a bride and groom.
By the late seventeenth century, the idea of romantic marriage is
fairly well established. Milton's *Paradise Lost,* apart from its depiction
of cosmic struggle between good and evil, is a tale of a romance
between a young man and woman who marry and proceed to
wreck their chances to continue living in the best neighborhood by
aspiring too greedily to upward mobility. By the end of the poem,
order is restored: Things are relatively quiet again in heaven and
hell, and our original parents have become a solid bourgeois couple
who settle down to a realistic domestic life of hard work, limitations,
and challenges to be met.

During the past couple of centuries, romantic love, no doubt al-

ways a deep inner impulse, now stripped of its aristocratic playfulness, became more purely a deep inner impulse. It then went on to
wage psychological and social warfare against older, more objective
reasons for marrying. Conjugal unions used to be arranged between
appropriate candidates by their families, at least in the well-to-do
classes, in order to combine households and make sure that the
wealth didn't slip through leaks in the class structure. By the nineteenth century, as business and manufacturing became the dominant
modes of production, this emphasis became somewhat less important. It has never completely vanished from parental and social concerns, however, especially among the wealthy, and the continuing
conflict between romance and social class as motives for selecting a
mate animates novels from Jane Austen to the Victorians. To the
extent that society succeeded in domesticating romantic love, keeping it within bounds through sexual taboos, perhaps parents felt that
they no longer had to intervene directly in mate selection; they
could begin to trust their heirs to fall in love with appropriate candidates and thus preserve the lineaments of social class. But like certain
breeds of dogs who behave as household pets for a while and then
suddenly turn on their masters, romantic love could never be completely tamed, a fact which will forever give it a leading role in
stories of both accommodation and rebellion, comedies and tragedies.

For generations of Americans during the first half of the twentieth
century, romantic love remained perhaps our most fervent secular
ideal, the one closest to our souls, capable of bringing us our sweet-
est joys as well as our deepest emotional pain. Its centrality in our
social life was supported at every level of culture—from the highest
to the lowest—from poetry and novels, which tended to treat it as a
blend of paradise and catastrophe, to the happy endings of Broadway
musicals and Hollywood movies, and on down to the cheap thrills
and dreads offered by soap operas and popular adolescent magazines
such as *True Confessions*.

Whatever turbulence of the soul romantic longings might engen-
der in adolescents and, perhaps one should add, in neurotics (which
is how those who repeatedly failed at love and marriage used to be

characterized), young people thought that the volatility would be laid to rest once one crossed paths under the stars with the right person of the opposite sex. But these visions of a peaceful and happy culmination in marriage are doubly threatened nowadays—both by the disappointments inherent in marriage itself and by the widening circle of sexual alliances outside marriage.

In our day, romantic love begins to seem rather incongruously nostalgic, like antique furnishings in an ultra-modern house. And though people will never stop falling in love, by now the romantic ideal, when used to explain our most private dreams to ourselves, looks as threadbare as a gorgeous Oriental rug worn to the nub, perhaps through too much coming and going in the foyers of intimacy. Nevertheless, its luster has by no means entirely disappeared, no matter how cynical our culture has grown. There is too much history at stake: Too much energy and grief have been expended by individual dreamers as well as the collective imagination on all that striving for the deepest and most mysterious of human connections. Romantic love still seems to haunt even the most lapsed of romantics among us, and we still struggle mightily with our disappointment over how it has failed us.

There are even signs of its return—antiques go in and out of fashion, after all—in the popularity of a movie like *Sleepless in Seattle,* or in the astonishing sales of a badly written, old-fashioned romantic potboiler, *The Bridges of Madison County.* Perhaps such recurrences are just another instance of our popular craving for the recently buried past—the lost frontier reappears as a theme park that looks like a set from *High Noon;* a group of promoters manages to crank up a sequel to Woodstock. This is a fashionable cultural tic that is as close as most Americans come to a respect for history. But it's also the case that we have yet to come up with a better way than romantic love to address certain spiritual needs for a sense of deep connection and belonging.

If so, the return of romantic love, at least in the form in which we used to yearn for it and apply it to our intimacies, resembles a deposed ruler returning from exile to a nation engaged in bloody civil war. Once a hope for rescue from the indifference or hostility of an impersonal modern society, the romantic ideal at present is hardly more than a tiny rowboat afloat on waters so storm-tossed and shark-infested that they make Matthew Arnold's imploring call in "Dover Beach" for love to stave off the ignorant armies clashing by night seem like trying to hold off a holocaust with a flashlight.

Of course we will always search for love; virtually all humans do. Why then do many of us start battering our closest relationships to pieces soon after we have formed them? The more monumental the hopes from love, the more devastating the fall into disappointment. With many marriages shattered by bitter, irreconcilable quarrels in which husbands and wives make continual raids on one another's character, it's no wonder that we are often left with two disturbing outcomes: Either the war gradually attentuates into a standoff, and the relationship, drained of vitality and meaning, continues to exist in a sullen climate of alienation and chronic discontent, or the two spouses head for the courts to redeploy their troops for the battle over a property settlement and visitation rights.

Thus the prevalence of intimate terrorism in our personal lives is grimly writ large in the surrounding society. The old sequence— falling in love culminating in a wedding followed by a secure life in the nuclear family—has been fatally disrupted, like the wedding in *The Graduate*. Just as the decline of romance has left us feeling abandoned with nothing much to substitute for it, the belief that the nuclear family would constitute the primary, if not the sole, source of an individual's emotional nourishment from enduring intimate contact has failed us also. The changing fortunes of one have gone hand in hand with those of the other.

Historians and social scientists generally agree that the Industrial Revolution brought about a major shift in the functions of marriage and the family. Before factories and corporations, getting married was considerably more than a way to meet people's needs for sex, security, and raising children in a warm and protective atmosphere. Besides running a household, the family tilled the fields, ran a shop, or plied some other trade at home, and it carried out a broad range of other social responsibilities. An American historian, John Demos, tells us that a typical family in seventeenth-century Plymouth Colony served as a vocational school training the young for occupations, as a church that held prayer sessions and gave Bible instruction, and as a hospital and welfare agency that ministered to the sick and often took in orphans and the poor.[4]

For all this apparent self-sufficiency, the early American family was also tied organically to the larger community. Even its emotional life was not wholly private and sealed off. Since the family produced so many goods and services, the surrounding society had a large stake in making sure that relations among family members ran smoothly. It would often intervene directly when they did not. Demos points to cases where the governor of the province sent in a mediator to straighten out serious discord between husband and wife.[5]

In the eighteenth and nineteenth centuries, both the family's responsibilities and the immediacy of its links to the social order were diminished. Of course this happened gradually and unevenly; even today in rural farming towns, there are still continuities with an earlier way of life. In such towns you can find families that combine relatively self-sufficient economic production with close-knit involvement in the community. But the drift of people and jobs away from the home, as well as the withdrawal of the household itself from society, has been the remarkable fact during the last two centuries. As the texture of urban life thickened, it became more efficient to create special institutions—public schools, state welfare agencies, large teaching hospitals, and so on—to take over jobs the family used to perform.[6]

In general, the space between the management of society and the family's private life widened as industrialization and urbanization progressed. Whatever the gains, there has also been well over a hundred years of protest and lamentation about the loss of community that these changes incurred. One major consequence is that the family curved in on itself: Close feelings between members of a family took on a new, urgent importance. In a study of the middle-class family in late-nineteenth-century Chicago, Richard Sennett has documented how a growing unease with the city and with work led people to begin spending nearly all their leisure time at home. Sennett calls this phenomenon "the evolution of family intensity." The individual's experience, once shaped by the diverse worlds of the city, he points out, has been replaced by "an overwhelming sense of intimacy within the house."[7]

If there was a sour-grapes attitude in this turning away from the life of the city one lived and worked in, behind it lay fear—a darkening sense of personal dislocation. Society no longer cuddled the family in its lap, so the family fled behind closed doors and became increasingly dependent on its own internal emotional resources.

This is one of the special burdens that the contemporary family has to bear. On the one hand, it is supposed to fill everybody's need for nourishing intimate contact. On the other hand, the family has come to exist in a social vacuum, compared to what was available in the past. Families are much more fragile entities than they used to be and are all the less able to carry the additional psychological load imposed on them.

This historical sketch is not a nostalgic plea to return to things as they were. It is tempting to edit a lot of unpleasantness out of our posters of earlier times: the fireside Bible reading; the artisan crafting a masterpiece of cabinetry aided by sons and apprentices eager to learn the trade; the farmer guiding his plowhorse at sunrise, while his wife churns butter in the pantry. These are images of stability— but it must have been a grim stability much of the time, bogged down in drudgery, intolerance, and sheer struggle for survival. I am by no means advocating a return to some pre-industrial bucolic way of life as the solution to our current marital plight.

It is important, however, to understand the unsettling long-term effects of the shocks which industrialism delivered to love and marriage. Relations between men and women in the past may have been overloaded with obligation and practicality. But they were also strengthened by bonds more durable than love by itself can forge. Such bonds fortified the erotic connection because they gave it purposes beyond itself. A man and a woman used to make love in a cosmos filled with widely shared communal and religious beliefs.

Now they make love only in a bed, to which they bring all their anxieties and dreams. That can be a fulfilling experience for a time, but it's still not enough to sustain a lasting intimacy. It's like being shipwrecked together on an uninhabited island, a good place to visit for a Hollywood romantic idyll, but would you want to live there? As the French writer and filmmaker Jean Cocteau once remarked about an acquaintance, "He doubled his loneliness by marrying."

Given the progressive thinning out of social roles both within the family and outside its confines, the intimacy between husband and wife became charged with too much undirected energy as well as too much dependence on one another. Both individual needs and changing social forces encourage this tendency to take root in each other. Then the emotional give-and-take between mates, already swollen with too many demands, gets further bloated by a self-conscious fear of failure or loss. What disappears is much of the natural, spontaneous affectionate connection between people that flows from their working together with a joint sense of responsibility not only for each other and their children, but toward a whole communal network of important relationships.

Such conspicuous consumption of intimacy is a poignant spectacle, at once tender and grotesque. What heroic performances the partners in a couple must feel they have to turn in! They have to be sexual athletes, parents to the child in each other, perfect friends, therapists to one another's symptoms. Carried to this extreme, the romance of marriage becomes a mode of salvation, almost a substitute for traditional religion. No relationship can carry so profound a burden. Couples who need so much from each other are bound to go under, uttering bitter cries of accusation at one another as things fall apart.

Before the nineteenth century, larger-than-life intimacies were not a common expectation; they existed mainly in literature and myth. Antony and Cleopatra, Tristan and Iseult, Héloïse and Abélard, Romeo and Juliet are among the best-known examples. Their grand obsessive passions for each other clashed dangerously with social obligations. For those famous pairs of lovers, too much absorption in one other person led away from society and into catas-

trophe. The stalemate produced by conflict between individual fulfillment and social norms was far too much of a mess to be cleaned
up by anything less than the lovers' deaths. It certainly didn't lead to
successful marriages.

If you listened to a group of hippies in the 1960s gossiping about
love, you might have overheard one tell the others, "Me and my old
man [or old woman] are real tight." The implication was that things
were okay on the sexual front. At the same time, this idiom made a
sardonic comment on our tendency to value overly intense, overly
dependent intimacy. "Old man" or "old woman" suggests that
one's intimate partner is like a parent, and the idea that feeling close
to someone is a kind of tightness is amusingly ambiguous, given the
live-and-let-live flavor of the whole hippie enterprise. "Tight" suggests closeness, but it can also mean tension, lack of breathing room,
insufficient slack around which to maneuver freely.

In the 1990s, we are more apt to call the experience of intimacy
"sharing," a sentimental word we usually utter in a sanctimonious
tone of voice, as though it enunciates a self-evident moral good. It
seems to me, though, that its goodness depends on what's being
shared. (The next time an acquaintance tells me that he is going to
"share" his anger with me, I think I will terminate the conversation
on the spot.) If the expression from the sixties hints at a child de-
scribing its relationship to a parent, this one smacks of parental in-
junctions against sibling rivalry, as when parents tell one child racing
another to the last piece of cake, "Now remember you have to share
everything, dear!"

Both expressions, although they reflect different cultural tonali-
ties some twenty-five years apart, imply a claustrophobic, overheated sense of intimacy, along with a considerable confusion of
roles from both adult life and childhood. At least there is an element
of parody in being "real tight"; the piety and self-consciousness in
the more current idiom make it the more sinister of the two.

The self-conscious intimacy practiced in many middle-class marriages is particularly lethal. Like doctors examining a patient's blood
pressure, couples check up regularly on the progress of the relationship. ("Relationship" is another word I don't much care for but

haven't been able to find a way around. It's a kind of pseudo-scientific abstraction. When I studied calculus in college, I learned that a relationship is something that holds between two variables that have an effect on one another. That is true of intimacy also, but people are not mathematical variables.) Many a couple's evenings, if they can still speak to one another at all in such a climate, are filled with anguishingly earnest diagnoses of each other's motives. They analyze the relationship as though it ought to be spelled with a capital "R." The poet Thom Gunn characterized this modern tendency in one neat couplet: "Their relationship consisted / In discussing if it existed."[8]

Once they climb in bed, there is apt to be more of the same, perhaps accompanied by massage exercises derived from Masters and Johnson or experiments with new sexual techniques and positions found in Oriental love manuals. I don't mean to dismiss behavioral sexology or Eastern sexual practices out of hand, but when you import them into an atmosphere already close to despair, they mostly add to the forces already turning love into labor. Under such conditions, initiating sex ought to be called "forework," not "foreplay."

The desperation comes from each mate's worry that if sex slacks off into something less than a marvel, the marriage has to be deemed a failure. In fact, under pressure to provide so many levels of fulfillment and meaning, modern marriages can hardly brook any disappointment without giving rise to internal feelings of failure. Feelings of that sort are not easy to tolerate by keeping them inside, so one way people try to relieve them is through persecuting the other partner as though the letdown is primarily the other's fault. It's easier to say, in effect, "You're not who I thought you were" than to take responsibility for one's own contributions to the decline. Add to this the tendency to replace diminishing affection with measures of control in order to maintain a facsimile of togetherness, and all the grounds for a campaign of intimate terrorism are established.

Thus we arrive at one of the more frequently traveled courses of contemporary marital collapse. When a husband and wife find themselves at an impasse created by their disappointed expectations, where do they turn? To therapists, a minister, an affair, a career, booze, a suicide attempt? All of these have been tried, of course, sometimes one after another, with varying degrees of success. Turning to parents, relatives, or friends rarely helps very much, because either they feel impelled to choose sides or their own anxieties get entangled in the couple's struggle. What's more, many people feel inhibited from admitting marital failure to their families and friends at the point where they could most use help with the crisis. It makes one wonder what it would be like if, as in the Puritan villages of old, representatives from the larger community were to step in, calm the two down, stress the larger social importance of their well-being, and offer support and help by redirecting the couple's energies away from mutilating each other toward something more cooperative.

When I speak of "community" in this context, however, I mean a good deal more than just bringing a lot of other well-meaning people into the marriage. The idea of community implies an integrated relationship between private life and society, in which there exists an exchange that nourishes both. It might be expressed through vehicles like extended family, close-knit neighborhood, larger social groupings, or even intangible expressions of the social will, such as values and myths, with which the individual or the couple interacts. As things are today, when intimacies get into serious difficulty, the outside world may still be invited in, but usually in the form of "experts" or professionals who supplant old-fashioned help from the natural flow between individuals and community.

Even though two people in a deeply disturbed marriage may act like victims of one another's neurotic manipulations, what history shows is how little help compared with the past they now get from their environment. If our dire marital situation could be explained simply as a lot of neurotic people having libidinal collisions that turn destructive, then the best bet would be to herd them all into mental-health clinics, the therapeutic equivalent of Republican "family values." But when 50 to 60 percent of our marriages break up and many of the rest do not look very promising, then the whole institution is called into question. The sequence of cultural and social developments I've been discussing has undermined its strength. Psychotherapy or counseling—at least as it's currently practiced—in such a predicament can provide little more than a soothing poultice for some individuals. I am not calling for an end to marital therapy any more than I am to marriage, but I do think that it is beyond question, if the quality of intimacy in America is to improve, that we confront the symptoms in the culture, not only in the individual.

Summarizing the evolution of the modern family, the social critic Paul Goodman wrote that "the Family was a bulwark of the private economy, and now it is a refuge from the collective economy."[9] It's as if the family became a refugee camp in an industrial and bureaucratic wasteland, the last resort of intimate connection. The trouble is that a sanctuary to which refugees flock all too easily turns into a ghetto. Besieged from without, ghettos evolve their own internal forms of oppression as well. It is well known that survivors of oppression or disaster often continue to be haunted by fear, guilt, rage, and feelings of impotence. These emotions then get played out in their subsequent social relations.

The romantic conception of marriage as a retreat—a "haven in a heartless world"—still carries some weight in our day, whether the source of heartlessness is perceived as the family one grew up in or an increasingly remote and complex technological society. One wonders, though, if there is anything really left except the residual shell of hope for this haven, which is based on an ideology of compensatory intimacy. The fact is that marriages in the United States, at least since industrialization, have never been calm or static. They have always been buffeted from within as much as from the outside, and the inner turbulence has only worsened.

By now marriage is far too battered and fragmented an institution to serve anyone as an emotional oasis. The marital ghetto is the human equivalent of a balanced aquarium, where the fish and plants manage to live indefinitely off each other's waste products. Intimacy, exiled from the embrace of a surrounding supportive community, feeding on itself, ultimately destroys itself. Humans do not flourish if they end up living off each other's anxiety and desperation.

4

Darwinian Love

I poked my head out of the office one evening and found a young couple holding hands in my waiting room. Since this was my first meeting with them, I hardly knew anything yet about why they wanted to see me, but they looked snug enough at the moment. They couldn't have had more than one or two years of marriage behind them; they were certainly not jaded veterans of countless bitter campaign. My first thought was that maybe they had forged a momentary alliance out of anxiety about what they imagined I might have in store for them. Some people arrive in psychotherapy for the first time as though it were a trip to the dentist, as though I will try to cure some hurting part of them by extracting it. On closer observation, though, I could guess that these two had already lost the ability to derive much contact or comfort from their touching. They held on to each other with stiff wrists, the way one holds the hand of an elderly relative in a hospital bed.

That their fragile, clutching appearance of togetherness concealed more than it revealed—that it was a kind of protest over what was actually going on between them—was soon confirmed by the story they told me. The husband, whom for the sake of convenience I'll call "Seth," was about twenty-five. He told me that he was currently finishing his medical internship in one of Boston's many teaching hospitals. He turned out to be the sort of gaunt, stern man whose romantic perfectionism springs from a lonely childhood. Having given up hope early on in the warmth of secure connections, such people often come to dwell in the stratosphere of a compensatory idealism. From this height they shine down on you with rays that feel like an accusation, as though they already anticipate that you will fail them. There is not a lot of room for error in an intimate relationship with a man like Seth. He could rather easily slide into fanaticism, were it not that he retained a softness and innocence despite his lean features and piercing glance, a boyish appeal that still reached out. He was still looking for love, even if not altogether on this planet.

People who are unsure whether they are worth anything and who thus continually doubt themselves at every turn tend to be attracted to men and women like Seth. These self-doubters frequently choose an intimate partner who has impossibly lofty standards because they need to keep taking a test to prove themselves. Doubting oneself is like being a student with a perpetual incomplete in a course titled "The History of My Feelings about Myself." Such was the case with Deborah, Seth's wife, whose dark hair framed a look of somber, startled thoughtfulness that made me hold my breath a little, as though I had stumbled upon a doe at the edge of the woods. Doubt seemed to leave her permanently poised for flight. She obviously had little problem with academics, however: She held a much-sought-after teaching assistantship in a local graduate department of linguistics.

Like Seth, she was dressed in earthy clothes that gave rise to images of European peasants, the Middle Ages, or the American frontier. In many university towns, the 1960s don't seem to have altogether disappeared, at least as a matter of style, and accordingly, I half-expected to hear that they practiced meditation together in a three-room Cambridge apartment and ate mostly grains and vegetables. Indeed, she was as slim as he was; taken together, they couldn't have totaled more than 240 pounds.

In one respect at least, their situation suggested an enviable simplicity and freedom: They were still a long way from taking on the burden of a large mortgage, the suburban pall, the worry about how soon to tell their kids to use condoms or to avoid the street pharmacists promising them a good time after school. Nevertheless, the pain they were causing each other turned out to be as severe as that among any of the more experienced warriors who enlist me to help them negotiate a cease-fire in their marriages.

Seth and Deborah had discovered one another a couple of years ago in the medical clinic of the university where she was working on her Ph.D. and where he spent two afternoons a week as part of a rotating team of young doctors who served students and faculty. She had come in with some sort of minor infection, and he wrote her a prescription. A spark of mutual recognition had passed between them underneath the usual polite phrases. Over the next two weeks, they went out first to lunch, then to the movies, then cooked their favorite recipes for each other, and in between meals and other entertainments, they went to bed together.

Each saw in the other an alluring reserve, an aloneness that they came to regard as a special quality that set them apart from other people. In their finding one another, it was as if a bolt had quietly slipped into place and enclosed them both in a haven of safety. Within its confines they felt they could surrender to the ideal hopes and longings that each had hidden away from the world till now. At least this is how they described to me their falling in love. In a matter of months, the new lovers decided to get married.

At first things could not have gone better. Their sex was steaming and splendid, affirming their decision in a way that seemed almost too good to be true. Being married made it official that they belonged to each other. They were cramped financially, but that didn't matter; both had the promise of successful careers stretching before them. And in marrying, they had found a way to retreat together into emotional insulation from a larger world that they both considered threatening and depriving.

Alas, it wasn't long before Seth's characteristic mistrust surfaced more and more regularly, and his bouts of criticizing Deborah began to wear on her. He would become coldly distant for no apparent reason or wax indignant over rather trivial differences between them, until she started to feel that she was always skating on thin ice around him. For days on end she couldn't seem to do anything right, as though she were the target of a vague but insatiable demand.

Whereas Deborah at first had felt secure and complete, wrapped in their physical satisfaction and idealized portraits of their future together, she now felt that Seth had demoted her for some crime she couldn't make sense of. Worse, she felt guilty anyway, a guilt to which she was vulnerable from being raised by carping, unhappy parents. She began to withdraw into moods of glazed depression. Seth responded to her growing silences less with concern than anger, apparently finding in them further proof of some unspecified betrayal.

They had contacted me, I learned, because this state of affairs had reached fever pitch. As their arrangement started coming apart, they found themselves with nowhere else to turn. They panicked and grabbed desperately at each other, trying to renew the relationship by forcing things back to the bracing idealism of their courtship. The very tactics of renewal, however, partook of the process that was already well under way: Each blamed the other for ruining the relationship and thus implicitly insisted that the other bear responsibility for fixing it. Even their caresses, once so confirming, now felt labored and mechanical, like their way of holding hands in my waiting room.

What happened to Seth and Deborah is typical of how marriage tends to bring out, sometimes with startling speed, our damaging dependence on how much love is supposed to accomplish. That it can happen so quickly to a young couple, hardly past the first excitements of exploring each other sexually and the adventure of looking forward to making a home together, shows how ill-prepared our society leaves us for absorbing the shocks to one's identity and beliefs that marrying entails.

A gap between appearance and reality that American culture has never closed continually subjects our expectations from intimacy to a potentially disastrous contradiction: We are taught to expect that love is abundant, but in practice we often find that it seems to be in scarce supply. This contradiction has only widened under the impact of the evolving social forces that I sketched in the preceding chapter.

The discovery of scarcity can sneak up on people in a particularly vindictive way after they marry. It mocks their fondest dreams. For what it tells them is that marriage consists of two people trying to make a go of it on emotional and psychological supplies that are only sufficient for one. As a result, they are liable to lapse into a barbaric competition over whose needs get met. The likelihood of this regression increases as marriages and families in America slip further from their moorings in purposeful connections to the larger society. "After all, there was good in the old ways," a forlorn Newland Archer says to himself toward the end of Edith Wharton's *The Age of Innocence,* as he contemplates the array of social duties and obligations one took on by marrying. Without them, he felt that marriage would become "a mere battle of ugly appetites."[1]

Of course, things don't usually start out this way. If the proposition that love is scarce was in the marriage contract, it must have been in the fine print that nobody bothered to read. The official attitudes that propel us toward love, marriage, and family are based on a promise of abundance, though, to be sure, it's an abundance defined within rather narrow limits. We are taught that the family is supposed to fill virtually all our early needs for love, a romance with an enchanting stranger our middle ones, and a family once again our later ones. We are taught that it is better to give than to receive, that when you give, you will get back more than you gave.

As we enter into collective arrangements, including marriage, it is with hope of reciprocity, such that close ties to others will enhance us through a give-and-take that brings out the best in us. In a marriage plagued by emotional famine, however, both people come to feel that the more they give, the more they are asked to give. Then their marriage comes to feel not only like a trap but a bottomless pit.

Our most influential theories of how humans develop in Western cultures have generally followed in Freud's footsteps. With respect to future troubles in adult relationships, Freudian-based theories tell us that the overheated libidinal atmosphere in the family deposits a simmering mixture of dependence on parents along with ambivalent emotional attachments and infantile sexual feelings toward them in the child's psyche, thereby producing inner conflicts that keep replaying themselves in disguised shapes throughout later life. I don't reject this view, but by bringing the issue of scarcity into the foreground, I find myself led away to some extent from Freud toward Darwin, who emphasized a basic *external* conflict—the struggle for survival—that occurs between members of a species whenever there is not enough in the environment to go around. The Darwinian perspective is a useful one for understanding how power functions in intimate relationships, a dimension mostly neglected by Freudians. And it makes clear why our intimacies are driven not so much by the unconscious as by willfulness, unconsciously or not.

Virtually all our theories of human development emphasize the bond between parent and child as the prototype of all later intimacies. There can be little question that this is a fundamental truth, but it's a partial one and susceptible to metaphorical fleshing out. Bringing scarcity to the surface suggests that infants and parents are not the whole story, especially when it comes to intimate power struggles and the anxieties between people that generate them. Darwinian love more nearly resembles sibling rivalry, another among the highly charged and ambivalent attachments within the family.

Indeed, sibling rivalry, even if one thinks of it metaphorically and applies it to such episodes as the tug-of-war between children's needs and needy parents (who can behave in this respect more like children), is the perfect model of a competition for scarce goods, a quarrel over whose emotional and material needs get met. Where there is sibling rivalry, anything one brother or sister gets leaves the others feeling deprived. If one child wants something and gets it, the others raise a fuss whether they want it or not because they feel in danger of being cheated. Then frantic parents respond to the increasing noise level by dividing everything up equally. Herein resides the origin of that dreadful contemporary idiom I mentioned earlier, in which people tell each other things such as "Thank you for sharing your feelings with me," as though genuine communication had taken place. The more people become viciously divided over their differences, the more isolated from each other they feel, the more they use the verb "to share" as a moral demand, disguising unresolved conflict as harmony, power as love. What is a troubled marriage, after all, but a grotesque version of sibling rivalry, in which two grown-up children, now out on their own, try to make each other into a more nurturing parent than the ones they actually had?

An underlying fear of deprivation helps explain why two intimate partners sooner or later are likely to treat their relationship as though it's a version of what social scientists sometimes describe as a "zero-sum game." In the simplest terms, this means that there has to be a winner and a loser, so that when you add up the outcomes, the result balances out to zero. Actually, such a marriage adds up to less than zero. Nobody wins—ultimately there can only be two losers, who wind up drained and diminished by the struggle over whose needs will prevail. An emotional climate of scarcity, perhaps more than any other factor, transforms marriage into an institution in which the whole adds up to less than the sum of its parts.

When two people fall in love, you might think of the event as the restoration of lost abundance. New lovers like Seth and Deborah often experience an unprecedented opening of possibilities, a sense that they have been suddenly blessed with endless reserves to meet each other's emotional requirements. The drama of this experience, which various cultures have compared to everything from divine revelation to psychosis, temporarily overshadows any question about either person's needs being met by the other. If anything, there is a sense of surplus: It's as if each can give all to the other without having to give anything up.

For most of the twentieth century, popular culture—in songs, movies, advertising, and romance novels—has conspired to portray this expansive feeling as paradise regained. Falling in love in a secular age, as I suggested earlier, took on a spiritual dimension: As a substitute for organized religion, it became the last frontier of our remaining hopes for salvation. The promise of paradise was incorporated into the act of marrying as well, through the ritual of the honeymoon, which probably explains why the first phase of married life frequently unfolds in the Caribbean. If the honeymoon is not quite a return to Eden, at least it can be an exotic vacation on a tropical isle, such as Martinique or the Bahamas.

One reason it is so difficult for us to get on in marriage after the honeymoon is that this romantic interlude, often wonderful in itself, partakes too much of our adolescent fantasies with their emphasis on eternal youth. From the images of ourselves reflected back from TV and magazine ads, for example, you would think we are a nation of perfect bodies romping in the surf and then in bed on an endless vacation from the ravages of time. Popular romance in America doesn't culminate in tragedy, as it did for the famous lovers of old, but in the denial of death. And this is only one of the ways in which intimacy in America stalls at adolescence.

Passion tends to cool or get complicated in the routine of domestic life, and when it does, the apprehension that love is scarce and time is passing may begin to darken the mood of a marriage, like storm clouds moving in. Summers eventually come to an end, even in our collective mythologies. The assumption of scarcity contains a self-fulfilling prophecy, because the resulting tension and anxiety that arise between husband and wife do in fact dry up their inventory of desire and support, appreciation and affirmation. At the point where competition over whose needs get met begins, the major issue in marriage becomes the survival of the fittest spouse. The brief marital history of Seth and Deborah is typical of this passage from the romantic model to the sibling-rivalry model of marriage.

As long as love seems plentiful, it's relatively easy to maintain faith in the relationship, even when there are momentary obstructions. During periods of difficult going, two partners can afford to give each other something essential to marital health: They extend to each other the benefit of the doubt, which means that a slight, a moment of forgetfulness, or some other behavior on the part of one that the other perceives as a failing is not automatically attributed to pure self-interest and therefore loss of love. Both still subscribe to the basic legal principle of democracy—innocent until proven guilty. After scarcity, however, intimacy is more like living under a dictatorship. Each assumes the other is guilty, and there is no way back to innocence. Intimacy comes to resemble life as Kafka conceived it—a surreal nightmare, in which one feels tried and judged without knowing exactly why.

The nagging anticipation of being deprived that scarcity breeds uses up all the slack between intimate partners, so that they have great difficulty finding enough breathing room to negotiate their differences or to tolerate periods of unease or conflict. Their treatment of one another inevitably gets aggressive and stingy, each requiring proof of love from the other while withholding declarations of his or her own. Scarcity is an acid that corrodes each partner's trust in the other's motives. It wears away the important belief that the other person has one's best interests at heart. One mate may start to interpret the other's adoring gaze as a pleading or angry stare and look away. Or an embrace may begin to feel too automatic to one, too grasping to the other. These are among the early portents of power struggle and war on the horizon. It probably won't be long before both partners begin overreacting to the slightest tug on the line that binds them together. Is it a distress signal or a hint of impending desertion? Either way, it makes them both anxious, feeling burdened by the other's demands, yet fearful of being left helpless and alone.

By the time a couple comes in for therapy, their days of snorkeling amid waving undersea grasses and exotic fish in the Caribbean are long gone. By now the two are more like deep-sea divers engaged in a difficult salvage operation. They grope toward each other in their bulky, armored suits, as though their oxygen supply is running low.

In the case of a couple like Seth and Deborah, the experience of abundance was particularly short-lived because of their perfectionism. The demand for perfect love can't extend generosity either to another or to oneself. It can't forgive doubt, confusion, or mistakes. In this sense, it is perhaps the purest form of scarcity. Those who drink in too deeply our idealization of achievement, delivered through middle-class parents and schools preparing kids for good colleges, are especially prone to believe that one has to be perfect to be worthy of love. Taken to an extreme, it is a culturally sanctioned message that produces dogmatism, feelings of emptiness or worthlessness, anorexia, and suicide.

Sylvia Plath, who was all too familiar with the curse of perfectionism, wrote a poem that begins "Perfection is terrible, it cannot have children."[2] One can see how perfectionism leads to a dead end in Seth's and Deborah's marriage: To enter into a relationship, he demanded perfect love; anything less constituted an injustice, a cheat or betrayal. And she felt that she had to be flawless before she would even consider herself adequate. Indeed, they were made for each other: a perfect couple in a sense, but perfect with a vengeance.

Thus the downward curve from idealism to disenchantment to despair allows scarcity to invade the life of a couple and wreck their intimacy. But that dreary slide is not the only factor that gives rise to each's fears that his or her needs will go begging, although it almost always plays some role in the proceedings. Here is an example of a marriage derailed by a growing sense of scarcity because two powerful individual wills turn against each other instead of working together.

In their mid-thirties, with six or seven years of marriage behind them, Laurie and Steven are both talented, forceful personalities, both moving ahead in careers, both able to make a splash in their respective worlds. They have a new baby, their first, which thrills them, but it also perplexes them because their careers are so important to them. Their story replicates in miniature our current cultural agony, in which the struggle over sex roles conspires with an entrenched legacy of individualism to make it extremely difficult to come up with inventive compromises for the sake of mutual growth.

Laurie, an unusually tall woman with close-cropped dark hair and a purposeful, almost aristocratic self-assurance that reflects her journey through expensive private schools, is a photographer whose work is highly regarded: She not only gets challenging commercial assignments, but also her more purely aesthetic work has been displayed in important galleries in Boston and New York. Steven is an electronics whiz with a background in both engineering and business administration. Vaguely blond, professorial, and a little overweight, he wears a frown of perpetual concentration. He and his partners have been instrumental in starting up two high-tech companies. Despite the risks such enterprises entail, the first of these, a data communications company, has done quite well, although he subsequently got bored with it and moved on to the second project, which he felt could be successful on an even bigger scale. The new project is in a state of considerable financial instability at the moment, and this is adding to the mounting friction between him and Laurie.

They met through mutual friends. What drew them to each other was their perception of each other's vitality and their common hunger for an adventurous life. Both came from well-to-do backgrounds, a circumstance which certainly helps pave the way for taking risks but also frequently means growing up under the rule of strong-willed parents. Like many people who possess high energy and whose native talents have been developed and affirmed in their youth, they are both aggressive, emotionally volatile, and quick on the draw. All these qualities fired their attraction to each other. Unfortunately, the same qualities now raise the temperature of their quarrels just as rapidly and intensely.

To take a typical scene: They came charging into my office one afternoon, her face still flushed with recent tears, his jaw clamped in the grimace of barely suppressed outrage. She had driven downtown, she explains (he is still utterly silent at this point), to pick him up at his office. On the way to the therapy session a fight broke out over directions. "Why are you following that truck?" he had yelled. "Turn left!" She replied that she had no interest in the truck, that she knew perfectly well when to turn left, and that he was yelling at her just to be deliberately mean. From this seemingly minor altercation over who is the most capable and in control, the firefight now spreads quickly to cover more and more ground: "He is always nasty to me when he is upset about work," she says to me. "Just like his father," she adds, delivering the clincher.

Steven begins gesticulating as her account proceeds; he wants the floor now. She looks at him menacingly as if to say, "Let me finish!"—they are always interrupting each other—but he counters her last blow with a lengthy, biting speech about her habit (as he sees it) of relieving her underlying unhappiness through swearing at both him and his family. Of course, he is able to draw on her use of his father—a sensitive subject—for immediate empirical evidence.

"When it comes to being mean, you are hard to beat," he informs her. The real issue behind their fights, according to Steven, is money, because she expects to continue living like a princess as she did growing up spoiled under the wing of her all-providing father. He is sure that this is why she is constantly on his back insisting that he get a steady job instead of embarking on speculative ventures.

"Nothing could be further from what I want to do," Steven states emphatically, "nor does she give me any credit for what I do best." Hasn't he always taken good care of her, their child, and their home? Part of the trouble, he continues, is that "she can't stand staying at home with the baby" and leaves the house all day, so that they have to shell out huge amounts for a full-time babysitter. Thus he returns her insult tit for tat by slipping in the intimation that she is a lousy mother. She bursts into tears.

I don't know who actually initiated this particular squabble, but if I tried to find out, it would end up in an infinite regress, and it doesn't really matter anyway. They are both enormously provocative and provokable, both theatrical by temperament, and both into overdramatizing being the victim of the other's foul play. Sometimes I am not sure whether such couples expect me to behave more like a trial judge, who is supposed to weigh the evidence and render a verdict, or a drama critic, applauding the best production. Neither role has anything to do with what this couple needs, however, which is help in understanding and gaining control over their hair-trigger defensive reactions to one another. These stem in large part from outdated expectations they imported into the marriage, so that by now each of them fastens automatically on the slightest sign of a negative comment from the other and responds in kind. Patterns like this cripple a couple's ability to negotiate basic questions about what they really need from each other. You often have to teach them to slow down and read between the lines, because the transition from a felt need to blaming the other person has become so instantaneous.

For instance, images of ghostly fathers, who had richly upholstered the domestic world of the past for dependent women, are very much involved in Laurie's and Steven's battle, driving them like two suburban Hamlets bent on revenge. They have reached an impasse in a contract dispute about male and female identities, and given their backgrounds, each of them has guilty, ambivalent feelings about changes that they are being compelled to face. In this respect, their personal tumult also reflects the cultural rumblings that surround them on all sides. Clearly the understandings and expectations each brought from their respective homes are no longer serviceable for a high-powered professional couple who need to work out a more flexible division of labor around commitments at home and at work. However, their current attempts to settle their differences have all the sophistication of a schoolyard brawl; their pop-psychoanalytic interpretations of each other's motives are tantamount to two kids who try to one-up each other by yelling " . . . and so's yer father!"

When it comes to ammunition, Steven and Laurie are truly a match for one another. Through the intimate knowledge each has gained about the other in the course of living together, they have become equal masters of going for each other's jugular. Each can demolish the other by hurling shorthand epithets like curses that condense a history of ill treatment at the hands of the other into a word or phrase. At one point, Laurie refers to Steven's "hybrid tulip schemes," a code phrase that he takes to mean that he is a hare-brained dreamer and a jerk when it comes to business and finance. Thus she expresses her insecurity and anxiety, not by enlisting his concern, but by dropping bombs on his character.

He, in turn, tries to make her feel lousy about both her maternal role and her photography when he puts it across in the space of two sentences that her demands are cheating him of his destiny and that her going off to shoot pictures is an outright abandonment of her baby and her household duties. (There is not even a ripple of suggestion, of course, that he might free her a little by assuming some of the child care or domestic chores himself. His attitude makes it clear that his mind is far too occupied with more important matters.)

They also, by the way, care quite deeply about one another and have every intention of staying together, though you might not notice it in what I have depicted thus far. The pity of their predicament is in the huge waste—"the expense of spirit in a waste of shame," as Shakespeare wrote—caused by the deployment of their psychological resources for attack and self-defense rather than for teaming up to invent new forms of support for one another. As in any war effort, the powers each possesses are aimed at destroying the other party to the conflict. But this is exactly the kind of spiritual drain that the scarcity premise leads to in marriage.

The pressing issue for Laurie and Steven, in fact, is not money, despite Steven's claim. They have always succeeded in bringing home more than enough between them, though neither has a fixed salary. Moreover, it turns out that there are family trust funds hovering in the wings for later security. Fights over money can be a screen or metaphor for doubts about love, especially when the warriors come from backgrounds where love was often paid out in dollars.

Indeed, conflicts can slip back and forth between issues involving income and love so rapidly in the scarcity economy of marriage that sometimes it's difficult for one mate to tell which one the other is talking about, a translation problem that leads to complicated misunderstandings. I recall another young couple that I saw—the wife was a business executive, and the husband taught in a community college—who recounted an after-dinner skirmish, which began as an episode in their ongoing debate about buying a house and ended with threats to separate. Why hadn't he bothered to call the brokers, the banks, etc., she asked him, was he going to leave all the work to her? He had more free time during the middle of the day, she reminded him. He took this to mean that she believes that he doesn't work hard enough because she contributes the larger portion to their income. Growing angry and defensive, he pointed out that he worked equally hard at a job that by its nature pays less.

Apparently what she was looking for was reassurance about their intimacy in the idea that they were truly teaming up to buy a house together—because once she sensed his anger, she went up to him and asked him for a hug. He remained stiff as a board. Confirmed in her fears, she felt vulnerable, rejected, and joined him in becoming angry and defensive. You can imagine how things continued from that point forward.

When I ask Steven and Laurie what one thing each most wants from the other person—I do this because they are so busy not only trading insults but also tossing a dozen related issues in each other's face at the same time, which makes resolution of any one thing impossible—both of them give essentially the same answer: They each want the other to take some responsibility for the viciousness in the relationship, instead of playing the innocent victim. But even more than that, each wants to feel that he or she is still a freely developing human being and a worthwhile one in the other person's eyes. Their quarrel over who is in charge of turning left expresses the desire to be perceived as competent and in control. On some level, they are both aware that they have a need in common for empathic and appreciative affirmation from each other. Without this, they will not be able to get on with balancing the diverse and complex concerns involved in building an intimate home environment, caring for a child, and supporting each other's professional ambitions.

Instead, Steven and Laurie have succeeded in locking each other into increasingly polarized roles, a characteristic pattern in intimate power struggles that I discussed in the first two chapters. It's a pattern that develops hand in hand with the assumption of scarce love. When intimate partners assign one another fixed roles, whether they be masculine or feminine, breadwinner or nurturer, lord of the creative self or keeper of domestic togetherness, they tighten the emotional purse strings in their relationship because both people feel personally diminished and cut off from experimenting with a range of possibilities in life.

Abundant love seems natural enough in human relations. In the normal course of things, for example, when an infant cries and a parent hears the cry, they are drawn toward one another like complementary parts of nature coming together. To some degree, all social existence, from the familial to the erotic to the political, is a hopeful elaboration of this natural magnetism between need and response. But if any social arrangement is going to flourish, there has to be enough to go around for everybody—or at least a system of economic and psychological compromises over how to divide up what is available.

In fact, many psychological complications can intervene between the child's need and the parents' response, frequently because the parents themselves are still smarting from insults and injuries they received as children at the hands of their parents. Residual wounds from their own childhoods may leave adults too preoccupied with their own needs and anxieties to be anything but distantly available to a child. In this way scarcity trickles down from generation to generation. When it does, children often absorb a mixed message: On one level, they might still dream that an unselfish mutual love holds out the greatest promise of fulfillment. On another, their experience growing up may be seriously, even profoundly, at odds with that notion.

Whatever they are told, children also discover for themselves that love is an uncertain commodity, hard to come by and even harder to hold on to. Since they are dependent for a longer time than any other species on fully grown caretakers, they have little choice but to remain emotionally attached to their parents, whether those two particular adults are capable of providing anything nurturing or not. Psychotherapists have long been aware that children are apt to equate whatever attention they get from their parents, no matter how painful, with love, if it is all that they can manage to get. Many children in this circumstance turn to tantrums, brutalizing their brothers and sisters, and other kinds of clamoring behavior, ranging from the merely noisy to the self-destructive, from failing in school to criminal acts, in order to attract *some* form of attention. For the rest of their lives, such children are likely to seek out similar forms of misery, still thinking that it is love.

The mixed message is not just an accident of children's innocence colliding with the wall of adult neurosis. It's deeply embedded in our social habits. Love and control are linked in America nearly from the beginning of an individual's development. We may preach that love is plentiful, but we use the principle of love's scarcity with considerable effectiveness to shape our children into good citizens. No doubt there are parents who give positive regard without strings attached, but in general our method of socializing children depends on bestowing love and approval for good behavior and socially sanctioned achievement. A common form of discipline is to withhold love, or at least appear to withhold it, when a child disobeys or fails to measure up to expectations. And although emotional rewards and punishments may proceed in an orderly fashion in many families, so that the children at least have a fairly clear idea about what makes them lovable and what doesn't, just as often they are distributed whimsically depending on the parents' mood.

Thus the traditional nuclear family and the values that support it offer a potentially unstable and confusing supply of nourishing emotional resources: They have to be won and they can just as easily be lost, sometimes for no apparent good reason. Some children fight for them, cling to them, hoard them when they get them. Some force themselves into ill-fitting postures of artificial obedience in the hope of obtaining more of them. Another common strategy children stumble upon, especially the more rebellious ones, is to learn to deny that they even need them.

The psychiatrist and developmental theorist Harry Stack Sullivan, who had an extraordinarily sensitive attunement to the currents of American family life, considered anxiety the motor of socialization, pointing out that anxiety is "utilized by all cultures, by some a little and by some a great deal, in training the human animal to become a person."[3] I don't know if it's true of all cultures, but it is certainly the case in ours that we commonly train children to become proper adults through teaching them that love is scarce, precarious, and closely associated with the deployment of power. One side effect of our childrearing is that many people grow up with what looks like an untenable choice no matter which way they turn: either loss of love or loss of self through being controlled by love. These threats hang like twin swords over the heads of children, fortifying the anxieties that can wreak havoc in their later intimate relationships.

The mingling of our two major myths of intimacy—the ideology of family emotional intensity with the ideal of romantic love—not only shields Americans from the perception that love is scarce, but it also leaves us relatively helpless to deal effectively with the embattled consequences of that perception by disguising power as love. Americans have historically treated "power" as though it were a dirty word, as though even to acknowledge its existence too explicitly would be unloving and undemocratic. As I have already suggested, this is nearly as true in our politics as it is in our intimacies even though politics is supposed to deal explicitly with the exercise of power in human affairs. As David Bazelon, a social critic, pointed out many years ago, in America "most political questions are argued on metaphysical grounds. . . . The issue here is seldom *how* power is to be used, but whether it is to exist in the first place."[4]

I assume that by "metaphysical grounds," Bazelon means such notions as that we go to war to "make the world safe for democracy," or to "win the hearts and minds of the Vietnamese people," to name two historical examples. But notice also that both these slogans imply we wage war out of a loving purpose—parental love in the one, courtship in the other. The analogous way in which we cloak power as love closer to home is to tell our children, "I'm doing this in your best interests" or "This will hurt me more than it hurts you."

The same sort of thing shows up in our adult intimacies, especially marital ones. We invoke romantic love in a context that elevates the sexual into the metaphysical—marriages, it used to be said, are "made in heaven"—and represses essential political issues, such as how to create breathing room for two people's differences or who makes what decisions. There is a strategy at work here: An effective way to preserve the established distribution of power between husband and wife is to deny that there is any distribution of power.

Our modern psychological theories of human behavior have often demystified the idealized and metaphysical aspects of sexual love, but they left matters pretty much in the realm of the strictly psychological, which is to say, in the interior of the individual personality. That emphasis does not lead us very far into the territory *between* people where power operates. But during the last twenty years, both the women's movement and the practitioners of family therapy have insisted sharply on the fact of power in all human relations, especially in sexual relations between a man and a woman and in relations between members of families. Family therapists treat the family as a self-governing power structure, involving political coalitions, enmities, and strategies, but they pay almost no attention to the impact of culture. The women's movement takes culture into account, but the only scarcity it interests itself in is the deprivation of women. I think we need a still broader framework than either of these provides to interpret the relations between power and love, anxiety and scarcity.

For example, our penchant to blend power with love and then deny the existence of power, it seems to me, springs from a misleading attempt to reconcile our individualistic bias with the claims of domesticity and community. This is a problem that American culture has never succeeded in solving very well. Individualism originally was part of a myth of abundance—the myth of America as an Edenic New World, a spacious society with limitless resources and prospects where self-realization seemed unconstrained. There is a venerable tradition in our culture, based on a utopian view of the frontier, in which the hero has apparently endless scope for self-fulfillment, as long as he can escape the clutches of the domestic world. An important strain in our literature, from Cooper, Melville, Whitman, and Twain to Hemingway and Kerouac, has devoted itself to exploring both the brightly hopeful and successively dark ramifications of this idea.

But in the much denser social landscape of the modern urban world, a fallen world where goods, including emotional goods, become scarce, individualistic self-realization begins to look increasingly greedy and self-aggrandizing, an exercise of power for the sake of the self. When the apparently unlimited possibilities for self-realization, for becoming whoever you want to be, are exported from

the wilderness to the city, you are more apt to get the terrible outcomes of Fitzgerald's *The Great Gatsby* and Dreiser's *An American
Tragedy,* novels in which romance and ambition merge disastrously,
than the optimistic expansion of the Whitmanesque self.

In D. H. Lawrence's words, "We need one another," and even
the most successful American individualists have to find some way
to get together. Romantic love is the perfect ideal of intimacy for
the individualist, since it promises togetherness without giving up
anything of self-realization—there are no obstacles to overcome,
conflicts to negotiate, compromises to make. This combination,
however, serves to hide the dark underside of both individualism
and romantic love—a potentially ruthless Darwinian struggle for
scarce emotional resources. We live in a culture that still believes in
a kind of frontier ideology, which promotes competitive self-realization rather than cooperative, empathic balance between self and
other.

There are any number of ways in which such sweeping cultural
forces translate themselves into how we live our everyday personal
lives. For example, we preach self-reliance as an important moral
attainment, yet a certain feeling of stigma surrounds doing things by
oneself or being seen too much alone. Some people, men in particular, carry around tales of sexual conquest like a driver's license or
passport as proof of being desirable. Many people cannot go to a
movie or a concert by themselves, as though the prospect of being
seen uncoupled is too shameful. This is especially true for women,
which in part, of course, is a holdover from Victorian notions,
where a woman alone is perceived as either a failure or available for
exploitation. Although that view may be changing in our era, it has
by no means disappeared. My patients complain about it all the time,
and not only women, even though it is more socially acceptable
(and these days, a good deal safer) for a man to make his way alone.
I hear complaints nearly as much from men as women in the privacy
of my office. Men simply learn to hide it behind a front of bravado,
adventure, or conquest.

The fear of scarcity and the related fear of being alone are among
the emotional forces (along with the economic forces—until re-

cently at least, especially for women) that often push people to choose neither wisely nor well when they choose mates. The early-twentieth-century American poet Edwin Arlington Robinson has portrayed this situation and the malaise it leads to with deft and graceful precision in his great poem "Eros Turannos," a poem that virtually condenses a novel into six stanzas. It opens:

> *She fears him, and will always ask*
> *What fated her to choose him;*
> *She meets in his engaging mask*
> *All reasons to refuse him;*
> *But what she meets and what she fears*
> *Are less than are the downward years,*
> *Drawn slowly to the foamless weirs*
> *Of age, were she to lose him.*

People don't usually come into therapy because they are in love. Either they are lonely, or their relationships aren't working. No matter how gratified the need for another's confirming presence might have been during a romance, the discovery that love is still scarce can turn the counterpoint of need and response into harsh discord once the knot is tied. The extent to which this sudden shift in perception exacerbates the anxieties that are likely to undermine a marriage can hardly be overestimated.

With both parents working in most families, kids today grow up having to draw support from shrinking inventories of intimate attention. Thus the effects of emotional scarcity become more pronounced in the next generation, even though we still subscribe to values derived from a premise of abundance: freedom to design your own life, equality, the richness of family relations, the American dream.

Such contradictions between professed values and actual experience set up some peculiar paradoxes. The women's movement, for example, labors to rectify ancient inequities in marriage, but its efforts are sabotaged by scarcity, which rouses anxieties that have not been adequately addressed by either sex. Often it seems that the more equal and democratic the structure of the marriage, the more its Darwinian or sibling-rivalry aspects are likely to take over. On an analogous note, a prominent divorce attorney told me that he believes that one of the most common reasons marriages fail is because the two partners are too close to the same age—which confirms the idea that marital problems often resemble sibling rivalry. Just as the movement toward sexual liberation during the 1960s and 1970s, for all its benefits, also freed sex to become more ridden with power struggles, so our more recent liberation from traditional sex roles has liberated the space within marriage to become even more of an arena for Darwinian quarrels.

The situation resembles that of an underdeveloped country dealing with the aftermath of revolution: A repressive ruling group is overthrown; censorship is ended and free elections are called for; a market economy is set up—and then everyone is filled with chagrin as near-chaos ensues and the crime rate rises. It takes a major change of consciousness, which entails cultural change as well as tinkering with social institutions, to ready a long-oppressed populace for democracy. People are only willing to share power, whether in intimacies or entire societies, to the extent that they have faith, based on some experience and some sense of community, that there is enough to go around.

Scarcity has oppressed both women *and* men. Because women have organized not only for political change but also for cultural change during the past twenty years, they may well be ahead of men in preparing for more egalitarian and cooperative intimacy. The violent reactions that men often have when the women in their lives exercise free choice certainly bear this out. The fact that men have for so long had the grip on the levers of power tends to make them blind to their actual plight. This means that a new culture for intimacy based on increased mutual empathy will have to capture the imaginations of men as much as it has women. But that will not be accomplished merely through political and economic threats.

Let me stress emphatically that I am not making a case here for a return to earlier men's and women's roles, with their socioeconomic rights and privileges badly skewed in favor of men—on the contrary. I am arguing, however, that as long as we teach that love is abundant and act as though it is scarce, more equal and flexible sex roles will continue to make long-term intimacies all the more beset by difficulty and the path to workable marriages more perilous. If society grants two intimates social and psychological equality, then they need the society to help them negotiate a different set of expectations from love.

5

The Fixed Diameter
of Eros

D uring a moment of acute insight into their deepening plight,
Lydia Tillotson, a character in an Edith Wharton short story,
tells her lover, Ralph Gannett, "Do you know, I begin to see what
marriage is for. It's to keep people away from each other. Sometimes
I think that two people who love each other can be saved from
madness only by the things that come between them—children,
duties, visits, bores, relations—the things that protect married people from each other. We've been too close together—that has been
our sin. We've seen the nakedness of each other's souls."[1]

Full face-to-face erotic intimacy is too blinding, like looking directly at the sun, for people who have been raised on a diet of emotional scarcity. They are forced to turn away from the nakedness of
each other's souls. They have to encounter one another from a distance, look at each other from the corners of their eyes or through
dark glasses. The main reason they can't tolerate the glare is that
many of them have lost the capacity to yield to powerful feelings,
which they experience as threats to their ability to remain intact and

in control. That loss is the price they have paid for developing the "strong character" that we venerate in America.

A colleague of mine once suggested that there are two kinds of offspring in the modern family—victims and survivors. Surviving too much deprivation or too much invasion with an intact sense of oneself entails becoming prematurely tough and self-reliant. If a child finds an absence of a loving, affirming community of support within its family, or if it endures being raised by anxiety-ridden, controlling, or punitive parents, the child who doesn't fall apart is likely to grow a thick hide, an armored independence that indicates a loss of faith in others. The cost of this kind of survival becomes especially clear when children grow up and begin to form adult relationships.

These people possess qualities that as a culture we admire. They are often decisive, ambitious, and successful. They get good grades in school and become corporate managers, accomplished professionals, or political leaders. They know what they want and go after it unwaveringly by overcoming obstacles and refusing to succumb to temptations or distractions. They are the self-motivated individualists.

The British psychoanalyst Michael Balint has brought out another side to our strong character types. He points out that their strength resides in rigidity not flexibility. In expressing themselves, they can only point in one direction, like a compass needle that always points north. This kind of strength operates through a reduction of possibilities. For example, it reduces the possible ways of experiencing pleasure and therefore of loving and being loved, because such character types can only tolerate pleasure and love along the path that they have established for themselves. Any exciting stimulation that comes in from any other direction or arises spontaneously from within causes an intolerable sense of anxiety. "If through external circumstances other possibilities of love alien to his character are offered to a man," writes Balint, "he will neither be able to love, nor—and this still less—to enjoy. *Character therefore means a limitation of the capacity for love and enjoyment* [italics Balint's]."[2]

In a family atmosphere of scarce love, it would be folly to remain innocent and trusting, to allow oneself to continue to anticipate a full quota of tenderness and warmth. A child learns early to protect himself against false hopes of gratification, joy, release. He simply shuts down his natural, spontaneous emotional responses to his environment. This is one implication of self-reliance: It suggests that one has given up on the intimate environment as a source of support and nourishment.

A series of famous research studies initiated by the psychiatrist René Spitz demonstrated that infants who had been installed in orphanages, hospitals, and similar institutions where they were left mostly alone cried at first, openly expressing their need for the warmth and immediacy of a mothering adult. After enough time went by, during which they received little or no response, they sank into states of uncommunicative apathy. The crying stopped. Their souls, to the extent that one can peer into an infant's soul, appeared to go blank.[3] If one grows up in an emotionally stingy or attacking family—too often the product of a culture based on emotional scarcity—the independence one develops may be like these orphans who have drawn the shades and locked the doors.

It's not necessarily that families in other cultures can provide so much more warmth and love than we do; it's that they don't add insult to injury by insisting that children grin and bear it by adopting our grim policy of self-reliance—square your shoulders, chin in, chest out. When I was teaching in Rome three years ago, some Italian psychologists told me a joke that was then making the rounds. It went like this: First God made Adam. But Adam complained that he was lonely. So God put him to sleep and made Eve from Adam's rib. When Adam awoke, he beheld a gorgeous female standing before him. Yet he still looked miserable, so God reappeared and asked him, "What's bothering you now, Adam? Look at the beautiful wife I made for you!" Adam replied, "Yes, but first I need a mother."

If this pokes fun at men's dependence on nurturers, it does so with a certain affectionate allowance. Consider also Erik Erikson's account of breast-feeding among the Sioux, who nurse their children for three to five years, a cultural habit that Erikson terms a "paradise of the practically unlimited privilege of the mother's breast."[4] It follows, according to Erikson's analysis, that generosity is among the most prominent of the Sioux's ethical ideals.[5]

The process of closing down in our self-reliant culture is not only psychological; it requires a good deal of physical alteration as well—a tensing, inhibiting, or deadening of the muscles and tissues that would normally go into full emotional expression. I recall a patient who came in with a wooden, quelled, slightly depressed quality about him. He said he felt empty inside and that women found him distant and inaccessible. I asked him to tell me the saddest thing he could think of, and he proceeded to talk about his immense loneliness through childhood and adolescence, the death, when he was six or seven, of a cherished grandparent, the disappearance even earlier of his beloved pet dog. His voice remained neutral and his expression didn't change. I found out that he couldn't remember the last time he had cried.

What we also discovered was that he experienced no feeling in the areas around his eyes and cheeks, as though the very skin that would carry the spread of sensation in crying were anesthetized or dead like scar tissue. He was a man whose family did not suffer its losses out loud. It suppressed them in order to keep up its image of well-being. Thus the possibility of grieving was thwarted in childhood for my patient. A child's tears of grief are a necessary letting go that begins the process of healing after an important loss, but they also call out for recognition, shared suffering, and consolation from its parents. Having no hope of this, he had given up on grief. The result was his emptiness and low-grade chronic depression, which was like a neutralized, ongoing minimal expression of feeling for what had been lost. I suggested that he massage the areas of his face surrounding his eyes every night before he went to bed, and as a result of his trying this, eventually tears came. Not until then was he able to go very far in therapy, which requires the music as well as the words.

This is one example of the kind of defensive spasm of body and soul that can occur during childhood, and it causes the self to harden into a set mold. To ask such a person to express or resonate to tenderness, passion, enthusiasm, empathy, or joyous gratification would be tantamount to playing a Beethoven sonata on a cello made of plywood. No matter how hard you try to express a range of feeling, all you'll get is a squawk.

In families where parents hold a monopoly on anger and punish their children if they raise their voices (love is not the only emotion subject to the scarcity principle), the children learn to turn their wrath back on themselves in order not to feel it or at least not to show any visible evidence of it. They often grow up to become "nice" guys or girls—the even-tempered passive-aggressive types. This revision of natural impulse, too, requires more than pummeling one's own psyche: To hide feelings of frustration, resentment, or rage, children have to tense up the muscles in arms and shoulders if they are to restrain the urge to gesticulate or strike out, and they have to restrict their breathing in order to deaden a chest cavity that would otherwise swell with hot emotion.

A woman in her late thirties named Victoria, an impeccably dressed executive, her hair already showing a few regal streaks of gray, came to see me, having just remarried. She was clearly a woman of strong character, in her determined presentation of herself, a determination amplified by an unmistakable quality of being pent-up inside—a woman precisely in the mold that I just described. Victoria announced that she had just come from a wonderful wedding and a terrific honeymoon in the Alps, where wildflowers were still in bloom and the air was both clarifying and rejuvenating. On the one hand, she now feels embarked on "a fresh start" after the prolonged chaos of her first marriage and divorce, yet getting married again, she tells me, "takes me back to feeling like a teenager in some ways." I reply that I hope she means it opens her again to relishing the adventure of a new intimacy, and she says, yes, partly, but also to the bad memories of feeling small, inadequate, and hampered in being herself. "I want to do things on my own, and yet I feel so damned dependent," she says, suddenly sounding weary and deflated, her torso appearing to cave in a little around her, until, indeed, she looks a little like a small girl.

One thing that wears her out, Victoria goes on to explain, is her internal battle over work: In a way she is comfortable with her current employer—a large corporation—providing her with assignments and telling her what is required, so that she doesn't have the sole responsibility for decisions. She has corporate support, secretaries, computers and a fax, complete medical coverage, a stock-option pension plan, and a check that shows up every month. She longs, however, to go out and start her own business, but she hasn't been able to muster the initiative to risk it alone. In social relations, she always feels pressed "to do the right thing," which in fact made her feel uneasy during the wedding, despite her love for her new husband, because it seemed so clearly that she was doing what she was supposed to do.

The underground rumblings of an old dissatisfaction, starting up just days after tying the second knot, scare her about the possibility that her new marriage will be a repeat performance. This is why she has come to see me. She is certainly not a woman who looks like she bends easily, yet in general she feels she has to be accommodating, trying to please others by meeting their expectations of her. People commonly think that she is a nice person, one whom they can rely on, though a little stiff and distant. Inside herself, Victoria feels distraught and in danger of spilling over with a resentment that slowly accumulates, like the drip from a leaky elbow joint under a sink. Every now and then, she gets fed up with laboring to please everybody, and at those times, she explodes with a volume of anger so great in magnitude compared to the annoying incidents that trigger it that those around her flee in shock.

Victoria is like a certain kind of midwestern landscape: It looks inviting and peaceful, with only the slightest perturbation from the breeze blowing through the long grass as far as the eye can see. You seem to know what to expect. Suddenly the sky darkens, and out of nowhere a tornado charges forward, mowing down everything in its path. Victoria's affect most of the time is as flat as those plains—she speaks in a cultivated, precise, but extremely muted tone; you have to lean forward to hear the whole sentence. She rarely exhales. But her anger when it comes is sudden and towering.

These outbursts destroyed her first marriage, and she worries that they will reappear to do the same to her second. She has good reasons to be a marriage wrecker, at least of her own marriages: She would have loved to have laid waste to her parents' marriage and thus to have finally put it to rest. For what I find out shortly is that her mother and father fought almost continuously throughout her childhood and adolescence, and each of them did the worst thing a parent can do to a child in that circumstance: Her mother tried to turn her against her father, and her father made it plain that if Victoria chose her mother's side, he would have nothing more to do with her.

They finally divorced but not until Victoria was in her twenties. As a youngster, she spread herself thin in endless efforts to find ways of pleasing them both. How could she have done otherwise? She could not afford to lose either of them. At times, it was as if she tried to become a tiny, premature parent to a pair of warring children; at other times, she tried to do the sort of job I do by intervening like a psychotherapist. Ultimately she felt like the infant presented to Solomon, about to be sawn in half. And at that point, she simply got herself out of the line of fire as best she could by tensing herself, becoming a quiet, studious girl, and making her emotions invisible.

Around the time Victoria reached puberty, the theme that loomed for her the most powerfully was her relationship with her mother. As she turned fifteen or sixteen, she began to feel more and more the need to discuss with an adult female that she could trust the confusing tides within her and the increasingly urgent business of womanhood. But the mother, infuriated at her own domestic situation, was the kind of woman who has slipped into a steady state of icy rage, and she radiated a continuous beam of animosity. Victoria walked on tiptoes around her; if she turned directly toward her, she felt afraid of encountering a blast (much like the ones she herself dishes out on occasion).

For a child (or, for that matter, an adult), being punished, criticized, or shamed out of one's spontaneous expression of emotion is a psychological crisis. Children respond instinctively as they would to an emergency, and if they undergo this enough times, emergency functioning settles in as a way of life. Many patients who enter therapy saying that they can't have a successful relationship, that they can't feel love, enjoy sex or much of anything else, live on a continuous emergency footing without knowing it. When you skid on the ice in a car, you instantaneously tighten all your muscles and hold your breath briefly in an unthinking concentration of personal forces. It's an involuntary response that helps one grapple with the immediate matter at hand. But imagine what it would be like to drive around town as if you were always skidding on ice. Owning a car would become a worrisome burden. And a Sunday pleasure trip through the countryside would be virtually out of the question.

Another middle-aged professional woman who used to see me in therapy could neither allow herself pleasure nor perform any task with ease and gracefulness because she was so overmobilized from living in a state of chronic emergency. Nothing she ever strove to do was good enough for her parents, who criticized and criticized her. You might describe her existence as a perpetual case of stage fright, the fear that her next move will send her down to a humiliating defeat. People who are chronically overmobilized in this way usually suffered too many traumas growing up at the hands of unpredictable or shaming parents or from other attacks on their self-expression. By now their radar is on automatic pilot, and they can't switch it off. Having looked around the present moment and finding it seemingly peaceful, they aim their senses and emotions toward the future in anticipation of a coming disaster. When somebody is so thoroughly ready to confront danger, their internal machinery is set for a hair-trigger response. As you begin to address them, they are already finishing your sentences, giving them a pessimistic or dire interpretation in the process.

Maintained over time, such tension-filled patterns of mind and body become one's identity, because a habitual posture and state of mind come to be what the self is. Often, it is a sense of oneself as a rigid shell coiled around a feeling of either emptiness or inner panic. The price paid out from the repertoire of human responsiveness and capacity to be intimate is extremely high. You can't love if you can't feel or express grief and anger or relax your vigilance, just as you can't say a full yes if you can't say an equally wholehearted no.

But hardening of the personality doesn't usually mean that the longing for intimacy itself disappears. The trouble is that people with strong characters can never fully surrender or tolerate anything beyond a preestablished quota of sexual excitement. They have to remain in control of their experience. They are more like the trunk of a tree, which remains steadfast, than the leaves, which flutter in the wind and register the impact of changing seasons.

When two people made of such material try to merge into an erotic relationship, they experience as much terror as pleasure in the closeness—a terror which is best understood as too much excitation for the organism to tolerate or manage. Sexual excitement under these circumstances is like a floodtide battering against a sea-wall. If a brittle structure is subjected to too much vibration, it is threatened with disintegration. "Terror," the philosopher Plotinus wrote many centuries ago, "is dissolution of the compound," and that is precisely what people with rigid characters fear will happen to them under the pressure of love. The result can be emotional inhibition, sexual impotence, frigidity, and a host of other similar miseries.

They do, of course, choose partners, form intimate relationships, marry, raise children. But a certain unconscious choreography that dominates their relations with each other bears importantly on the concept of intimate terrorism. I can best illustrate how this works with a geometric analogy. Imagine a circle with a diameter drawn through it. At the two points where the diameter intersects the perimeter of the circle, locate the two intimate partners. Now they can travel around the circle, one in pursuit, the other in flight. They can reverse directions. But they can't leave the rim, nor can they move along the diameter in order to get closer to one another.

The length of the diameter is fixed early in their relationship through a secret collusion. It represents the compromise between staying together and staying safe. If they came any closer, their intimacy would become too hot to handle. But if they tried to get further apart, they would fly off the circle into the surrounding void—for example, the void of divorce. It's a cozy arrangement—a buffer zone—that they have cooked up, most likely without being aware of it.

The tactics of intimate terrorism, based on provoking each other's abandonment and engulfment anxieties, are in one respect a means of keeping this arrangement going. One sees this regularly in therapy with couples: One mate keeps claiming, "You never give me enough. I want more of you," and the other replies, "You always want too much. Give me some space." At some later date, the one in retreat may decide to stop and say in effect (usually after a good deal of therapy), "All right, I give in. I'm yours." And oddly enough, the one who had been so urgently seeking this outcome acquires a dubious frown and begins to back off. Their love seems always to be painfully asymmetrical, but the distance between them remains constant. Like planets, they stay in orbit.

Once, in a Machiavellian mood, I told a patient of mine, an older woman who complained and complained that her second husband was forever on her back pounding her with accusations that she didn't love him enough, to go home and instead of complaining to me, say to him in an aggrieved tone, "I just don't think you love *me* the way you used to." Theirs was a blatant case of a sibling-rivalry marriage: He would become almost insanely jealous whenever she saw her fully grown son and daughter from her first marriage, which had been over for fifteen years, because he felt that any time spent with them subtracted from her love for him. He couldn't even stand her taking her grandchildren out for ice cream. The two would explode into shouting matches over these issues, which typically terminated with her going off to a corner of the kitchen and getting slowly and methodically drunk for the next few days. Meanwhile, he would develop an acute depression or somatic symptoms, such as an immobilizing bad back, that made her feel pinned to the house with guilt and worry.

My directive to her was a calculated gamble, like sacrificing a knight to consolidate a position in chess when your opponent pushes forward aggressively. But I believe I was on to a usable truth: With the husband so preoccupied with being loved, how could she know whether he still loved her? So I was trying to give this intuition a little practical and strategic implementation.

Sure enough, turning the tables on the husband worked quite well. She came in the following week to announce its effectiveness:

Her husband, after protesting in surprise that yes, of course he still loved her, not only retreated a little but began behaving in general more independently. I soon realized that she was not altogether pleased, however. She felt ambivalent about his new autonomy. Maybe he won't really care about her so much, she intimated with a frown, if he discovers that he can get along satisfactorily on his own.

The preceding little vignette illustrates how various unpleasant emotions that two people stir up in each other, such as jealousy, anxiety, depression, and guilt, can work as gravitational forces to hold them in place on the fixed diameter of apprehensive intimacy, even if they are very active there, turning and twisting this way or that. Symptoms, including phobias, addictions, and physical problems, also have similar strategic value in regulating the degree of being tied together yet far apart: A spouse threatening suicide or bedridden with psychosomatic infirmities can keep his or her mate off the streets while remaining self-preoccupied; an alcoholic spouse can hang around the house in a state of numb removal. And these are just a few of the destructive, complicated tricks that keep a couple safe from too much closeness and too much aloneness. Some couples, for example, will maintain the safety zone by carefully editing their intimacy, perhaps allowing close, companionable affection with infrequent or no sex. In a similar way, others have lots of sex with little or no demonstrable affection out of bed.

Psychotherapists have known for a long time that people rarely give up their so-called neurotic symptoms willingly, no matter how vociferously they may proclaim their intentions to do so. Symptoms are useful in too many ways: They can contain a person's life within a familiar structure and thereby provide a sense of security. Of course they are painful, but at least they narrow anxiety down to the known territory in the face of life's larger unknowns. Someone who is paranoid doesn't have to guess what comes next; he already *knows* it will be bad news. The fixed diameter itself is a shared symptom, a kind of *folie à deux* that creates a sense of certitude and security about love.

In therapy, you have to practice a kind of psychological judo and go with the energy of symptoms, not simply blast them out of the water. Patients have every reason to resist a direct assault on their symptoms, given their effectiveness in binding anxiety. And if the therapist wins that battle, so much the worse; he will probably succeed in amputating the patient's personality along with the symptom. Or to put it another way, you have to sail your way into the patient's heart on the wings of resistance, as a former teacher of mine once suggested to me. But sometimes you fail anyway, as in the following case where the anxiety is too great to be converted into exciting but unfamiliar possibilities.

Dennis, the handsome, curly-haired husband in a couple I used to see, was about thirty years old, with the cool blue eyes of a young Paul Newman. He had modeled himself after a long line of American heroes. A former addict himself, he worked with adolescent kids in a drug rehabilitation center, an extremely difficult, wearing job, and he was good at it. He was a streetwise loner, whose tough vocabulary and attitudes showed he had matriculated in the school of hard knocks. It's an inner-city style, but it has antecedents in those figures, frequently haunted by mysterious outlaw pasts, who rode the plains and single-handedly mopped up the lawless towns of Hollywood stage sets—Jimmy Stewart, Gary Cooper, Randolph Scott.

Such men are on their own and seem inaccessible, yet there is something beseeching about them—a touch of awkwardness in their stance around a woman, despite their uncanny athleticism under fire, a glint of sadness in those eyes that can sight with such accuracy down a gun barrel. Like the Byronic heroes of nineteenth-century Romantic poetry, they bear the traces of hidden wounds inflicted long ago. Somewhere beneath the protective coating they wear, the self-containment, there is a softness waiting to be evoked by the right touch, which makes them irresistible to women with a penchant for maternal programs of restoring them to family life.

Sometimes the smitten rancher's gorgeous daughter or the cultivated schoolmarm from the East manages to recruit this kind of man for this therapeutic form of marriage; more often, she fails and he kisses her goodbye and rides off into the sunset, as she, left behind on the front porch looking wilted and imploring, watches him disappear over the horizon. I guess this must be our version of Ulysses and Penelope, but it offers no assurance that Ulysses will make his way back home.

The same hard-bitten pathos appears in a wide variety of American fictional figures. For good reason: They epitomize certain American ideas about manhood. Humphrey Bogart was another archetypal representative; he could transmit the tough guy with an appealing hint of melancholy, whether he was playing a cynical detective, a haunted racketeer, or a cosmopolitan expatriate. The lonely, inwardly tormented Jay Gatsby, in Fitzgerald's novel, leaning with studied casualness against the side of his ostentatious automobile, one foot on the dashboard, also radiates these qualities. So do Hemingway's heroes.

No matter how weathered by hard times the faces of these men might look, an eternal adolescence shines through. The blend of yearning, toughness, and untouchability, with the adolescence made explicit and given the modern touch of alienation, comes across in Jimmy Dean's films or from a youthful Marlon Brando in *The Wild One* and *On the Waterfront*. All the lesser men—wealthy, crooked cattle barons with sheriffs in their pocket, scheming or petty-spirited bureaucrats, union leaders, or district attorneys—are out to destroy these guys at the same time as the beautiful women are out to make love to them. (Though in the latest versions, the male aloneness and avoidance of intimacy is often postdivorce rather than premarital. Thus they are likely to include an unsympathetic, sometimes greedy ex-wife who has kicked them out of the house or run off and betrayed them. How many recent films have opened in a shabby bachelor apartment with an alarm clock going off, and a depleted-looking, obviously hungover male lead staggering to a filthy refrigerator that contains nothing but a carton of orange juice? There is about as much domesticity here as in *Moby-Dick*.) Mel Gibson, who plays a reformed drug dealer in *Tequila Sunrise,* is a recent addition to this masculine elite, although by the time that movie appeared, the image of women had changed sufficiently that his female counterpart, Michelle Pfeiffer, also bearing the scars of old betrayals and hidden wounds, is even more able to maintain her cool and her personal strength and integrity than he is.

Dennis had this tradition down so perfectly that it must have come instinctively. He managed to keep his slouch intact and his hands in his pockets even while sitting in my office. Absurdly good-looking, battle-scarred, and inaccessible, he fixed his gaze neither on Carolyn, his wife sitting near him, nor on me, but on the futility of life located somewhere in a corner of the room. Central casting couldn't have chosen a more fitting female lead than Carolyn. Maybe two years younger than Dennis, she was nowhere near as dramatically attractive, but she was as tall as he, willowy and chic. She spoke with a hushed, urgent expressiveness that drew one instantly to her.

At the moment, though, she sat as still as a bronze figurine, hugging herself and looking down at her feet, in order to damp down her anger. After four years of turbulent marriage, in which she had held things together while he struggled to kick his habit, she now wanted a baby. He appeared to be totally uninterested. On this account, they had been referred to me.

Brought up in a working-class New Jersey town by parents who had torn each other to shreds only to slink away after a messy divorce to opposite corners of the state, Dennis had devoted his life to warding off his childhood losses and disappointments. I believe that he was in fact drawn to Carolyn's strong presence and its intimate appeal, that he was grateful to her as well, and that on some level, he would love to become a father. But he couldn't show her any of these things. There is a way in which these strong, silent men, these movie hero–like characters, still furious about something that happened to them in the past, are brimming with a childish form of resentment commonly known as spite. Spite is the anger of the powerless: It grows from the feeling that you can only get back at the other by doing yourself in. Dennis's drug habit had been a spiteful one-upping of his parents' violent estrangement. His current treatment of Carolyn's having long stood by him and now wanting a child with him was filled with spiteful denial. He had built a hard shell around any soft or vulnerable emotion, as though making sure he is unavailable for intimacy.

It comes as no surprise to find that Carolyn felt exploited, unloved, and rejected, especially in light of all that she had put up with, although one could raise questions about why she had put up with it for so long. There is no question that she continued to be the victim of both Dennis's desperate problems and his methods of covering them up. But just because I may have given Dennis a hard time in this account, don't let me leave the impression that he is solely responsible for their misfortunes. Holding intimacy at bay is by no means restricted, like sports used to be, to male prerogative. It takes two to create geometry, which occurs in a plane, not at a single point. Carolyn had her own share of childhood pain to contend with. Even if it were not so dramatic as what Dennis had been through, her background, combined with her experience of Dennis's withholding denial of her, made her almost as leery as he is of the very intimacy that she sought from him.

Carolyn had grown up in a large midwestern family of prominent attorneys, some of whom had become judges or politicians. It was a family that not only turned its face outward to society and placed most of its energy there, but that for evident reasons had a large stake in its public stance of uprightness. Carolyn felt severely restricted in how she was allowed to conduct herself. She experienced her childhood environment as at once suffocating and remote. Above all, she had been a little girl who had slipped through the cracks amid a crowd of preoccupied family members. This left her feeling useless and unable to raise herself up to the others' level of eminence from whence she might command their attention.

Having graduated from college in liberal arts, Carolyn had recently landed a position in an on-the-job management training program. This, plus the nature of her marriage, had an uneasy look of moving in two directions at once. On the one hand, management training might be her final bid to make it in the eyes of her family, which had virtually disowned her for marrying Dennis. On the other hand, it wasn't difficult to make out why she was attracted to a working-class rebel like Dennis, and even in some measure why she stayed with him. But was she ready to seal her fate? Did she really want his baby, or was that an idea in her scheme to prove that someone really cared about her and that she could actually be useful?

Carolyn was caught in ambivalent nets of her own.

I first noticed her part in preserving the stalemate through a series of small gestures that regularly took place between them. One of them would look at the other somewhat expectantly, hopefully, apologetically, or searchingly. But only one at a time. I virtually never saw them look at each other at the same moment. When she turned toward him, Dennis blanked out, his eyes locked on the corner of the room. But when she became active, mostly in animated discussion with me, he would watch her with an almost wistful concentration. She, however, seemed oblivious to his changes of mood. Perhaps she even deliberately or punitively ignored them, as though she might have to soften her statuesque posture in response.

Theirs was a simple but important way of remaining disconnected. To make contact with others requires seeing them in their fluid moment-to-moment particularity, seeing them see you, and so forth. However minor and, at times, ambiguous these visual cues may seem, they are real, immediate, and form part of the accompaniment, when people deal with each other over complicated issues, that nourishes their background sense of connection and trust. Perpetually troubled couples, people fearful of intimacy, however, rarely look at each other at the same time. If two intimate partners don't see each other in the here and now, all they have to go on is their projections of each other—mainly the historical ones based on how they experienced each other five minutes ago or five years ago.

Any blank space in seeing, hearing, or otherwise experiencing another person can constitute a projection screen for one's old movies—period pieces based on fantasies, anxieties, specters, dreams, and past experiences. This is precisely how people like Dennis and Carolyn clamp each other into molds, usually adding to those the stamp of important intimate figures from their early experience, especially parents. And there the relationship stays, stagnating at best or, more commonly, sinking ever deeper into the quicksand of mutual hopelessness.

For Dennis, there's the risk of Carolyn seeing the full extent of his hurt and longing through the barrier of his numbed-out anger and, maybe even more difficult to handle, of his having to respond to her seeing it. And for her, there is the danger of being taken in once again by looking directly at those sudden openings when his vulnerability leaks through his armor. Perhaps the footing in such uncertain territory strikes both of them as more treacherous than they dare attempt.

As T. S. Eliot wrote in "Burnt Norton," part of his *Four Quartets,* ". . . human kind / Cannot bear very much reality," and like any number of couples, perhaps Dennis and Carolyn don't want to bear too heavy a load of each other's reality. So they conduct their relationship as though it's preferable that she keep him a rebellious, rejecting tough guy with a beautiful profile—the kind that she must have doted over in her wishful thinking when she was seventeen amid the stiff adults around her—and that he treat her as a demanding, invasive mother figure trying to pry loose his secret pain and trap him into a new version of the hurtful family life he witnessed growing up. The obvious adolescent themes at play in their reductive distancing of each other is an important point I will return to later.

Thus they circle each other warily, avoiding direct contact, harboring inner thoughts and longings that neither expresses, their "safe" distance from each other like the sword between the sleeping lovers forbidden to touch each other in medieval fables. Dennis and Carolyn were a strong-willed couple, thoroughly hooked to one another, and ultimately scared to death of each other. I felt I could only go so far with them in working toward shortening the diameter that bound them and held them apart. The issue from session to session always turned on who would give in first. When some melting took place, their anxiety grew more rapidly than their excitement or relief. After a time, they left me. I heard later that Dennis finally gave her a baby, but not until the marriage had almost come apart at the seams. I feared that they were probably doomed.

Perhaps the sexes will always circle each other suspiciously, even if their classic battle grows quiescent, though one can hope that they might learn some day to do it playfully as well, more like a ballet than a duel, a *pas de deux.* Whenever a man and a woman find each other interesting, there's a crackle in the air between them of the not yet known—an anticipation or apprehension of exciting possibilities that also contain dangers. When this tension becomes too momentous, because it's saddled with too many old anxieties, then it turns into a question of whether there is going to be lovemaking or the spilling of blood. One function of the struggle for control between them is to make sure that neither takes place too dramatically.

Learning to play with tension and doubt in relationships is very important. The psychoanalyst and pediatrician Donald W. Winnicott has pointed out that children's games are an essential way through which they learn to master anxieties that would otherwise become debilitating.[6] Playfulness in intimacy doesn't entail a loss of respect either for the other person or for the power of sex; if anything, the contrary is true. This is a point that the courts of love in the Middle Ages understood very well; their careful balancing of decorum and passion was held together by what the Dutch historian Johan Huizinga called "the connection between culture and play."[7] Such serious games—in ancient times they were frequently sacred games—play a central part in the flowering of culture and art, as courtly love indeed did in the medieval period. (Huizinga, who thought of playfulness as a civilizing virtue, also says, quite beautifully I think, that "seriousness seeks to exclude play, whereas play can very well include seriousness."[8] Sex, in particular, is a delicate and spontaneous tension, unresponsive to willfulness, and readily obliterated when it is subjected to the querulous interrogations of fear and anger.

But sex can also build into a tide that sweeps people away with demonic force. "A stairway to the sea / Down which the blind are driven," Edwin Arlington Robinson called it in his magnificent poem "Eros Turannos." We have tended to lose sight of that side of it, as I suggested previously. The old American Puritans were certainly more cognizant of it than the liberated hedonists of our own day. In some respects (though only in some), repression was closer to the truth of sex than free-wheeling liberation, as any true romantic knows perfectly well. One could argue that there are very real reasons, not merely neurotic ones, for passionate lovers to keep some protective distance between them, to touch gingerly the force they generate—at least a good part of the time. It used to be the case that we had ways of holding each other's raw animality and its deep-seated darknesses somewhat at bay. Now that we have disinhibited ourselves—I am not ready to equate that with "freedom"—we have shed everything that protected us from having to deal too directly with each other's souls pouring through the naked body. And that way lies madness, as Wharton's Lydia suggests.

With old taboos cast aside, we have created the possibility of looking at one another in a far deeper nakedness than emerges by just taking off our clothes. It's as if we might come face-to-face with each other's unmediated, spontaneously deconstructed human existence, and this is intolerable. This event in modern culture—who knows exactly when it transpired? thirty years ago?—was like another Fall from Eden and for similar reasons: pride that led us to want to know everything, to achieve certitude, to be like gods and yet not be bruised by such knowledge. After all, Cupid is a god, and the depictions of him as a cute imp with wings on Hallmark valentines are enormously deceptive. In one of my favorite books on love, *Eros the Bittersweet,* a study of passion in ancient Greece, Anne Carson explains the concept of *aidos* or "shamefastness," a sense of modesty which visits the new lovers' eyelids and lowers them against the rising heat of desire. She describes *aidos* beautifully as "a sort of voltage of decorum discharged between two people approaching one another for the crisis of human contact, an instinctive and mutual sensitivity to the boundary between them."[9] One might add that *aidos* expresses reverence and humility before the god of love, the divine demon, appearing as a potential playmate one moment, a predator the next.

If you want to tackle passion, first gird yourself with poetry, for heaven's sake. Read Robinson's "Eros Turannos" and Wallace Stevens's "Re-statement of Romance" and "Soliloquy of the Interior Paramour," read Rilke's "Orpheus, Eurydice, and Hermes" in Robert Lowell's translation, read the poetry (and novels) of D. H. Lawrence and Thomas Hardy, read John Webster's *The Duchess of Malfi,* the Gretchen episode in Part I of Goethe's *Faust,* and all of

Shakespeare. Before one flirts with shorter diameters, one does need to be aware of the risks—being singed by anxiety, suffering defeat or the pain of loss in the encounter. Poetry warns us of these matters but also often invents ways to convert them into a less disintegrative force. As Harold Bloom, a literary critic much influenced by psychoanalysis, has explained in his book *Agon,* "By showing us that anxiety is a mode of expectation, closely resembling desire, Freud allows us to understand why poetry, which loves love, also seems to love anxiety."[10] Sex *is* power, which one can make an unpredictable ally, if one doesn't try to control it along with the other person.

One thing that helps people take such risks is remembering that the worst has already happened—in childhood when one is least equipped to fend off its consequences. As an adult, one has the resources to tolerate anxiety and survive painful experiences. For example, humility in an adult is not the same as the humiliation that crushes a child. Rejection in adult love hurts, but it doesn't kill. And an adult can say no to the invading will of another without destroying the other or being destroyed as a result. Admittedly there are circumstances in which none of these things is true, but that is another matter, involving serious pathology both individually and culturally, and the subject of a later chapter.

We could certainly benefit by importing the idea of *aidos* from ancient times, in order to introduce a measure of humility and respect toward Eros, as well as sensitivity to the boundaries between people, into our intimate proceedings. Love is not merely a question of wild surrender or a transcendent merger of two perfect beings who take each other for granted. On the other hand, neither does one flourish by approaching it—or avoiding it—in a suit of armor with the visor down. The ideal approach to love is analogous to taking your own or someone else's pulse: If you don't come into contact with the skin, you feel nothing; but if you squeeze the wrist too hard, you shut off the circulation and feel nothing. Moments of surrender and transcendence are among the deeply gratifying possibilities that erotic intimacy offers, and they yield lasting meanings the more that people move into them, which is to say, toward one another, with a delicate tread, even when their hearts beat in a spirit of play or adventure. Ideally, one always ought to approach love as one would approach the unknown—with cautious excitement.

A patient of mine, a woman in her forties, summed up her seventeen years of marriage as "a truce with sporadic intimacy." It's a perfect description of what life is like for a couple tied to a wheel that turns them through the years holding them at once apart and together on its rim. For one thing, it keeps them busily, sometimes frantically, occupied with each other, despite the fixed distance. Such a couple is likely to travel through cycles of changing moods, but it is change that resolves nothing. They might live in relative quiet, more side by side than face-to-face, for a while; then go through fluctuating periods of quarrels, affairs, confessions and reconciliations, bouts of weeping and hurling ashtrays, drunken episodes of intimacy, even passion. If one withdraws, the other, pulled along by the receding tide, follows in pursuit until their motion, like all things impelled by currents of anxiety, reverses direction. Then they may find themselves back to parallel lives again, but more bitterly and despairingly this time, sometimes not speaking for days, both of them silenced by fury or resignation.

Cycles like these tend to keep repeating themselves, but not without at last depleting the two individuals' resources, because the experience is so emotionally corrosive. How long a couple can carry on probably depends on each person's sheer will to endure. Certainly some continue till death do them part, each partner having died in spirit long before, like the couple in Willa Cather's *My Mortal Enemy*, which I discuss in the next chapter. Sometimes the marriage rusts out so thoroughly that it finally cracks into pieces, and the two divorce as though they were abandoning a piece of machinery that has ground to a halt, beyond repair. Other marriages die a violent death, like a car smashing into a telephone pole, flinging two bodies free, which land in the contorted postures of people with broken bones.

In *Too Far to Go,* John Updike has assembled seventeen related short stories, all of them involving a couple whom he calls the Maples, into an extraordinary novel about contemporary married love. Up-dike manages, through concentrating on a series of crucial turning points in the history of the Maples' long marriage, to evoke its entire course from its first glow of wonder till it flickers out in divorce some two decades later. To my thinking, Updike is our wisest chronicler of modern marital failure, and in this novel he conveys with great poignancy and depth how the Maples' desperate need to keep each other at bay eventually erodes their capacities to make the relationship work. Yet it is obvious that they love one another quite deeply as well.

Each of the seventeen tales is a brilliantly but delicately illumined glimpse, a cameo by a fine miniaturist. What those lit moments reveal is how acrimony and tenderness, betrayal and loyalty become tangled and cancel each other out when the fear of being too close is sufficiently powerful between two people who are infinitely close despite themselves. The Maples' marriage, as it passes through an apartment in Greenwich Village, suburban homes in New England, children growing into young adulthood, European vacations, cruel-ties inflicted on one another, numerous infidelities, and finally sepa-ration, is an endless succession of missed opportunities.

"We sense everything between us, every ripple, existent and nonexistent; it is tiring," Richard Maple thinks to himself, as he watches Joan puttering among the children after seven years of mar-riage. "Courting a wife takes tenfold the strength of winning an ignorant girl."[11] He's right, of course, but what finally exhausts these two is the unceasing and anguishing confusion as they whirl each other through alternate rounds of desire and hostility. In a word or a gesture, Richard and Joan can transmit the full scope of a deep em-pathy for each other, but they can't seem to stop themselves from adding equally economical, equally knowing barbs that cut each other to the quick.

They are passionately, even yearningly attracted to one another yet go about deliberately spoiling the magnetism between them by having affairs with all the other wives and husbands in their neigh-borhood. Then they stage unforgivable confession scenes far into the night, in which they try to treat each other's infidelities with

cool up-to-date ironical acceptance that merely disguises their underlying mutual terror. Every now and then, they break out into
ferocious assaults on one another. Whenever feelings, negative or
positive, run too high between them, they douse them with bourbon or brandy, and wake up the next morning sick, preoccupied,
and depressed.

Driving together to Boston the day after a party, they go at each
other because Richard had spent the evening flirting on the dance
floor with another woman. He now tries to vindicate himself by
pretending to be jealous of a mutual friend at the party, one of the
"little fat men," as he puts it contemptuously for dramatic effect,
whom Joan had sat and talked with for a long time. ". . . Every time
I looked over at you last night it was like some pale Queen of the
Dew surrounded by a ring of mushrooms." He brushes aside the fact
that he had blatantly abandoned her, thus depositing her by default
in the hands of the friend. "You're too absurd," Joan tells him.
"You're not subtle. You think you can match me up with another
man so you can swirl off with Marlene with a free conscience."

That she can read him so accurately makes Richard turn mean,
and he replies, "You're right. . . . But I want to get you a man your
own size; I'm very loyal that way." When she silently rises above
this bit of nastiness, Richard, flushed with being so deeply in the
wrong, loses all restraint: "It's your smugness that is really intolerable. Your stupidity I don't mind. Your sexlessness I've learned to
live with. But that wonderfully smug, New England—I suppose we
needed it to get the country founded, but in the Age of Anxiety it
really does gall." And Joan, looking over at him after this with an
"uncannily crystalline expression," ends it by staying cool: "I asked
you not to talk. . . . Now you've said things that I'll always remember."[12] Knowing full well he has gone in over his head, Richard
changes the subject to a discussion about their baby, who has a fe-
verish cold. Their mutual concern about their children always soft-
ens them and leads them to reconciliation.

Excruciating flurries like this—with sometimes one, sometimes
the other taking the initiative to dig the terrible chasms they tumble
into—are always followed by fumbling acts of forgiveness, rescue,

sex. At one point, Updike tells us that Richard "wished her to be happy. . . . So he dried the very tears he had whipped from her eyes."[13] These recurring episodes bind them more and more tightly together at the same time as they push them ever closer to separation. For most of the novel, it's a perfect standoff, a maintenance of their fixed diameter.

In a particularly touching account of the Maples on a desperate vacation, a kind of dismal honeymoon at the wrong end of the marriage, Updike shows us the full pathos of two people trapped at an intensely intimate, painful fixed distance from each other: "Their conversations, increasingly ambivalent and ruthless as accusation, retraction, blow, and caress alternated and canceled, had the final effect of knitting them ever tighter in a painful, helpless, degrading intimacy." Talking endlessly of separating, they continue to make love "like a perversely healthy child whose growth defies every deficiency of nutrition." They struggle to be away from each other, and the very effort brings them closer. "Burning to leave one another," Updike announces, "they left, out of marital habit, together. They took a trip to Rome."[14]

The trip to Rome comes late in the game. It's close to a last fling or final turn in the Maples' agonizing dance, which throughout the novel is characterized by immensely intricate, grotesque steps and twirls, yet goes nowhere. They might as well have been standing stock still in each other's arms on the dance floor for twenty years, heads a little bowed as though from shyness, wondering when the music will start.

Until very late in the novel, when Richard decides at last to leave and marry another woman, the adulteries that they simultaneously turn to for self-protection and to beat each other over the head with are advanced symptoms of the disease more than they are serious alternative intimacies. They don't yet snap the diameter between Joan and Richard; if anything, they help maintain it. At the same time, they keep weakening it like an old rusty axle increasingly pockmarked with infidelity. Indeed, adulterous affairs commonly play a key part in keeping marital fixed diameters intact; they drive a wedge between husband and wife that also serves as a buffer of safety from intimacy. "It's sad, to think of you without a lover,"

Richard says to Joan at one point, as though there is a blank space between them best filled in by going to bed with a neighbor.[15] But in the long run, infidelity is a disastrous strategy, because neither spouse can tolerate its ravages very long, or because one or the other, whatever the intent, becomes seriously involved with someone else.

In divorcing at last, both Richard and Joan bleed, as Siamese twins connected by vital organs bleed when they are surgically severed. After living apart for a year and a half, Richard wonders, "Can even dying be worse than this?," and he perceives Joan's body as "a great unhealed wound crying, *Come back.*"[16] But the Maples don't bleed to death; they grow apart, and strangely enough, freed from scapegoating each other, they finally grow playfully affectionate with each other. Driving together to divorce court, they are almost like new lovers. Richard marvels "at how light Joan had become; she sat on the side of his vision as light as a feather, her voice tickling his ear. . . . He no longer blamed her: that was the reason for the lightness. All those years he had blamed her for everything."[17] Next to each other before the bench, surrounded by their fidgeting lawyers and all the grim apparatus of the legal system, they feel as weightless as rainbows; when it's over the judge smiles and wishes them good luck, they step back, and Richard turns and tenderly kisses Joan.

Too Far to Go is a wondrously sad tale, an important fable for our times, full of ambiguous destruction and lushness. Updike himself has come too far to be cynical or condemning toward the Maples. He knows that even the most painful marriage contains mutual glorying in the children, cooperative enterprise in laboring over a home, and lasting moments of tenderness and longing woven through its betrayals and other brutalities. So he guides us through the decline of the Maples' marriage with a sorrowing lyricism that rings the most complex notes of modern love, until it all ends like the fading sound of distant church bells at a wedding or a funeral.

If the Maples' divorce sounds like a wedding ceremony run backwards, it is no more than what Updike, perhaps in a mood of mocking compassion so ironical as to be perverse, fully intends. In the end lies the beginning, as T. S. Eliot's *Four Quartets* repeatedly suggest—but the beginning of what? Certainly of freedom from compulsion, for the marriage based on anxiety and scarcity, the power-driven sibling-rivalry marriage, the marriage of two people longing for each other but frozen a diameter apart rolls its forlorn way down labyrinths of compulsion. Updike may end *Too Far to Go* in a parody of intimacy, but it's a parody that discloses a deep truth: Desire can flourish only in a climate of freedom, freedom from blame and deliberate intimidation at any rate. And if love cannot altogether be free from anxiety—anxiety, after all, to recall Kierkegaard's definition, is "the dizziness of freedom"—let it be anxiety that each person has learned to tolerate well enough, such that all freedom to choose one another does not disappear.

One comes away from Updike's novel almost ready to believe that a sweet-tempered, empathetic divorce could become our new model of romance after the fall—the fall into a marriage that dies of its wounds. Most of the wounds occur in the first place because when a man and a woman marry, swept away with the sense of miraculous possibilities at the outset, they have to encounter the pitfalls of everyday life together. Why are these so hard to face? Why do the two so often tumble head over heels down the slope of fear and disappointment? Partly it's because they blame each other for the fall. And partly it is because they come to know each other too well; they become hypnotized by every quirk or tic of one another's personalities. A hypnotic state usually means either that you are on your way to sleep, perhaps out of fatigue and boredom, or that you are paralyzed, like a small animal about to be caught by a bird of prey. The Maples, like various patients I've described, suffered from both these conditions. Waking up to a fuller, more adventurous and therefore more unpredictable intimacy for them is too anxious-making, too much to bear, "too far to go."

In fact, Richard Maple resembles my patient Dennis in that neither of them dares give voice to the powerful feelings that go begging somewhere inside them. Even waiting up alone late at night, in the middle of one of their countless adulterous crises, Maple chokes on his own atrophied emotions. Downing bourbon for lubrication perhaps, he tries to get angry, but "anger had never been easy for him." He tries to cry, "but produced only the ridiculous dry snarling tears of a man alone." And then there follows a scene that is heartbreaking in what it reveals—as he paces the house near midnight, agitated, close to desperation, Joan finally returns: "By the time he looked she was walking toward him, beneath the maple tree, from the deadened car. She was wearing a white coat. He opened the kitchen door to greet her, but his impulse of embrace, to socket her into his chest like a heart that had orbited and returned, was abruptly obsolete, rendered showy and false by his wife's total, disarming familiarity. He asked, 'How was it?' "[18]

In a couple like this, like Dennis and Carolyn, like virtually all the couples I have presented, the men are stifled—by fear of being hurt or shamed, of losing control, of appearing weak or powerless. And the women, if they are not already stifled in similar ways, are stifled by the men's being stifled. Often, it takes a serious crisis, especially the crisis of imminent loss of the relationship, to snap them out of it. Then the withheld love and need may press forward with enough force to break the dam, and they begin to let each other know how much each cares. Surely this is the final joke, at once terrifying and poignant, in Richard's and Joan's kiss just after the divorce. (Ironically, he had forgotten to kiss her after the marriage ceremony.) Like all far-reaching jokes, it only pushes a little further toward an extreme the reflection of what so many of us have been experiencing all along. How sad to think that we can only express our love for the other in marriage at the point of losing one another forever!

Love returning to express itself as an intimate relationship breathes its last, as a home is destroyed and children scarred—such is often the last gasp of a marriage based on a safe compromise between distance and closeness, a final desperate balance of forces to keep the diameter the same length just as it breaks into pieces. Because their habitual pattern is disintegrating under so much pressure, this might have been the point at which two people could renew their affection, their desire, their light-heartedness with and appreciation of one another—because, like the Maples, they no longer blame each other. Once in a while it works out this way, though more often, if they do get back together, the old patterns start up again after a short time. This is one reason so many couples go through repeated separations and reconciliations. We need to begin much earlier with a different point of balance, a different compromise than the fixed diameter to deal with the anxieties in being together. What is the secret, then? Two themes of D. H. Lawrence's taken together, provide at least a hint: He wrote an essay titled "We Need Each Other." But he also teaches everywhere in his writings that we have to learn to give without giving ourselves away.

6

Failure and Disappointment in America

There is a short novel by Willa Cather that in the interval of a hundred or so pages manages to reveal quietly yet devastatingly "the whole drab compass of marital disillusion," as Evelyn Waugh once put it neatly.[1] That a novel about marriage bears the title *My Mortal Enemy* is almost as neat: The story is about the gradual, corrosive transformation, when a marriage becomes burdened with maintaining unfulfillable romantic expectations, of love into unspoken hate.

Myra Driscoll, the heroine of *My Mortal Enemy*, had fallen in love with a dashing youth named Oswald Henshawe when she was a beautiful and brilliant young woman, the cream of her social world. The guardian who raised her, an extravagantly wealthy great-uncle, is utterly opposed to the alliance. Eventually Myra elopes with her lover, and just as he had threatened, her great-uncle cuts her out of his will. She thus voluntarily gives up the vast fortune she was due to inherit. Twenty-five years later, this romantic tale of great sacrifice for the sake of passion has become a legend in the small southern

Illinois town from which Myra had so abruptly departed. That winter night when she strode for the last time through the iron gates of her guardian's magnificent estate and climbed into a waiting horse-drawn sleigh is still the talk of the townspeople.

Myra herself, however, now in middle age, has become a disappointed, bitter woman. Her husband appears to be a decent if rather ordinary man. The prospect of an ardent life together has ended for them; what began as a passionate adventure has dwindled to meaninglessness in the stale, claustrophobic air of their marriage. On the surface, they are still an attractive, well-dressed couple, admired by society, living in a handsome apartment in New York. Underneath, they are destroying one another in a "long, silent duel with invisible weapons," as still another novelist, Ford Madox Ford, once described the subterranean carnage that, like termites, can eat away the foundation of trust in a marriage.[2]

Cather never tells us anything very specific about the nature of the Henshawes' mutual failure—whether it might be due to misunderstandings or boredom or secret infidelities, for example, although there are intimations of all these things. The point is that they feel compelled, through most of the novel at least, to uphold the facade of continuing romance not only in public but even in their private life together. They cannot acknowledge that their grand, rebellious merger has failed, so they have no way to grapple with it, to resolve anything, to learn from it. Myra and Oswald feel simply defeated by one another. They have become, in Willa Cather's chilling phrase, each other's "mortal enemy."

If the realities of power have often been denied in America, failure has not been treated with much respect either. We have never considered it a tolerable possibility, much less one of the available, perhaps inevitable paths to self-transformation and further understanding of the human condition. American history is, above all, a success story. We have plenty of fables and cultural myths, which we are taught from early childhood forward, that exhort us to succeed and tell us how to achieve success—in sports, in business, in love. We have a few homilies on the need to persist in the face of failure: "If at first you don't succeed, try, try again." "But then quit!" added

W. C. Fields. "Don't be a damn fool about it." Our culture offers very little to help us fail gracefully or fruitfully, little to teach us how to recover from failure, almost nothing to support our putting our disappointments and failures to use in order to learn from them.

No wonder so many people live through their marital disappointments with gritted teeth and keep up a cheerful facade, like the Henshawes. Or, nowadays especially, they simply give up and divorce with an eye to the next marriage, like trading in an old car for a new model with sleeker styling and a sun roof. With regard to our romantic successes, we have our whole culture to cheer us on, but when it comes to our failures at intimacy, we are mostly on our own and have to struggle as best we can to squeeze some insight from them. Appearing in public as a happy couple is still a badge of success. That is why so many people, especially women, as I suggested earlier, regard showing up alone as a sign of failure, as being forced, so to speak, to wear a scarlet "F."

Even one of our more popular conceptions of rebound from failure—the thoroughly American myth of the Comeback Kid, a story in which the heroes are usually scarred prizefighters, forgotten political losers, and aging actors and actresses who have kicked alcohol or drugs—is ultimately about success. This theme probably has its roots in the first settlers' hope that America would be a New World, a second chance at utopia. Our notion of the comeback is an attempt to recapture original glory; it hardly chastens one for an acceptance of a life with diminished or different prospects.

Most of our newsworthy tales of actual failure emphasize a failed expediency, as though one simply used the wrong tactics or had lousy luck, whereas in our literature, failure usually ends in tragedy and death. During the Iran-contra hearings in 1987, Robert McFarlane was interviewed on CBS by Barbara Walters shortly after his suicide attempt. She asked him, "Why try suicide, what drove you to such despair?" McFarlane replied, "I felt I had failed the American people badly. . . . My pappy taught us children responsibility for success." Walters: "So it was the sense of failure?" McFarlane: "Yes." Not a word about the laws that were broken, the deception of the populace, the other moral issues involved. One has the sense that if the clandestine operation had succeeded, he would have felt that he had lived up to his father's principles and would have continued to pursue politics with zest.

Similarly, when the first insider-trading scandals broke on Wall Street a few years ago, it seemed clear that Ivan Boesky, Dennis Levine, and a group of young investment bankers with Harvard MBA degrees had operated according to an ethic of success, measured in terms of unending gains achieved by any conceivable means. One wonders whether the suicides during the Great Depression were more due to the trauma of lost wealth and a luxurious standard of living or to the sense of having failed.

Pointing to the war with Iraq pursued by the Bush administration, a spokesman for the Sojourners, a peace group, pointed out that Americans equate success with moral good. No doubt this helps explain why our failure in Vietnam has had such a devastating impact on our sense of ourselves, as well as why we don't know how to respond to our slackening industrial power except to curse at Japan. Our culture gives all its support to winning, which is evident across the widest scale—from the Horatio Alger myth, an account of how hard work can carry one from rags to riches, which used to be one of our standard morality tales for individual success, to our recreations, which can get so competitive that they are no fun for the loser; from our airline and car rental ads ("We're Number One" or "We Try Harder") to our foreign wars, which we are supposed to win since the Divine Spirit inhabits our trigger fingers.

Many works of serious literature, such as *Moby-Dick, An American Tragedy,* and *The Great Gatsby,* spell out darker possibilities, in which the terrific drive for success turns into hubris that precedes a tragic decline or a catastrophe. But even in these more critical appraisals of our urgency to conquer, the drama is in the push for success. Only by implication do they teach us how to accommodate disappointment. *The Scarlet Letter* is a rare exception in that it takes a startlingly different tack from most classic American fiction: Through the lonely spiritual strength with which Hawthorne endows her, Hester Prynne rises above the pinched society, made bleak by its narrow moral vision, and converts an apparently disastrous failure into transcendence.

Today, when the romance turns sour in a marriage, the couple no longer feels, like the Henshawes, quite so compelled to remain stoical about their pain and endure it to the bitter end. Many disillusioned couples struggle for a long time to fan the dying embers or at least to work out some accommodation, especially if they have kids, that makes staying together tolerable. Many try individual therapy, marital therapy, sex therapy. But statistics show that at least half of them end up throwing in the towel. This, of course, is one way to acknowledge failure, and sometimes no doubt it is the best way. Unfortunately, a great many divorces are like having a fire sale before the flames have been put out: The marriage is terminated amid desperate heat and fury.

Such premature divorces tend to repress the deeper, more complex meanings of each mate's disappointment by obliterating the most palpable source of it—the other person. Then both individuals may imagine they have freed themselves from misery, and they sail off in opposite directions to brave new worlds, dusting off their long-shelved dreams of success and fulfillment in order to invest them in the next marriage.

Those who never really question their defeated romantic agendas enter their next relationships and marriages with renewed fervor till they are once again wrung out, as though tossed through the cycles at a Laundromat. Others may labor to revaluate the romantic aspirations that culminated in divorce but find themselves unable to climb back out of their bitterness. Given our taste for victory, the absence of cultural support for learning anything from one's mistakes makes it easy to slide from realism into cynicism.

Falling in love is one of the high points in life, and it can plant the seeds of what will turn out to be a satisfying and lasting intimacy. Nevertheless, there remains a lot to accomplish between the intimation and the realization. The most hazardous decisions to marry upon falling in love probably come about when two people, seduced by the intensity of their infatuation, presume to make nearly irreversible commitments hastily because the requirements of the romantic ideal appear to have been met. And indeed, such romantic passion may well hold them in good stead for months, maybe even years on occasion, but it is both too fierce and too fragile to support four or five decades of married life. When couples at some later point encounter the usual domestic messiness, they are likely to experience their second fall—this time not into love, but into disappointment, restlessness, boredom, and finally into rage and despair.

Thus we have developed an approach to love and marriage that begins in a haze of sweetness and proceeds almost inexorably to disillusionment and maybe divorce. Those of us who escape cynicism go to the other extreme and, as though restored instantaneously to some pristine condition of innocence, start the whole cycle up again with someone else. In broad outline, this pattern resembles our restive tradition of the frontier, which helped get the nation under way but finally became obsolescent because it encouraged us to hit the trail in search of new horizons just when we needed to settle down and complete what we had already established. In his *America's Coming of Age,* a study of our culture at the turn of the century, the literary critic Van Wyck Brooks gives a poignant rendering of the fate of the American dream in the hands of such a nomadic impulse. He describes the look of villages and towns that were founded in an enthusiastic fit of enterprise and quickly abandoned when the citizenry encountered hardship and disappointment, grew impatient, and moved on. "Round about," writes Brooks, "lie heaps of ashes, burned-out frames, seared enclosures, abandoned machinery, and all the tokens of a prodigal and long-spent energy."[3] After divorce, the psychological landscape for two people is usually left as scarred and desolate as the physical one that Brooks describes.

There can be little doubt that disappointment is an inevitable developmental stage in marriage. Contemporary psychological theory has concluded that humans continue to develop virtually until they are swallowed by the grave (in contrast to the older psychologies, which thought that development ended with childhood). Such theories could do well to add marital disappointment to the phases of adult development.[4] One could argue that mature love—the birth of a new, more wistful, limited romance, and thus the possibility of flourishing in marriage—can occur only *after* the two suffer the loss of their initial idealism and the fall into disappointment. Our waning popular ideal of romantic love took us only a relatively short distance anyway: It offered a simplified if beautiful version of love to a society that is fixated at the phase of adolescence, a time in human development when idealistic enthusiasms are especially appropriate and when the primary developmental task, one that makes for a great deal of anxious unease and awkwardness, is to discover how to maintain a sense of personal identity and then risk it in the fires of sexuality and intimate closeness.

One could summarize a great deal of thinking in the field of adolescent psychology by pointing out that adolescence is the phase in growing up during which young people arrive at full physiological erotic maturity and find themselves struggling psychologically with the often competing claims of power and love—power, in the sense of experiencing that they can assert an individual self and have some impact on their world as well as be affected by it; love, in the sense of trusting themselves to surrender to a deeply meaningful give-and-take between themselves and others to whom they are attracted.

Insofar as American culture tends to be arrested at adolescence when it comes to social relations, especially intimate ones, it obstructs more than it paves the way for individuals to work out a balance between the need to feel powerful and the need to love. Strands of power and love are inevitably interwoven with one another in people's lives, but in our lives they remain more entangled than integrated and reconciled—thus our tendency in so many areas to confuse the one for the other, especially when anxiety is aroused. The confusion creates, for instance, a merging of the stimulation of sex with a sense of threat and an urge for control. In general, this is because the essential, delicate work of balancing the claims of autonomy and intimacy doesn't get completed. People grow up overdeveloped in one direction and weak in the other, so that their relationships readily push them toward the extremes of abandonment or engulfment fears.

It takes considerable discipline that combines risk with restraint, aggression with patience with oneself and others, and bravado with tact to make one's way through the labyrinth of sometimes mingled,

sometimes contending claims that assail the passage through adolescence. With respect to intimacy, falling in love is not so much a fall
as a grand leap of faith, a leap for unity and meaningfulness that
mysteriously soars beyond all these difficulties and labors. Like the
psychedelic trips of a previous era, this improbable, thrilling event
can point toward the far horizons that love and sex can reach for a
spell—the realm of the extraordinary. No wonder that it captures
the adventurous idealism of youth, including the youth that remains
(one hopes) in all of us later in life. No wonder that it offers the
promise of an ethereal food for intense hungers as well as a balm for
equally intense anxieties. It would help if there were the net of a
more seasoned, empathic culture under people when they eventually fall from such heights.

To the extent that our aging culture of romance, based on extraordinary erotic experiences, brushes by the problems of two people leading an ordinary life together, it has not served us well.
Youthful ideals won't necessarily help people deal with the crises or
even the pleasures of later life. The adolescent battles with identity
and intimacy ought to be largely done with before marriage. Or else
we need to evolve a different set of expectations from marriage—
ones that actually assist two people in supporting each other's growing up instead of encouraging them to regress. Unfinished business
having to do with the adolescent anxieties about being oneself and
being with others in a climate of unlimited romantic expectation
helps set the stage for intimate terrorism. Where this prevails, one
would have to say that Romeo and Juliet, a pair of adolescent lovers,
were lucky. They drank their poison in one gulp and died with their
ideal love intact, rather than watching it drain away over the years
with nothing to replace it in the slow toxins of suburban married
life.

In the realm of work and other achievement-oriented arenas,
Americans are willing to apply discipline—to practice, to be methodical, to seek solutions, to concentrate, to labor and sacrifice as
much as necessary to reach the goal. This is evident in the lives of
athletes and musicians, research scientists and founders of corpora-

tions. They brook failure all the time and find ways to do battle with it, especially if the battle involves disciplined courses of action, like building physical strength and speed or working long hours to develop virtuoso technique. Americans are usually delighted to tackle a challenge if it can be cast in the form of a problem to be solved; this is a major source of our technological prowess.

But the same criteria do not apply when it comes to matters of the heart. Love refuses to model itself after all those pursuits amenable to problem-solving techniques, although a good number of lovers and spouses try to grapple with their difficulties in those ways. In part, the recalcitrance stems from the fact that intimate troubles strike at the core of our deepest and fondest dreams of personal fulfillment. Love and sex are so thoroughly and immediately bound up with one's sense of identity—as a man, as a woman, as a competent and lovable creature—that failing at them can raise not merely anxiety but existential panic. (Not that work doesn't involve an intimate sense of one's worth for vast numbers of people also; but even there I would argue that the question of being lovable is at the root.)

When intimacies come apart, it often seems that all discipline, restraint, and willingness to work it out patiently fly out the window, and what's left in the relationship is icy paranoid silence, depressed withdrawal, or a hysterical battle. In other words, disturbances in love are unmatched in their capacity to bring on an instantaneous regression to infanthood. Psychoanalytic theory argues that neurotic behavior results from defensive responses to anxiety. Boiled down to essentials in the furnace of intimate warfare, most neurosis does in fact look pretty much like what frustrated infants do: They either sulk or throw tantrums. When troubled intimates run from the trouble or lunge for the other person, it's as if they were headed back to the crib.

Our refusal to allow room for failure also leads to the widespread belief, often held to the point of delusion, that when things begin to fall apart in an intimate relationship, you can find your way back to the way things were before the trouble began without suffering loss. "The Way We Were" theme not only expresses a nostalgic lament for a golden age, as in the song made famous by Barbara Streisand, but it also frequently expresses a longing to return there and a stubborn insistence that the journey back can reach its goal. I hear it sung in therapy all the time by couples contending with marital catastrophe. One or the other spouse says to the one intent on leaving, "Can't we just go back to the way things were?"

The tragic dimension of experience, as serious drama and poetry conceive it, asserts that mature knowledge is hard won through experience that includes grief and pain caused by losses suffered. Tragedy may lead to dying—it always does in literature—but it also leads to wisdom in the face of human failure; it is the most extreme form of learning from experience. A wise man or woman bears many scars inflicted by life.

Tragedy acknowledges that something has happened. It survives the worst and moves on. The American myth of romantic nostalgia, however, cries out that nothing has really happened. It demands that an appearance of well-being be upheld no matter what, thus practicing both self-deception and deception of others, as in *My Mortal Enemy*. Or it insists that one be given a second chance without having to labor painfully to earn it. Both these demands involve a denial that time has passed, which implies that our ideal of romantic love ultimately comes close to the denial of death.

There is a well-known short story by John Cheever, called "The Swimmer," that illustrates how far into madness this kind of denial can carry one. Cheever, like Updike, is one of our true poets of failed suburban romance. Both writers render with great bemused sorrow the waste that wrecked marriages strew everywhere within their vicinity—on friends, neighbors, and children, as well as on the terrorized and terroristic spouses. "The Swimmer," published in 1964, must have hit a certain cultural nerve, because it was later expanded into a feature-length movie starring Burt Lancaster as its ill-fated protagonist.

We first see Neddy Merrill, Cheever's swimmer, lounging after a swim with his wife and friends around the edge of a neighbor's pool. It's one of those hungover Sunday afternoons in the suburbs in the middle of summer. Neddy is "a slender man," athletic with "the especial slenderness of youth," though far from young. His own house lies eight miles away in Bullet Park, that mythical suburban development in which Cheever set so much of his fiction. Soaking up the sun, he imagines his four beautiful daughters at home having lunch and playing tennis. Then he pictures the string of swimming pools stretching from this one all the way to his house, and it strikes him that he could travel home by water.[5]

Neddy is an expansive late-twentieth-century American individualist to the core: "He was determinedly original and had a vague and modest idea of himself as a legendary figure."[6] Like all such men, he passes immediately from conception to action and, shedding the sweater over his bathing trunks, dives in. Crossing backyards through hedges, traversing vacant lots, garden paths, and driveways full of parked cars, he stops at each familiar house along the way in order to swim the length of the pool.

Neddy's journey is as allegorical as Dante's but in reverse: He begins in an alcohol-saturated heaven of beautiful, affluent people and flowering summer landscape, of catered poolside parties and sociable hugs and kisses, but as he proceeds, it grows late, and the sky gradually turns leaden with storm clouds. There are now hints of autumn in the air; oddly, some of the backyards he reaches are overgrown and deserted, and one pool has even been drained dry and left behind. These are among the signs that significant changes may have occurred long before, but Neddy is taken aback—weren't he and Lucinda, his wife, over for dinner at some of these houses just a week ago, he wonders. "Was his memory failing or had he so disciplined it in the repression of unpleasant facts that he had damaged his sense of truth?"[7]

Painful experiences begin to accumulate. Crossing a highway in his bathing suit, he is jeered at and beer cans are thrown at him. Lifeguards order him out of a chlorine-filled public pool because he has no identification disk. And at the next pool, on a sprawling estate belonging to an extremely wealthy elderly couple, the melancholy owners, who sun and swim in the nude, express their regrets about his recent misfortunes, though Neddy replies that he has no idea what they could be talking about. He leaves feeling unaccountably depressed. He's exhausted and cold, his arms and legs now feel lame, and he appears to have lost weight. Leaves are falling, and, strangely for this time of year, there is the smell of woodsmoke in the air.

Time continues to slip and slide more and more drastically. At the next house, three years of events seem to have eluded him. And at the next, where a party thrown by people who used to covet his attendance is in progress, he is treated as a gatecrasher. The one after that belongs to his former mistress, who used to weep for him to stay but now responds to his unannounced appearance in her yard with cold contempt. Swimming across her pool, Neddy can barely haul himself out of the water. At long last, he heads up the driveway of his own house. It has turned into night, and somehow the wrong constellations are in the sky. The house is dark. When he tries the garage doors, they are locked, and their handles have rusted. Pounding frantically on his front door, he looks in the windows and discovers that the house is utterly empty—no wife, no daughters, no home.

Obviously this story flirts, and it does it brilliantly, with the far edges where the real blurs into the hallucinatory. It is a kind of black fairy tale, a vision induced by alcohol or psychosis. It takes the shape of Neddy's slow descent by water from a false heaven into the hell of his actual life, and that is exactly the point the story wants to make about the loss of a grip on reality produced by clinging for dear life to a failed ideal. Everything has changed for the worse in the world of Cheever's hero; to keep it the same, to stop time in its tracks, he has hurled himself, as into a pool, over the brink of madness. In thus linking a romantic delusion with the denial of death, Cheever's fable reminds me of a much earlier famous American short story set during the Civil War that, in a sense, makes the connection the other way around.

Ambrose Bierce's haunting "An Occurrence at Owl Creek Bridge," written around 1891, is another small piece of fiction that was not long ago turned into a relatively short but exceedingly powerful film. "The Swimmer" concentrates on total domestic failure—financial ruin, the loss of home, wife, and children. It gives us the awful picture of a man reduced to nothing, held by a mere thread of delusion to his belief that he still possesses a haven in a world that becomes more heartless by the moment. This is all the reprieve from decay and death that he has left. "An Occurrence at Owl Creek Bridge" puts imminent death in the foreground and shows how far a man's mind will stretch fantastically in order to convince him that he will be saved if he can escape into the arms of his beloved wife.

Bierce's strange fable covers in its entirety no more than the span of a fraction of a second. But we don't know this at first, for its narrative unfolds slowly with a hallucinatory sharpness and magnification of detail. A young southern planter, taken prisoner as a saboteur by federal soldiers, is being hanged on a railroad bridge over a stream. We see the noose around his neck and the rope's end tied to a beam over his head. An unmoving company of infantrymen faces the bridge with the butts of their rifles on the ground. The condemned man closes his eyes to think about his wife and children, as the captain nods to the sergeant and the plank supporting the man is released.

Miraculously, the rope breaks as he falls so that he hits the water. He is nearly unconscious from strangulation but still alive. Upon coming to, he seems to have acquired almost superhuman strength, and his senses and mind have become incredibly keen. Indeed, he is able to hear each separate ripple of water land on his face as he surfaces. A shouting company of soldiers fires volley after volley at him, but he dives again and is swept downstream, pursued now by grapeshot from a cannon, until he is flung up on a gravel bank, where he weeps with delight at sand that looks to him like heaps of jewels.

Then there follows wild flight through an endless stretch of woods that become darker and thicker as he flees. But he emerges at last onto a wide, silent roadway which he is sure goes in the right direction, until he finds himself, as if transported, standing at his own front gate. Descending toward him from the veranda is a noble and lovely woman, his wife, clad in a gown that shimmers in the morning sunshine. She smiles with ineffable joy that transfigures her beautiful face. He runs toward her, his arms reaching out, but just as he is about to embrace her, he feels a stunning blow on the back of his neck, there is a blinding white light, and then all goes dark. Immediately, we are back at the creek, where we now see his dead body swinging from the bridge.[8]

One has to take a few deep breaths before it sinks in that this poor man had never escaped at all. Bierce's ingenious stroke in this little gem of a story was to take the conventional notion that your life passes before your eyes in a life-threatening emergency and convert it into a dying man's last gasp of fantasy—the fantasy that even as he expires, he can still be rescued by love from the clutches of the grim reaper. Taken together, Cheever's and Bierce's stories, coming at intimacy and death from opposite directions, span nearly the whole of our culture's collective dream of love.

In my judgment, our finest, most exemplary American parable of romantic tragic failure is F. Scott Fitzgerald's magnificent novel *The Great Gatsby*. It reaches out to explore the possibilities of passionate love in the first half of the twentieth century, the era of burgeoning erotic hedonism, as fully as *The Scarlet Letter* did the residual sexual puritanism of the nineteenth century. In both novels, a solitary larger-than-life figure loves heroically and thus rises above the mediocrity of his or her surrounding social milieu. There's also an important difference between them: Hester Prynne's compassion and capacity for forgiveness, both toward herself and, more profoundly, toward her far weaker companion in adultery, Arthur Dimmesdale, become a mode of redemption. There is no redemption for Jay Gatsby, a more limited creature spiritually, although a man of great decency and splendid will, who is brought down by his total immersion in the ideals of his time.

Partly, of course, the difference stems from the closing down of redemption in the modern world. The idea of sin, a religious conception of failure, contained within it the idea of a higher forgiveness. But a large enough mistake in judgment in our day can turn out to be, as it was for Gatsby, simply a fatal error. Gatsby's demise hovers between the tragic and the pathetic; there is something almost blind, almost as random as natural disaster, about the sheer moral stupidity of the surrounding characters' actions, which finally succeed in crushing Gatsby to death.

What makes *The Great Gatsby* so powerful and so important a map of its contemporary social landscape is the lyrical precision with which Fitzgerald, through his narrator Nick Carraway, a perpetual bystander who rarely loses his patience with the ambiguities of individual life, lays open layer upon layer of the American dream and, without sacrificing what is beautiful in it, demonstrates its inevitable, disastrous failure. Its beauty, though, is the beauty of adolescence, enchanting to behold, poetic and meretricious at the same time in how far it will go, in what sublime, almost insane risks it will endure, to realize its stubborn belief that pure wanting can make the fantastic happen. The daring in this youthful journey is awesome, but the product at its end can be so thin—much too thin to cover the blunders of conflicted, imperfect adults as they try to get by and love one another. No other piece of writing about our culture has penetrated as deep, or with such a mixture of sympathy and distaste, into the pulsating interior organs of this dream.

At the end, even Nick turns away in disgust and hopelessness, appalled at what he has seen, what he has been called upon, despite himself, to participate in. For the American dream, as Fitzgerald conceives it, is ultimately the romantic dream of becoming whoever you want to be, of good fortune, if you crave it hard enough, of unlimited, renewable promises, of vast loves inextricable from vast material successes. The allure of romantic culture is a hypnotic beckoning light on the remote horizon or across the dark bay, but when you get too close in broad daylight and try to make it too real, Fitzgerald tells us, much of it turns out to be just tinsel, a cheap glitter.

There are various facets to the glowing image that drives Jay Gatsby to the verge of a seemingly impossible success, only to have it shatter into failure at the last minute. In the first place, there is the combination of discipline, charm, and just plain good luck with which Jay Gatsby, née James Gatz, a poor immigrant farmboy from North Dakota, is able to take himself by the bootstraps and revise himself, fitting himself into a role that he has for so long envied and fantasized about. Opportunity knocks at the door of those who are prepared to make full use of it—this is the premise by which he conducts his life. We learn only after his death and in the most touching way how early in his life Gatsby's fierce resolve to get ahead had swelled in his breast, when Henry Gatz, his father, shows Nick a copy of *Hopalong Cassidy* with his son's spartan schedule and list of good intentions hand-printed on the rear flyleaf. It's the new liberalized Puritan ethic, in which living by austere rules and good works *does* earn you a place among the elect right here and now on earth; one no longer has to pray for rewards in the next life, which are contingent upon the unfathomable will of God.

Of course, in our secular version, we have replaced God with the venture capitalist, a wealthy investor willing to place his faith in someone with empty pockets but a brilliant, marketable idea. And indeed, Gatsby finds his venture capitalists, even though his only brilliant idea is his self-made personality, a gorgeous "unbroken series of successful gestures" and a "heightened sensitivity to the promises of life, . . . an extraordinary gift for hope, a romantic readiness."[9] First, a millionaire from the Far West named Dan Cody discovers him at seventeen, takes him aboard his yacht as his right-hand man, and sails off to distant ports, showing Gatsby the wonders open to the very rich. When Cody dies a few years later, Gatsby is penniless again, but now his fantasies are fleshed out with palpable experience. After serving in the army, he is forced to turn to the gambler Meyer Wolfsheim, who found him hungry and broke in a poolroom and picked him up on the basis of his charm. Wolfsheim enables Gatsby to become fabulously wealthy through making him a partner in shady deals—bootlegging, illegal maneuvers in the financial markets, and other criminal ventures.

In one sense, all this adds up to nothing more than a darker and more colossal version of the bourgeois hope that one will accumulate enough to own a bigger house, buy a flashy car, and have a great social life. In portraying Gatsby's royal mansion on Long Island Sound, his dazzling yellow Rolls-Royce convertible, his bureau drawers spilling over with expensive shirts, and his outrageously generous parties, Fitzgerald has inflated this part of the dream to a grandiosity of baroque proportions. Whatever shabby means it takes to get there, at moments the glories of material opulence turn into pure song. As Nick describes the settings of Gatsby's lavish parties,

"There was music from my neighbor's house through the summer nights. In his blue gardens men and girls came and went like moths among the whisperings and the champagne and the stars. . . . On weekends his Rolls-Royce became an omnibus, bearing parties to and from the city. . . . Every Friday five crates of oranges and lemons arrived from a fruiter in New York. . . . On buffet tables, garnished with glistening hors-d'oeuvre, spiced baked hams crowded against salads of harlequin designs and pastry pigs and turkeys bewitched to a dark gold."[10]

But to Gatsby, these riches have become by now almost incidentals; they are the means—as if courtship were a matter of conspicuous consumption—by which to impress and win the great romantic love of his life, the belle from Louisville, Daisy Buchanan. This is the final, almost religious meaning of Gatsby's quest. In the most refined versions of medieval courtly love, passionate commitment to the idealized other, resulting in the performance of sacred duties and services on her behalf, built the stairway for a spiritual ascent. *The Great Gatsby* borrows some of this and converts it into an epic poem of American upward mobility wedded to romantic love. It doesn't matter that for a flash in the gray aftertaste of the next morning, it all looks suspiciously like little more than a teenage boy, in the heat of his first infatuation with the most popular girl at school, who drives by her house in his new car hoping to capture her interest.

Dreiser's *An American Tragedy,* published in 1925, the same year as *The Great Gatsby,* diagrams much of the same territory, although Dreiser views the relations between love and material success with a much more cold-blooded eye than Fitzgerald. The Darwinian bare bones stick out in *An American Tragedy,* since there is hardly enough romantic coverlet to disguise the hero's naked ambition, and he cynically exploits his two girls—the first for sex and a bit of solace for the lonely life that goes with working in a factory; the second, a rich man's daughter, whom he intends to marry mainly as the vehicle for finally achieving status and power. Most significantly, the emphases in these two novels are practically the inverse of one another: Whereas romance is only the means to wealth in Dreiser's tale, wealth becomes both means and end, inseparable from romantic fulfillment, in Fitzgerald's. Both novels show us that the holy quest for success, driven by whatever force of impulse, must come to grief—the more driven, it seems, the more dramatic the final failure. Both Gatsby and Dreiser's hero, Clyde Griffiths, aspire with terrific will. But because his idealism transfigures the crass materials provided by his culture and because he is fundamentally decent and sensitive to others, we mourn Gatsby's pointless, misguided execution more deeply than that of Griffiths, whose punishment comes much closer than Gatsby's to being what he deserved.

The other central theme of romantic adolescence in *The Great Gatsby* is that you can always go back and retrieve what appears to be irretrievably lost. Gatsby has dedicated his entire life to an idyllic month five years earlier when he and Daisy met and fell in love just before the army sent him overseas. That month for him is frozen in time forever. When Nick tells him that you can't repeat the past, Gatsby answers, "Why of course you can!"[11] Gatsby's faith is the consummation of romantic culture's unshakable belief in the second chance at a great love that has been lost: Clinging to it is supposed to lead the way back through the gates of paradise, a journey that will end in the very arms of the idealized lost beloved.

Vacillating between her marriage to an abusive, unfaithful husband and the lure of Gatsby's ferocious love, Daisy Buchanan is simply no match for the myth that Gatsby has constructed. When he insists that she return his perfect loyalty to their original meeting, she replies, "Oh you want too much."[12] From that instant forward it's clear that Gatsby is doomed. Daisy has moved on, not to something more wholesome or mature, but to a confused and torn resignation from which she spends her time distracting herself. She has given herself up to a dependence on the secure power and wealth of old money, thus conforming to the upper-crust values she was born to, and she is not about to risk it now for the suspicious new wealth of Gatsby, even though her security takes the form of Tom Buchanan, her brutally dominating husband. Daisy is not being inconsistent at all: In love with Jay Gatsby five years ago, and probably still in love with him, she is simply repeating what she did last time, when, no longer able to wait for Gatsby's return from the army, and not wishing to go against her parents' and her society's expectations, she married Buchanan in the first place.

The Great Gatsby, for all its wonders, offers us little besides two alternatives for intimacy and marriage, two polar extremes by which to measure how to love, both unsatisfactory, both destined to failure. Take your choice: either Gatsby's impossible, illusory adolescent ideal of romantic perfection, or the callous disregard for others and resignation toward one another that characterize the self-centered Buchanans, who are far worse than Willa Cather's Henshawes in that they are beyond either illusion or disillusionment. Our hearts go out to the poetic, self-created Gatsby, but how can we believe in him or make use of his almost fanatical adherence to an impossible dream?

The failure of virtually everyone in *The Great Gatsby* is not merely human nature; it's largely due to the blight—and Gatsby himself is by no means uncontaminated by it—that they have absorbed from their culture, that strange fusion of greed and idealism, power and sexual love, that too often exemplifies America's greatest aspirations as much as its lowest. Fitzgerald's dissection of it displays the sickness at its heart. In a way, Jay Gatsby is an American descendant of Emma Bovary. He is just as filled as she with yearnings to break through the restrictions of his background, the gray destiny his social class would have afforded him, just as intent on acquiring the freedom and power that wealth, status, and romance combined seem to provide for self-fulfillment. If he bears a family likeness to Emma Bovary, however, it is Emma crossed with Captain Ahab—a Darwinian, inevitably male version of Emma, an Emma who grew up in the vast empty spaces of North Dakota and who brought the myth of the frontier to Long Island Sound.

Both *Madame Bovary* and *The Great Gatsby* present us with fascinating characters who refuse to settle for the given limits of the social or even the human condition. Both Emma and Gatsby feed in adolescence on popular images of romance to inflate their hopes. And both use this imagery to create new selves, as though the self is all surface and appearance—the manners, expensive clothes, and paraphernalia that their cultures treat as the stuff of being desirable.

But think of the difference between the dreams of a lonely, poor immigrant boy growing up in the empty spaces of North Dakota, inheriting the myth of the frontier, and those of a beautiful young woman raised among the petty bourgeoisie in a cramped and busy French rural town. Flaubert's *Madame Bovary* is also about the aspiration to status and wealth through fantasies of romantic love, but it takes place in a society thickly textured with social class and thus with less of the underground raw Darwinian power struggle.

The fixation on eternal youth, the belief that there is always another chance, the feeling that time doesn't really pass, so that life is conceived as boundless opportunity, the struggle to make love last forever—these are the major themes of the culture of romance, a culture arrested at adolescence. It's a potent but unreal myth of infinite abundance, perhaps our most fervent try to make up for underlying emotional scarcity. But it has brought us to an unfortunate pass: Most of us marry out of enthusiasm, which in a way is one of our most heroic gestures. But we travel too lightly for so momentous an expedition. Carrying enough psychological equipment for intimacy only to the point of adolescence, we stop there, and the values of our popular culture help us stay there. After the enthusiasm begins to wane, there is not much left over to deal with the laborious part of it—differences that are hard to reconcile, mistakes and other letdowns, old anxieties that have to be absorbed and metabolized into something useful instead of destructive. Having started on the top of the mountain, we are suddenly deposited once again at the bottom and can't find the inner momentum or external help to work our way back up.

Outfitted with high ideals along with a good bit of zeal, Americans have always been good at getting things started—love affairs, political campaigns, presidencies, wars, high-tech companies on a shoestring—but not always so good at sustaining them. Freud, for instance, worried about two things in particular: the skepticism of Europeans, who rejected his new ideas for a long time; and the almost immediate acceptance by Americans, who he feared would vulgarize psychoanalysis through their premature enthusiasm for anything that offered the promise of improving their lives. Utopian proposals, and heaven knows, marriage is a utopian proposal, eventually have to be tempered and thus modified in the heat of friction generated by obstacles and other disappointing realities. That is the direction a journey beyond adolescence necessarily has to travel. Its basic prerequisite, of course, is learning from experience. As a society founded on the ideal of a new beginning, however, we love fresh starts and second chances, but we don't care at all to be lectured to by history.

Above all, our ways of ending things are generally dreadful. Especially these days: Political careers, as well as athletic and professional ones, more and more frequently seem to climb rapidly to the heights of celebrity, only to plummet suddenly, burnt out or nearly so in the flames of defeat or infamy. Think of the Johnson and Nixon administrations; think of Janis Joplin and Jimi Hendrix, Gary Hart, Geraldine Ferraro, Ivan Boesky, Jim Bakker, Mike Tyson, Leona Helmsley, Michael Jackson, Woody Allen, Kurt Cobain, Bob Packwood; think of the eminent scientists, including Nobel Prize winners and heads of national institutes, who have been allegedly caught covering up falsified research data. Leaving aside for the moment the questions of a general moral decline and the role of the media in all this, what sort of model for bowing out gracefully do these figures present? It's as though Lear, Othello, and Macbeth had taught us how to say goodbye.

When it comes to intimacy and marriage—and I'm of several minds about where to draw the line on ending marriages as readily as we do nowadays—we leave with our children probably the most searing image of all of how badly things can come to an end. Torn to shreds in barbaric divorces and custody disputes between parents who pay all their savings for the kids' college tuition out to lawyers, children commonly learn that marriages indeed end, love ends, traumatically in a bloodbath. If love has to end, we might at least learn to do it with some measure of civility, as did the Maples. It was that shrewd and brooding philosopher Kierkegaard who wrote concerning the male seducer (the only kind he recognized) that to make a woman fall in love with you is a work of art, but to make her fall out of love with you gracefully is a masterpiece.

If marriage and other important intimacies are to succeed in the long run, it is essential that we resurrect disappointment and failure from the disgrace to which we have consigned them. We need a framework which, if not exactly putting failure in a positive light, helps lift some of the pressure from couples suffering from disillusionment and a sense of personal failure when their initial hopes for marriage begin to fade.

There are useful lessons about failure in earlier periods of Western civilization. For example, one strand of medieval theology, which influenced Milton in *Paradise Lost,* called the Fall a *Felix Culpa,* meaning a "Fortunate Sin." The idea behind this view was that life in the Garden of Eden, being perfect, was static and ultimately boring. There were no obstacles to overcome; the skies were always sunny; the emotional seasons never changed. So Adam and Eve were left without questions or adventures. In effect, God introduced the apple and allowed in the snake to test the first couple's ability to manage perfection. Their failing the test introduced pain and difficulty into the human condition. Not the least of it was that Adam's and Eve's sexual relations became troubled.

But there was also a fringe benefit—their failure also brought challenge and growth into the conduct of life. If the Fall introduced malaise and death into the human condition, it also brought hope, flux, and the possibility of a hard-won redemption and transcendence. Disappointment in marriage after romantic love fades may be our current version of the Fortunate Fall, presenting us with the challenge to become more than we were. Each of us who goes through it has to struggle against the odds with the sinking feeling of having failed as a woman or man. But persisting in that struggle is the kind of life experience that can lead to maturity, even wisdom.

Part III

Eros at Twilight

7

The Age of Abuse

According to an article in the *New York Times,* the commander of the U.N. forces in Bosnia used to refer to the nightly roar of machine guns in downtown Sarajevo during the summer of 1993 as "domestic violence."[1] This is a rather sick joke, but if anyone is entitled to practice black humor it is a professional soldier assigned to "peacekeeping" duties in the middle of a nightmare such as Bosnia—which is a job sort of like being a family therapist on an apocalyptic scale. Moreover, the U.N. commander's quip ought to give one pause for serious thought. Although there must be a thousand wisecracks based on the battle of the sexes, this one gives the worn, venerable metaphor new life by standing it on its head. It suggests that our already tattered image of married love has taken a sinister turn for the worse.

Judging from the statistics, marriage does indeed seem well on its way to becoming one of our most violent institutions. Social scientists and other collectors of such numbers have noted for years that an unusually large proportion of mayhem and murder cases occur between people living together, but the situation has become more worrisome every day. In a column that appeared in May 1994, titled "Homicide Begins at Home," Anna Quindlen cites the surgeon general's office to the effect that domestic violence is the leading cause of injury to women between the ages of fifteen and forty-four.[2]

Those are appalling figures. For one thing, they suggest that domestic violence is a euphemism for the fact that more and more men are maiming or killing their wives. Last year, though, we were given the Bobbitt case as a grotesque warning that wives can retaliate. In a recent issue of *The New Republic,* writer Katherine Dunn adds that women are perfectly capable of initiating violence as well. She cites several studies which show quite clearly that assaults on husbands as well as mutual physical attacks between spouses are much more frequent than we generally suspect. If these findings have not been paraded before the public, Dunn points out, it's because violence by wives has not thus far been defined as a significant problem.[3]

Yet the spread of violent, even lethal resolutions to marital conflict is only one part of a larger story. How people treat their intimate partners cannot be usefully separated from the cultural milieu in which all our relationships are embedded. Intimacy, love, and desire, whatever their roots in the mysterious swamps of instinctual life, are also social constructs. They are shaped by the collective imagination, and whether people would rather rape or cuddle each other outside of culture—a condition known as the "state of nature" in classical political theory—is probably unknowable. Even an orgasm, shorn of all the meanings we infuse it with, may be little more than a pleasant sneeze in the loins, as Alan Watts once proposed. For that matter, Freud's ingenious attempts to find universals of human intimacy in the ebb and flow of children's attachment to parents probably say less about our nature than about the excitations as well as tensions inside the late-nineteenth-century patriarchal family.

After dominating our culture for some eight centuries, romantic love no longer seems to serve our need for sexual ideals. It might be hard to determine whether romance has worn us down because its demands are too transcendent or we have failed it because we are growing more incorrigible. Either way, it no longer commands the same force it used to, especially in shaping our expectations about marriage. To be sure, the old romantic themes still abound in popular culture—as nostalgia, as camp, as conservative backlash, as decoration for selling beer and cars, as early-evening TV sitcom, none of which disguises a growing lack of conviction. But one thing is certain: We have not yet formulated a more inspiring conception to replace this ideal.

As romance fades from the electronic screens of the American cultural imagination, its departure leaves a blank space, a gaping hole in our values. Culture, like nature, seems to abhor a vacuum, so it is not too surprising that raw images, derived from current events, rush in to fill it. They are proving to be not very uplifting ones. In place of the old fictional Hollywood romances—Humphrey Bogart and Lauren Bacall, Doris Day and Rock Hudson, Spencer Tracy and Katharine Hepburn—our attention is captured by ugly depictions in the news media, no longer staged by actors though just as theatrical: visions of harassment and molestation of their employees by a senator, a Supreme Court judge, and even a former governor turned president; allegations of rape, wife-beating, and domestic slaughter by sports superstars; confessions of having been brutalized during childhood or in marriage by leading figures of stage and screen. It used to be the romantic roles that movie stars played out that fascinated us and taught us what to hope or expect for ourselves. Now it's the actors' offscreen erotic behavior, especially if it appears sufficiently morally defective or perverted, that competes for the limelight. What it is teaching us to expect remains to be seen.

Nor is this just a matter of the latest revelations about misbehaving celebrities: From the flood of both national and local news reports, it would appear that all of our closest and most private relationships are suffering from an epidemic of moral blight. The guidance and support, nurturance and protection that parents, relatives, teachers, clergymen, and daycare workers are supposed to provide for children prove to be riddled with increasingly sickening discoveries of sexual trespass and violence, until all such relationships have become suspect. There is a disheartening feeling that our adult relations with one another are going down the same path. It is difficult to enter into any kind of relationship these days without misgivings. You could say that the paradigmatic relationship between self and other in our time is expressed in the idea of abuse, to the point that it has become a cliché.

Indeed, it begins to look as though the whole of society, from the White House to the playground, from the master bedroom to the executive suite, from the classroom to the back alley, has turned into a stage upon which a new cultural drama of sexual good and evil is unfolding, one that resembles a medieval allegory of sin, confession, and retribution. Nearly every day the front page and prime-time news add a few more sexual horrors, sandwiched between the roll call of congressmen for and against health-care reform and the body counts from distant lands. Having turned over rocks in high places as well as low, we find ourselves staring with growing bewilderment at stranger and stranger specimens of abusive lust crawling out into the light. As the culture of romance draws to a close, it is already being replaced, by default as it were, with a new culture—the culture of abuse.

What can this development tell us about the fate of our intimate relationships, whether casual flings or lifelong alliances, courtships or marriages? Is it all we can muster by way of a new myth to guide our sexual lives? Are we on our way to becoming a society like that of the Dobu Islanders of New Guinea,[4] who based their intimate arrangements on sexual danger, jealousy, and paranoia?

Of course, it is hard to get one's bearings in the middle of so perplexing a cultural transition as this shift from romance to abuse. Its outlines are hardly firm; its long-run consequences are unknown. But everything suggests that its implications may well be momentous. And there are at least a few things about its impact that already can be made relatively clear.

To say that abuse has become central in our culture is to say not only that it represents a change, a decline in fact, in our actual intimate behavior but also that it has reached the level of a shaping idea.

That means it has considerable power to influence the way people perceive, think, feel, and act. In this sense, romantic love was one of the most powerful ideas ever to arise. By "idea" in this context, I don't intend something so abstract as the word might suggest at first glance. The kind of overarching idea that gives shape to culture is not a set of propositions; it is more like an attitude, a sensibility, a pattern of expectations and motives. One might think of it as the style of consciousness for a particular time and place.

There is a vast difference in how these two formative ideas exercise their influence. Romantic love was a unifying force. Many people may have quarreled with it or rejected it for personal, religious, or other reasons; but on the whole it pervaded the fantasies and aspirations of an entire civilization. It expressed itself throughout the widest spectrum of cultural productions, from sonnet cycles to shampoo commercials. Its message was positive—if anything, more than positive; indeed, at its core was the promise of the deepest harmony between two people, which could approach the ecstatic or transcendent. Even when circumstances took a tragic turn, as with Romeo and Juliet or Tristan and Iseult, one felt that the expiring lovers would be reunited forever on some more ethereal plane. At its most profound, romantic love seemed something worth dying for.

Abuse, in its worst aspect, turns love and sex into something worth killing for. Abuse has no conceivable redeeming features; its meaning is totally negative. This may explain in large part why its effect on our culture, as it becomes a pervasive cultural idea, is fragmenting, even polarizing. The harmony promised by romantic love might have been elusive, but everyone could gather around its meanings. The romantic feeling was one of melting, if not with joy then with sorrow. It could move you to tears, as in scenes in the movies of lovers reuniting after long, ordeal-ridden absence or of their parting forever although their two hearts beat as one. And sorrow, like desire or affection, inclines people to move toward one another. But sexual abuse inspires horror and anger, emotions that rigidify and repel. When such abuse rears its head, lovers, husbands and wives, even parents and children are set against one another, often to an extreme degree, and families are frequently shattered beyond repair. If the pinnacle of romance is an ecstatic merging, like a climactic duet in an Italian opera, a corresponding image for the culture of abuse is a courtroom with intimates pitted against each other in a criminal proceeding.

On the level of consciousness, the ascendancy of abuse also reflects how profoundly our thinking has changed about the relationship between love and power. When intimacy between men and women was ruled by romantic decorum, the distribution of power between them was not seriously in question. It's only in looking back through jaded contemporary eyes that one can make out the extent to which power, chiefly the power of male domination perhaps, was humming away behind the scenes, disguised by various ideal tableaus of what courtship, marriage, and sexual union were supposed to be. Both our erotic conduct and our ways of making sense of it over the course of the twentieth century have gradually exposed the secret power politics of romantic love.

In this respect, the dismantling of romantic love began quite some time ago. Early in the century psychoanalysis initiated the process, demystifying romance by dissecting its idealism into more earthy components—a mix of animal urge, incestuous projections, and sublimated anxiety. Modern feminism has taken this reductive tendency in another direction and argued that romantic ideals work mainly to enlarge the scope of men's control over women. For example, a woman on a pedestal may look as though she has been elevated to a lofty position, but we now tend to focus more on how she is effectively trapped there, prevented from freely developing her own sexual, economic, and creative potential. These have been among our most valuable modern insights. But it could be that the pendulum has swung too far. Power conceived now as abuse—the exploitation and violation of one intimate by another—seems on the verge of conquering love in our view of the relations between men and women.

One consequence is that our feelings about sexual contact are drifting far beyond questions of who wields the power when two people get together. In the age of abuse we are starting to treat love and sex as though they are a hazard to one's health. Older generations of Americans, however they may have behaved, used to believe that sexual love was an oasis of safety and protection, pleasure and fulfillment in a tumultuous world. That belief is changing into a vision of love that resembles a private version of life on our disastrously violent city streets. One used to walk the streets of our great cities with a sense of warmth, excitement, belonging, and the adventurous prospect of making larger connections. Now one barely ventures out the door without a pang of fear.

So pessimistic a transformation is no commonplace historical event, for love has traditionally been the repository of Western civilization's most cherished aspirations, from Plato's time till our own. It is true that ancient societies often held a dim view of the passion that we came to know as romantic love, sometimes dismissing it as madness, as C. S. Lewis has pointed out.[5] But in part this was because they tended to compare it unfavorably to other ideal versions of erotic intimacy.

On the other hand, a gloomy attitude toward erotic love is not wholly foreign to the American sensibility: One can find among the Puritans ancestral forerunners of the culture of abuse. And now there is a sense in which the culture of abuse has evolved into a return of the repressive—a swing back to puritanism after decades of sexual liberation. I will return later to the ramifications of this unsettling reversion.

Of course, it hardly comes as news that friction, struggle, and furious moments occur between intimates. "Is there a love, then, that can also hate?" asked Wilhelm Stekel, an early follower of Freud.[6] Either this question is purely rhetorical, or it deserves to be answered with another question—is there love that doesn't hate, at least some of the time? Given the willfulness of the human animal, the urge of each member of the species to have its own way, and the brute fact that every one of us is different in important respects from every other, how can the best companionship not be punctuated by sparks of irritation—or even threats of disintegration—generated by the sheer rub of another's existence up against one's own? Anger wells up spontaneously when there is an obstacle in one's path, and lovers or spouses will always become roadblocks to each other now and then, at times without doing anything except just being around. It reminds me of a patient of mine who said of his wife, "Sometimes I wake up, and she is always there." His weird grammar itself speaks volumes.

These are among the reasons that I think a successful intimate relationship resembles a work of art: They are both ingenious constructions in which satisfying and enduring form comes from the laborious work of reconciling or integrating conflicting tendencies. In the case of intimacy, some of these tendencies draw people to merge with each other, while others threaten to pull them apart. When it comes to making an intimate relationship, therefore, you also have to factor in anxiety. There are obviously deep anxieties involved in producing art—stage fright, the encounter with uncertainty, the frustration and sometimes torment of self-expression. But the anxieties inherent in love and sex, the ones discussed throughout this book, tend to assault one's very sense of identity and well-being, bringing up all of one's early childhood fears in the process.

The disintegrative and destructive aspects of love, the ones that give rise to particularly virulent anxieties, are where our myths and values—in other words, our cultural forms—play a particularly important role. That intimacies can last as long as they do beyond biological necessity is a tribute to a singular human capacity to live by ideals that restrain our wilder impulses. As the anthropologist Edward Sapir once pointed out, knocking on the door to signal a desire to enter is a slightly inhibited and symbolic form of kicking the door down.[7] This combination of consensual inhibition and symbolic expression is called civilization. Sexual violence, however, is neither inhibited nor symbolic; it represents breakdown, and its prevalence suggests that civilization might be losing its grip.

The late literary and social critic Irving Howe made a useful distinction between this kind of social trouble, largely cultural and psychological in origin, which he called a "crisis of civilization," and the more common social crises, which have to do mainly with institutional arrangements. Whereas a social crisis, Howe pointed out, "signifies a breakdown in the functioning of society: it fails to feed the poor, it cannot settle disputes among constituent groups, it drags the country into an endless war" and thus calls for economic and political reform, "a crisis of civilization has to do not so much with the workings of the economy or the rightness of social arrangements as it does with the transmission of values, those tacit but deeply lodged assumptions by means of which men try to regulate their conduct." Therefore, Howe concluded, "a social crisis is expressed mainly through public struggle, a crisis of civilization mainly through incoherence of behavior."[8]

"Incoherence of behavior" says it well. For years, aided and abetted by the media, we watched Hollywood celebrities commit infidelities and break up their marriages till we were just about inured to the whole business. We looked on with prurient fascination that tacitly gave these famous, larger-than-life intimates special exemption from our stricter sexual codes, as though the very nature of their profession entails less stable libidos. Perhaps their activities fed our underground fantasies of letting the id have freer rein, but they certainly didn't overturn our official beliefs and hopes about romantic love. Nowadays there is a radically different quality to such incidents. When the breakdown of the twelve-year-long, apparently tranquil love affair (almost more domestic than marriage) between Woody Allen and Mia Farrow hit the front pages in the summer of 1992, it left us deeply shocked, asking unanswerable questions: Did he or did he not molest their youngest daughter, Dylan, who was seven at the time? Or was Mia Farrow using the unforgivable charge of sexual abuse as the ultimate weapon of vengeance or as a ploy to get total custody of their children? What were we to make of Allen's infidelity with Soon-Yi, Farrow's twenty-two-year-old Korean daughter adopted during her marriage to Andre Previn?

The incoherence and confusion, especially over the abuse charges, proceeded to spread rapidly. Farrow took her charges of child molestation to the police and other authorities, and tried to document them, an unsavory task at best. Everyone from friends and attorneys to therapists and policemen got involved in holding press conferences and taking sides. It was related in the *New York*

Times that poor Dylan had been interviewed and examined by medical staff from Yale–New Haven Hospital on nine separate occasions and several more times by the Connecticut State Police, a period during which she alternately confirmed the charges of abuse, retracted them, and then retracted the retraction.[9]

Allen, of course, denied the charges of sexual abuse, but affirmed his affair with Soon-Yi in glowing romantic terms. It sounded awfully much like a typical case of a middle-aged man, grown weary or afraid of a middle-aged relationship, seeking renewal through infatuation with a winsome, nubile young woman—only the young woman happened in this case to be Farrow's adopted daughter. Exactly where does the transition from falling absurdly, even stupidly, in love to committing a crime of abuse occur?

In the custody trial that followed, Farrow squared off in court with no fewer than five attorneys, including Alan Dershowitz, and Allen shielded himself with four. Dershowitz, a Harvard Law School professor, had already acquired his own celebrity status in matters of unusually notorious and dramatic domestic warfare in the trial of Klaus von Bulow, who was charged with attempting to murder his wealthy wife; Dershowitz's role was later dramatized (and publicized) in the film *Reversal of Fortune*. From von Bulow to Farrow versus Allen: We have managed to create a world in which reality can turn almost immediately into cinema and cinema into reality, until we can barely tell which is which. It's as if the concept of virtual reality, arising from computer technology, has become the new basis for intimacy, marriage, and family life. The same thing holds for therapy and reality. When the Allen–Farrow custody trial got under way, it emerged that this peculiar family was virtually riddled with therapists: According to Peter Marks, a *New York Times* reporter who covered the trial, Allen had been consulting two therapists of his own; Farrow apparently had the more usual number—one; Satchel, their biological son, age five at the time of the blowup, had been seeing a therapist for about two years; Dylan had begun therapy at five; and Soon-Yi, Allen's new lover, had been sent to a special school run by psychiatrists when she was a child. All in all, Marks reports, the names of eight psychologists and psychiatrists came up in the courtroom.[10]

My own favorite example of the expanding incoherence glut came, naturally enough, from a member of my own profession. When the judge asked her whether Farrow might regard Allen as a "bad person," Dr. Susan Coates, a therapist of Satchel's and on occasion an adviser to both Farrow and Allen, replied, "The issue for me is, could Miss Farrow find a way to empower what has been and is good in her relationship with Mr. Allen, while also holding him accountable for it?"[11] I have no idea what this means, or even what the antecedent of "it" might be. Subsequently, however, Dr. Coates added what I guess must be the definitive diagnosis of all this smoke and heat, the only lame conclusion that we can draw with a measure of certitude about the demise of this couple: "The amount of non-agreement between them was so great . . . that it led me to ask why they were together."[12] I don't know if "non-agreement" in the mind of a psychotherapist means something more portentous than the tried-and-true English word "disagreement," but I assume it means that Allen and Farrow had irreconcilable differences. If their mess, then, represents anything at all about our evolving sexual habits, it stands for how pathetic we have become.

This sad emblematic couple, Allen and Farrow, gave us a new and spectacular version of the battle of the sexes, played out between two celebrities on a national stage, at a pitch of complication and intensity that carried across a substantial slice of American culture. In a sense, our elevation of abuse to the level of culture is the next logical step after an era of mounting divorce rates. In the culture of romance, it is easy to get together. There are just the two of you, and all that is absolutely required to get married is one other person endowed with the authority to make it official. Divorcing is totally different; the bitterness of departure requires a lot of costly legal apparatus. In the culture of abuse, the relationship, broken and bleeding from having been unforgivably violated, winds up in the criminal justice system, encumbered with an entire corps of professionals, agencies, bureaucracies, and state and local officials. And if the wreckage is dramatic enough, you get reporters and television crews as well.

Cultural change rarely takes place in a methodical or uniform fashion. It begins with the stitching together of what may seem at first like vaguely related events in various parts of society: minute as well as dramatic differences in the way people behave; a shift in the breeze that carries popular opinion, rumors, gossip, daydreams, and news reports from one person to another; a new slant in speculation about both public acts and private ones. Ordinary people may begin to comport themselves differently; but so do celebrities, who establish the new conduct as a style or fashion, and you can't tell whether the regular folks do it first and the celebrities pick it up, or vice versa. As a rule, no one can make out the overall pattern until, like an old-fashioned quilt, its fabrication is pretty far along. And then the cultural makers and shapers, the communicators, come along to give it coherent imagery and form. Art and literature begin to embody the change, but so do soap operas, movies, the top ten pop songs, cartoons, and advertisements.

The invention of romantic love involved gradual transformations of this type. The upper classes began to idealize certain kinds of sexual and intimate behavior during the Middle Ages. Eventually these changes were codified, frequently in allegorical lyrics and writings, and conveyed throughout European aristocracy by the troubadour poets who circulated from castle to castle. Our current troubadours work for the media—journalists, correspondents, and camera crews sent to the scene to report courtroom trials and senate hearings; singers and comedians who formulate our latest slogans and epigrams; news anchors, columnists, and talk-show hosts who process confessions, revelations, and indictments.

Romantic love may have started as poetry and ended centuries later as spectacle in Hollywood. In certain respects, however, it was always about keeping secrets, whereas the culture of abuse is about publicizing them. This is an important distinction, ultimately leading to radically different interpretations of love and its place in the social order. A romantic relationship between lovers was *supposed* to be private, even tucked out of sight as long as possible. Lovers sometimes went to extravagant lengths to keep their intimacy out of the general social arena, at least until they married. Its meanings were special and belonged to them alone.

The romantic imagination looked with a special fondness upon the beginnings of young love—its innocence and tentative losses of innocence, its thrilling (though anxious) furtive and exploratory fumblings with zippers and skirts. All this now seems quaintly charming, as though on its way to join convertibles in the museum of American nostalgia. There used to be a respectful holding back as one went forward in sex—or so we thought, and most of us practiced it that way. Desire was still considered a force to be reckoned with, one that left people trembling at the gates between either entry into paradise or a fall into guilt. This hesitant doubleness has been one of the great motifs in almost all the famous tales of romantic love; think of Tristan and Iseult, for example, sleeping together with a sword between them. Perhaps the idealization of sex and the darkness of sex have always been traveling companions.

Today, however, we act as if we already know where erotic experience will land us—in murky ambiguity, accompanied by disclosures of violence and violation, charges and countercharges. Our attention is concentrated at the dead end of romance, carried forward into the realm of abuse by therapists, lawyers, and the media. We have become so alert to evils lurking under the covers alongside romantic intimacy that nothing seems innocent any longer. Romantic love took place behind closed doors with the lamps turned down low. Nowadays it's as if Eros, caught redhanded in a criminal act, stands exposed, looking shamefaced under the klieg lights.

These themes—the uses of exposure and publicity, the attraction to the demise rather than to the beginning of intimacies and marriages, the hidden violation suddenly revealed in a way that shatters relationships and families, the corruption of sexual desire—are widely affecting how couples and families respond to their troubles. Intimate terrorism, which I formulated in Chapter 1 as a kind of metaphor to describe the regulation of anxiety through a battle for control, no longer seems so metaphorical. Of course, the tangles of love, power, and anxiety go on plaguing close relationships as they no doubt always will. But our thresholds for frustration about these matters seem much lower than they used to be. Intimate terrorism in the era of abuse thus passes more quickly into physical or sexual assault. It more often infects other family members besides the couple. And then it spills over into the public arena, where state or county family services and similar agencies, along with the police and the courts, get into the act.

When a new couple phones me for an appointment these days, they are apt to tell me that one of them has just been arrested for domestic violence, or that a child went to see a therapist and returned accusing one of them of sexual abuse. A couple came to me recently under orders from the guardian ad litem in a divorce proceeding because they were charging each other with abusing their children as well as one another. Each spouse hoped that the court would decide that the other one was the more malevolent abuser and therefore deserved to lose custody of the children. For its part, the court had thrown up its hands and shipped the two off to therapy in the hope that this might disentangle truths from lies or at least calm things down enough for negotiations to begin again. (It didn't.) I have been in private practice for twenty-four years. How can it be that for most of two decades I rarely, if ever, got a call like this, yet now they are almost commonplace?

A historian, Leon Botstein, writing about modern political terrorists who hijack planes, take hostages, ambush athletes, and the like, pointed out that "if terrorism, in general, has a rationale, one aspect is the dramatization of a cause to the world."[13] Since disclosures and confessions now make up so much of our cultural reality, it might be that both terrorists and the terrorized among couples and family members are more often going public to dramatize their causes to the world. Where there is actual domestic violence or sexual abuse, the growing support for coming out of the marital or family closet to make known the horrors taking place therein is a curative social development of major significance, an opportunity at last for victims to get out from under their victimizers. But intimate terrorists can also turn into hijackers and hostage-takers—of each other's lives, the marriage, the kids—by taking advantage of abuse charges. So we have also acquired still another class of victims—people who are falling under a curse of exaggerated or even completely false accusations of abuse, a phenomenon that might well be called the abuse of abuse. And this phenomenon is having major social implications as well.

Presumably no one questions that there is more *actual* abuse, even taking into account the fact that we are more determined than ever to expose it. We live in a social climate conducive to physical and sexual violence at every level. One day we may finally decide to control the purchase of guns or soften movie and television violence and pornography, but neither of these measures will begin to solve the problem: They tackle symptoms, not the disease. We have become a careless society, by which I mean not only that we do not take care of each other but that we do not take care *with* each other. The fundamental respect with which one ought to approach or treat the existence of another person seems to have become lost. It used to be called civility. Violation of one another has become part of the polluted air we regularly breathe in America, and people will resort to it more spontaneously when they feel frustrated or helpless as temperatures rise in lovers' and marital quarrels. I suspect that every therapist has seen indications of a more rapid movement from violent words to violent deeds, from primitive sexual fantasies to impulsive acts of rape, molestation, and the like.

But if abuse has become a more common form of intimate terrorism, so is the abuse of abuse on the rise among intimates out for vengeance, vindication, or the upper hand. Both these trends have brought children more directly into the pitched camps of intimate terrorists, whether as pawns of husbands and wives trying to do each other in, particularly in custody suits; as patients of therapists who have their own axes to grind; or on their own as avenging angels in the ancient wars between generations. Terrible dilemmas around guilt and innocence, truth and falsehood, are being generated, and they are grinding many families to pieces in addition to exacerbating our general social confusion. The abuse issue has established its own peculiar set of epistemological as well as ethical problems: How do you know what really happened, followed by what do you do about it?

During the last few years, I've stumbled across people stuck in this cognitive and moral quagmire a number of times in my own professional life, as I imagine nearly every psychotherapist has by now. In one chilling case that a colleague told me about, an elderly woman was suddenly approached by her middle-aged daughter with an astonishing accusation. The daughter now claimed that her mother, her father, and another couple some forty years earlier had been running satanic cults that practiced regular sexual abuse of children and other horrible rituals. She was referring to a distant time when the two couples were graduate students who had teamed up to help each other with caring for their young children. It seems that the daughter's own marriage had recently broken up, and she had fallen into a serious depression. One of the therapists she saw convinced her that she had been sexually abused as a child. The same therapist urged her to confront her mother.

The narrator of this tale did not know whether the satanic dimension was introduced by the therapist or the daughter. What she did tell me, however, was that the therapist informed the mother that her daughter could only get well if the mother admitted her guilt. Still reeling with shock, the mother was given the choice of corroborating the charges that she had indeed subjected her children to satanic abuse rituals or abandoning her daughter to indefinite mental illness. If this seems an extraordinary approach to psychotherapy, it is by no means the only time I have run across the notion that the parent's confession of culpability is the only road to curing the child.

I suppose that I am in no position to pass judgment or even to know whom or what to believe in these instances. According to the sexual abuse recovery movement, the parent's denials in cases like this are generally part of the family collusion to cover up one or more members' evil deeds. It is almost as though the more vehemently parents, spouses, and others deny charges of abuse the more evident their guilt, which is a sticky web to climb out of. If their denials seem particularly convincing, so the argument proceeds, it is probably because they have succeeded in deceiving themselves along with everyone else.

Psychiatrist Judith Lewis Herman has written eloquently and profoundly about a historical turning point, in which a convergence of the women's movement, long and laborious clinical work, and cultural evolution has at last given the victims of traumatic abuse a language to tell of the unspeakable things that have been done to them (made unspeakable because society consigned them to shame and silence).[14] I don't question the important social value of this development.

But neither do I know exactly what might have gone on behind the scenes to culminate in horrible messes like the one I described above. I suspect that *something* happened in these families, but how would one get to the bottom of whether it was sexual abuse or not? It could be that a grown child's early memories of having been touched coldly or too anxiously or even not at all might now be recovered as a memory of abuse, especially when cheered on by abuse experts in the present cultural atmosphere.

It is becoming increasingly difficult for anyone to be sure about what to believe—with the exception of those therapists and others who are currently staking out claims in the fundamentalist regions of absolute truth. Painful, disorienting uncertainty of this magnitude is not easy to live with. As a result, the whole business is turning into a clamor of polarized certitudes. Although our two major political parties, no matter how opposed their rhetoric may make them look, usually begin to melt into each other during the heat of elections, it is striking how often our social, cultural, and moral concerns end up in an inconclusive clash of mutually exclusive positions.

People tend to gravitate toward ideologies based on righteous indignation to the extent that they cannot tolerate waiting or remaining curious when faced with complexity and uncertainty. And though we have never been a priestly country—Americans prefer the power of technique to the power of faith in miracles—we have evolved a secular substitute for priesthoods, known as "experts." One always has to be skeptical in our society about experts who come forward with claims to special knowledge. An added complication at the moment is that such special knowledge has become equated with being a victim of oppression. Robert Hughes has pointed out that our new criterion for weighing the validity of historical truth is that "some victim know it in his or her bones."[15] Presumably that explains why so many therapists who advertise themselves as experts on recovering from sexual abuse also let it be known that they themselves are survivors. This is a new gimmick in mental-health marketing: In the past, therapists did not promote their own depressions, say, to the public as certifying their competence to work with depressed people.

Insistence that the cure of the son's or daughter's ills depends on their parents admitting the truth of what they deny with all their hearts, on their accepting devastating accusations, goes against the spirit of a principle that Western civilization fought long and hard to implement. Liberalism and democracy sought to protect the accused from premature destruction of reputation and good name, as well as from unjust sentencing, through the concept that one is innocent until proven guilty. This is an ethical principle as well as a strictly legal one, for it demands that one treat the accused on faith as a full citizen in good standing, until found guilty of a crime beyond any conceivable doubt.

The emphasis on abuse in the practice of psychotherapy, and increasingly in the general culture as well, is in the process of overturning this principle. Some abuse therapists act as though they possess the techniques for extracting absolute truths out of the dim, convoluted labyrinths of mental life. In contrast, the best psychotherapy since Freud's time has insisted that the most valuable prerequisite for self-discovery is a nonjudgmental and openly curious state of waiting on the part of both therapist and patient, given the many-sidedness and ambiguity of human experience. But these traits are being scrapped as unnecessary or irrelevant by some of the abuse experts. To the extent that such therapy succeeds in swaying law enforcement agencies and juries through its claims to expertise, we have cause for profound alarm. Bringing abuse into public view has no doubt succeeded in dredging up many a scoundrel as well as promoted the mental health of traumatized patients. But even if one were tempted to write off as a mere side effect the innocent citizens who find themselves accused because they are relatively few in number, those few often end up stripped of their jobs, their reputations forever ruined. Some are presently languishing in jails. We need safeguards in the form of accountability from any psychotherapy that can have such consequences. It is not much different in principle than when psychiatry was used during the Stalinist period in Russia to imprison political dissidents in mental asylums.

Faced with so much confusion about knowing what "really" happened and what might be at the root of abuse charges in so many cases, one doesn't know quite how to respond—whether with unadulterated outrage or with a few molecules of allowance for their pathos—to those individuals, mostly men, who manage to get caught between two cultures with their flies unzipped. At one point after the custody trial ended, Woody Allen gave a press conference in which he issued a call for Farrow to join him in a truce, adding that "if the Arabs and Israel can do it, we can."[16] At least this remark recognizes a relationship between love and power; it even raises the battle of the sexes to new geopolitical heights, hinting at border clashes between nations, exchanges of political prisoners, signing of treaties, and other intricate diplomatic negotiations.

Ultimately, though, Allen was either being naive or disingenuous about missing the point, as he tried to fight off the new culture with the materials of the old. In invoking romantic love as the justification for his affair with Soon-Yi and jealousy as an explanation for the depth of bitterness between him and Farrow, Allen is just plain out of date. A lot of people, again men especially, seem just plain out of date in this way, which doesn't mean that their desperate or dumb behavior is forgivable. Passionate feelings are no longer an excuse; they have become a symptom. Lovers' quarrels can no longer be readily patched up because, in the inevitable tangles of love and power from which they spring, the workings of power nowadays so easily vanquish whatever there might have been of love. Once charges of sexual abuse have surfaced, things have usually entered the realm of the unforgivable. The blackest allegation that Farrow hurled at Allen—that he molested his seven-year-old daughter—may never be fully settled, which is a disturbing problem inherent in our society's preoccupation with abuse.

Senator Bob Packwood is another well-known figure who has dropped through the cracks between the old and new cultures. Here is the case of a man who had achieved a high station, who had maintained a decent voting record in the Senate, particularly in the area, ironically enough, of women's rights and concerns. But he naively, if not wickedly, drew upon an outdated prerogative that he must have thought he was still entitled to. A recent *New Yorker* profile portrayed him as having been a shy, unattractive, and rather wimpy young man through his adolescent years, one who had trouble getting a date even in college. So what is a guy like that supposed to do? Why, get rich or gain a powerful position! replied an underside of the old culture. Thus an adult and successful Senator Packwood felt (one speculates) that he had earned the right at last to grab for himself some of what the other guys got.

When I was an undergraduate, this was no big deal. All of us knew about our classmates who had made it big in football or who had a certain social charisma that enabled them to get—or maybe take—all they wanted. And we never knew whether the girls involved were really willing or not. The word *no* had not yet been invented for women. If they said it, by some curious dialectical twist, it meant yes. (And now, on the outlying flanks of militant feminism, a woman's yes means no—even though she may not realize it, she is being exploited by submitting to intercourse.) I am not trying to make light of the serious moral issues or even the culturally induced masculine pathology involved in this. I am simply trying to emphasize that times have changed, and some people are having trouble figuring it out.

Another eminent figure, indeed an epoch-making one as things turned out, among the legions of men being toppled from pillars of respectability by the culture of abuse is Supreme Court Justice Clarence Thomas. Perhaps he, too, like Allen and Packwood, got trapped unsuspectingly in the new atmosphere of outrage. But he lost the chance for much sympathy when he tried to vindicate himself by implying that he was the victim of a racist lynching. One of the least appealing devices in our era of blaming and buck-passing is when the accused fight fire with fire and try to defend themselves by claiming that they are in truth the bigger victims than their accusers.

Moreover, one ought to be skeptical of conservative claims that

Anita Hill was simply the pawn of white Democrats behind the Senate Judiciary Committee, which conducted the hearings on Thomas's nomination. Granted that could have been what some associated with the committee had in mind. But whatever political machinations might have gone on, why not assume the broader picture—that she was willing to speak up after so much time had passed because the culture now supports such speech? This aligns her situation with other related recent developments in the sexual sphere, such as gays who have come out of the closet because cultural change has freed them to do so without anticipating terrible repercussions. The same sort of thing likely applies to the women who have "come forward," as the current saying goes, one after another, to report on Senator Packwood's pawing at them over the years.

From all these incidents one can make out a number of salient features characteristic of the culture of abuse. First of all, we no longer know whose truths to trust—the alleged abuser, who, if not a celebrity, is often a pillar of the community and speaks with sanctioned authority, or the accuser, who speaks with the authority of victimhood. Nearly all established authority (which usually means that men are in charge) is coming to be regarded with suspicion, because, if not already infected, it is considered vulnerable to the spreading sickness of using power for sexually exploitative purposes. And indeed, the news seems to provide ample signs that this habit might be on its way to reaching epidemic proportions, although questions arise over whether it was not there all along.

Just for starters, take a single day in the newspapers a few years ago—namely, October 23, 1991. There were stories in the *New York Times* concerning the investigation of charges that an ex-president of the University of South Carolina had made sexual advances to four male students; the indictment of a former national "father of the year" by a Manhattan grand jury for sexually abusing and endangering several of his thirty-five adopted children; and the arrest of a fifty-two-year-old handicapped man in a Brooklyn apartment loaded with guns on charges of using dozens of young girls as models for pornography. That same day, the *Boston Globe* reported that the congregation of a Catholic parish in western Massachusetts was in shock following the arraignment of its priest for the alleged assault and rape of two teenage children, with the added suspicion that he may have also been involved in the sexual murder of an altar boy twenty years ago. These incidents are all old hat by now, because there have been so many more, and far worse, since then.

I picked the fall of 1991, though, in part because that was also the period during which the culture of abuse first seriously entered high politics. Until Professor Anita Hill, a former employee of Justice Clarence Thomas, showed up at his confirmation hearings to testify about his crude sexual advances toward her, his appointment seemed to be little more than Washington-as-usual: the selection by a Republican president of an undistinguished jurist with a record of no outstanding or decisive opinions about the crucial issues of the day, who also happened to be both conservative and African-American. Neither was the content of Professor Hill's testimony really all that shocking. Who could have doubted that an exploitative fusion of power and sex goes on behind the closed office doors of men in high places? What was shocking—and in fact sufficiently dramatic to keep the country's eyebeams hooked to TV screens for days—was its being spelled out in great detail on every major network. We might have taken such a sexual soap opera in stride, as we always had before, if it had remained rumor or innuendo; but witnessing it made explicit on so grand a scale was new for this country (in contrast to Britain, for example). And it couldn't have happened without television, which communicates across our society with the force and scope that the tragedies of Sophocles or Aeschylus must have had in the Greek polis.

The debates continue to this day about whether Hill or Thomas was telling the truth. That there is any debate at all is another part of what is so new: The very idea that the sexually abused and the relatively powerless (and in the culture of abuse these categories begin to merge) had any truths to tell—that they could speak out against their oppressors after years of silence—had now penetrated the highest levels of government. Such speaking out had, in fact, been gathering momentum for quite a while—in the recovery movement, in the revelations by celebrities in popular magazines, in confessions on television talk shows. For that matter, sexual harassment itself, which is what Thomas stood accused of, as Packwood also would be shortly, was a relatively new invention as a subspecies of abuse. It had been made an effective issue in the courtroom only a few years earlier by the increasingly prominent activities of feminist law professor Catharine MacKinnon. Appropriately enough, MacKinnon appeared on the cover of the Sunday *New York Times Magazine* (although the profile inside didn't mention Thomas) during that same month—October 1991. Meanwhile MacKinnon and her compatriot-at-arms writer Andrea Dworkin had moved on: They were hard at work trying to get cities to pass ordinances prohibiting all pornography, not simply on the basis that it might be conducive to but actually *is* abusive male violence aimed at subjugating women.

Thus the categories of abuse have been rapidly multiplying during the last few years. At the same time, the news of abuse has burgeoned, cutting wider and wider swaths across the social landscape. A year after the Thomas hearings, the *Boston Globe*'s coverage of Derek Walcott winning the Nobel Prize for poetry wove in an explanation of why Harvard had not renewed his teaching contract. According to the *Globe,* there were reports that a female student had complained to university officials when Walcott confronted her with a choice of sex with him or a bad grade. This unseemly footnote—a professor using grades to coerce a student sexually—would not have even made the school paper when I was in college. In fact, I doubt that it would have been permitted to appear, yet everyone knew it was going on. The most striking thing about the *Globe* article, as least in its cultural implications, is to come across the sexual harassment issue appearing in an announcement of a distinguished writer winning a Nobel Prize.

Disclosures such as those I have discussed—one could go on listing them endlessly, drawing examples from every social institution—have spread across social classes, generations, racial barriers, and sexual preferences. And with a mischievous or maybe vindictive effectiveness, they have instantly converted esteem into notoriety,

bringing people down to earth from the stratosphere of show business and other celebrity arenas. Abuse first became a noticeable topic
in the late 1970s when a growing number of women and a few
children broached conspiracies of silence, threats of humiliation, and
other retaliations to reveal the damage that had been inflicted on
them. These were acts of rebellious courage. But no society has ever
turned rebellion into fashion faster than America. We begin with
housewives and children struggling to escape sexual enslavement
and brutality, and we end up with Madonna and Camille Paglia.
This cultural trait is a mixed blessing: On the one hand, it has been
known to pull the fangs of radical movements agitating about important issues by ignoring their point and adopting their style. On
the other hand, it can at times also spread the message with great
efficiency. Thus the disclosure theme was picked up by media stars
such as Oprah Winfrey, Janet Jackson, and Roseanne Barr, who
announced in interviews or articles that they had suffered sexual
violations in their families or at the hands of spouses. Confessions
like theirs had an air of self-promotion, but they also helped create
the atmosphere of accountability in which Mike Tyson was found
guilty of raping a young beauty queen and William Kennedy Smith
was barely acquitted of similar charges brought by a date he picked
up in a bar.

This new climate of personal accountability may have prompted a
speech Senator Edward Kennedy gave in 1992 at Harvard's John F.
Kennedy School of Government. In the midst of denouncing Republican policies, Senator Kennedy suddenly changed course in
order to apologize for the conduct of his private life, and though he
gave no particulars, everyone knew that he was alluding, among
other things, to his numerous affairs and other sexual indiscretions.
Senator Kennedy is often in the position of apologizing for something, but this was his most fetching apology yet, not least because it
was unconnected to specific episodes such as Chappaquiddick. And
what's more, now he has plenty of company.

One thing emerges quite clearly from all this: The culture of abuse
challenges power by challenging, among other things, what was

often dismissed as normal or only slightly aberrant male sexual behavior in the 1960s and before. Many men felt free to grab whatever part of a woman's body intrigued them, to "cop a feel," as schoolboys used to say, to regard a woman's refusal as a coy invitation. Anyway, so the argument sometimes ran, what's wrong with a little sexual pressure, given that males naturally have to express their lusty, vital nature, and given that women don't always know what is good for them until they get it? If a woman rejected these approaches too vigorously, some men felt additionally licensed to enforce their wishes with everything from threats of job loss to physical harm. Even the worst of the lot, those who proceeded from a pat on the ass to rape, felt relatively safe: If they got caught, they could always insist that the woman provoked or otherwise invited it. Despite two decades of feminist protest, there are courtrooms and other forums where this insane notion is still treated as plausible. It doesn't hold water the way it used to, though. Alan Dershowitz failed to convince a jury with the old-fashioned argument that Mike Tyson was the real victim, namely the victim of the beauty queen's guilt after she had consented to sex.

For a time, there were flickerings in our culture that hinted at the coming of a new kind of man, the "sensitive male." He was supposed to be more willing or able to express emotions, more content to cook, clean, and help rear children, in resonant counterpoint to the women's movement. Above all, he was more empathic, less power-hungry. He would initiate sex more tentatively and tenderly or hand the initiative over to his partner. This new man did arise to some extent, even on the marital scene, enough to exert some minor influence, but he appears to have declined just as swiftly. In light of the unmistakable rise in domestic violence, rape, and sexual murder, one is moved to ask whether there may be a punitive masculine backlash against women's recent gains in social and political independence, an effort to reassert control.

With abuse assuming such prominent forms nowadays, one is also liable to forget how comfortably the social fabric, which gave men considerable sway over women, used to absorb behavior that we now regard as criminal. "The Husband's Right of Correction" in

Volume 1 of *Blackstone's Commentaries,* the standard compendium of English common law dating back all the way to the Middle Ages (and the precedent for much of our own body of law), is unequivocal on this issue. It states that "the civil law gave the husband the same, or a larger authority over his wife; allowing him, for some misdemeanors to beat his wife severely with scourges and sticks." Our idiomatic phrase "rule of thumb," as every law student knows, derives from a decision attributed to an English judge, Sir Francis Buller, who supposedly concluded that a husband can beat his wife as long as he uses a stick no thicker than his thumb. This may or may not be apocryphal, but it certainly reflects a deeply engrained attitude.

When I was growing up in a rural part of northern California, the standard lore among the boys was that if a real man found his wife in bed with someone, he could fill them both full of bullets on the spot, and no court in the land would convict him. Whether it was true or not, tales that confirmed it somehow reached our ears, usually from a land of strong, silent men, like Texas. We didn't yet have Arnold Schwarzenegger or Bruce Willis, so our heroes still included cowboys, and emptying a six-gun into an unfaithful wife and her lover seemed like an appropriate form of cowboy vengeance. Premonitions of O. J. Simpson, perhaps. On the other hand, no one suggested that it might be equally appropriate for a betrayed wife to do something similar. Not so far in the background, though, hovered the fearsome image of "castrating bitch." Behind the violent methods all too many men employ to keep women in their place, there appears to be a good deal of fear over what might happen if women's full sexual anger got loose. Premonitions of Lorena Bobbitt.

There are plenty of signs that the belief that women invite abuse is on the wane. Nevertheless, we still tend to preserve a modicum of cowboy vigilante justice for women who don't knuckle under by muting their sexual hungers, anger, or other forms of independent assertion. It's just that we have grown more subtle: The up-to-date method for getting our lumpen vigilantes off the hook is to condemn their actions and then give them therapeutic sanctuary through insanity pleas, "crimes of passion," and, perhaps the weakest one of all, special dispensation for the abuser or killer because his own childhood was deprived and abusive or because he has obliterated his mental capacity to make moral distinctions with alcohol or drugs. Harvard Law Professor Duncan Kennedy has argued that all men benefit (in maintaining patriarchal rule) from male sexual violence directed at women. A sufficient sprinkling of rapes and murders here and there extends a warning to every woman that she had better watch what she says, how she dresses, where she goes, or whatever other freedoms she might arrogate to herself.[17]

From another standpoint, one could also consider sexual abuse the sin of the nineties. In an age when sin is hardly a fashionable idea, except in certain sectors of the religious right, our intensifying concern with abuse comes as close as the post-therapeutic world has yet come to restoring a sense of evil. Every society has evolved its own list of distinctive sexual taboos. Sexual abuse is the perfect erotic or intimate evil for our society, in part because its primary ingredient is the violent exercise of power by one person over another. In this respect, it differs from the majority of sexual sins in past eras, such as masturbation, obscenity, promiscuity, homosexuality, premarital intercourse, a variety of perversions, and so on, which have often had more to do, at least explicitly, with pleasure than with power. The denunciation of abuse, both real and imagined, represents the extreme of our modern heightened sensitivity to exploitation and power. From this perspective, the culture of abuse is an outcome of a somewhat paradoxical tendency that I mentioned in the first chapter. While we have lost faith in the political process itself, our private conduct has been more and more defined in terms of political meanings. And as this has occurred, politics and morality have tended to converge.

Now that the conservative right has lost communism as a source of all social evils, and now that we no longer need a radical student movement to tell us that all established governments, all structures of authority, are corrupt, it seems logical to turn to a scrutiny of our private behavior. And it follows from this emphasis that the penetration of culture by the abuse movement is a Protestant revolution. In large part, it's a secular Protestant revolution, led by feminists, against all signs of sexual decadence in the citadels and cathedrals ruled by male authority.

The early American immigrants, an austere and hardy group, were Puritans who had taken Calvinist self-scrutiny and vigilant alertness to signs of the devil's work as far as it would go. In certain respects, we have come full circle. Regarded as a symptom of evil, abuse is a sin with a therapeutic dimension. There are intriguing connections to be made here. Psychotherapy and Puritanism have a common denominator—both stress the importance of looking inward—just as Puritanism and militant feminism both abhor what they perceive as a blend of power and sleaze. When psychotherapy turns moral, as much of contemporary therapy certainly has done in its encounter with abuse, some schools tend to harden into a kind of puritanism or fundamentalism. Although I have already discussed some consequences of this turn of events, there is another that bears consideration. In responding to the messiness of abuse cases, psychotherapists are dividing down the middle, and neither wing is helping much to resolve the mess.

Until recently, social science, psychological theory, and psychotherapy, in their public roles, had all contributed to the dissolution of traditional distinctions between good and evil, especially when it came to assigning individual responsibility for crimes. As a result, we have tended to look rather more benignly than most epochs upon wrongdoers. We came to regard them, for example, as traumatized, deprived, driven crazy either by genes or by parents, or otherwise victimized by circumstances beyond their control. Instead of making complex distinctions about who is responsible for what, we have tended to point the finger at general and inescapable circumstances. As Mary Midgley, a moral philosopher, puts it, "public wickedness vanishes into a social problem, as private wickedness does into mental illness." This outlook, she adds, effectively "slices off all our power of self-direction" because it leaves us without an inner moral map for orienting ourselves.[18]

One wing of psychotherapy, even in the age of abuse, still clings firmly and somewhat absurdly to this kind of ethical neutrality through employing, for example, colorless diagnostic euphemisms. This is quite different in spirit from the suspension of hasty judgment that can enable the therapist and patient in an actual session to discove. something. When one of Farrow's attorneys, for instance, intimated during the custody trial that Allen's behavior might be construed as "evil"—it wasn't clear whether he was referring to the affair with Soon-Yi or the charges concerning Dylan, but he was clearly coming from the perspective of abuse—a therapist on the witness stand responded that perhaps Allen had acted with "impaired judgment."[19] It is difficult to tell whether she meant this to qualify as a moral, psychological, or legal defect. Such innocuousness leaves us standing exactly where we were with our vision a little more blurred than it was. (Unfortunately, this kind of blandness is what liberalism often sounds like when it goes up against puritanism.)

In addition, there is a very significant way in which the poor old romantic ideal has proved to be particularly weak in confronting the violence and impulsive self-gratification that become more apparent almost daily in every area of social life. For all its sweet hopefulness, romantic idealism glosses over the predatory and other dangerous possibilities that often travel under the name of love. We are being forced to learn from bitter experience (and thus might be learning too well) the cautiousness that Midgley urges when she declares that "perhaps every human motive, including love, can on occasion be sinister, if it is not properly watched and understood."[20]

The culture of abuse certainly encourages wariness by inclining us toward a much darker and more dangerous view of sex than the beautiful wistful one encouraged by the old ideals of romantic love. But there are many indications that our absorption with abuse is becoming a kind of fixation or obsession, and the danger in a fixation is that the forest becomes a bunch of undifferentiated trees, the ability to discriminate thus lost. With respect to abuse, the important truths about child abuse and domestic violence become swamped in the general atmosphere of indictment. One of the signs that American culture tends to be stuck at adolescence is its inclination, like a teenager, to oscillate between extreme polarities—to swing from idealism to cynicism, from infinite hope and optimism to alienation and despair, from isolation (self-reliance; hands-off foreign policy) to merging (romantic love; we can make the world safe for democracy). The problem here is that just as love begets love for the sake of community and intimacy, power begets power for the sake of self-preservation or having one's way. This can lead to a Machiavellian view of intimacy. Machiavelli points out that in an essentially bad world, "it is necessary that the prince, who wishes to maintain himself, learn not to be good."[21] For "prince" in this quote substitute *husband, wife, lover, child,* whatever.

What the present change in attitude ultimately reflects is the degree to which we now assume that violence and violation are almost inevitably part of family life, intimacy, and all social relationships. Like all cultural myths, abuse, beyond the fact of its increased presence, has also come to stand for how people *feel* in general about their families, intimacies, and other relationships. Behind the transition from romance to abuse lies an even more fundamental historical development that is quite terrible indeed. At its root is the evolution of a state of mind that can best be described as carelessness toward the existence of others. Carelessness is the proper term here if one keeps in mind two essential aspects of caring, one of which is usually left out these days when people in therapy and recovery groups go around informing others how much they "care" about them. On the one hand, caring implies an emotional or empathetic sense that others matter; on the other—and this is the connotation that commonly gets ignored—it also means a respect for the differentness of others from oneself, the difficulty of getting to know them, expressed in the idea of being careful in how one approaches another person. I have seen enough so-called therapeutic caring dished out on the fringes of my professional life to conclude that indiscriminate caring is just another kind of carelessness. The worst part of it is that we have grown careless with one another's lives to an unprecedented degree, more willing to take each other for granted, more able to destroy one another on almost any pretext of meeting a need, from wanting sex to wanting someone else's Nike basketball shoes.

And this is the basic state of consciousness, or unconsciousness, that underlies abusive relationships.

Modern history has provided ample influences to push all of us, from every social and economic category, toward becoming careless with each other. Although the twentieth century is a story of technological progress, one of its main subplots has been a deepening barbarism in the form of mass slaughter generated by intolerance of differences. The Holocaust was, of course, the definitive modern event in exhibiting how far supposedly enlightened modern societies could sink. Subsequently we have had to assimilate the use of the atomic bombs to wipe out whole cities in Japan, followed by the napalming of villages in Vietnam. Now there is Bosnia, Somalia, Rwanda, Haiti. How much carefulness about the well-being of others in particular and human existence in general can one manage to sustain faced with mountains of corpses?

Not that one needs to look so far abroad or only at such monumental manifestations of carelessness. We have plenty of more homely examples directly underfoot: children carrying weapons to school by the age of ten or twelve, even in the middle-class suburbs, while others barely into their teens are gunning each other down on the inner-city streets with automatic weapons. A little parable for our times, comparatively mild yet one among thousands of instances of singularly uncharming stories about our kids, appeared in the *New York Times* recently. Two twelve-year-olds stood at the end of a line of fourth- and fifth-graders waiting to go on a school picnic. The teacher had collected $4,000 for food, travel, and expenses. When he got to the end of the line, the two children, who turned out not to be part of the group, pulled out guns and took off with the entire proceeds.[22]

It is impossible that such cruelty and indifference toward human life as we have been forced to witness for the past half-century, both on a global scale and at home, could do other than affect our intimacies and our sexual feelings. One reaction might have been for us to become more caring in our close personal relations—the theme of "Dover Beach." But perhaps it is hard to say where carelessness begins—on the level of government and large social institutions, and then in a kind of trickle-down effect into our individual private relationships, or the other way around. A version of romance's last stand to society's cruel indifference was portrayed in the flood of espionage novels that became extremely popular during the cold-war years. John le Carré's novels, such as *The Spy Who Came In from the Cold,* are excellent and typical examples. In *The Spy Who Came In from the Cold,* a jaded and bitter English agent falls in love with an innocent immigrant librarian, who is then used as a pawn in the course of carrying out a complex espionage scheme in East Germany. By the end of the novel, both of them have been exploited, betrayed, and finally slaughtered by the utterly indifferent bureaucratic machinery of intelligence services on both sides of the iron curtain. The message seems to be that there is no longer any escape or safety even in another's arms.

The late Isadore From, one of the founders of Gestalt therapy, took up the question of how most of us could go on during the cold-war era living ordinary lives under the precarious equilibrium of nuclear stalemate. What kind of psychological mechanisms would enable us to carry on daily activities as if all were well, he asked, despite our knowledge that missiles containing the capacity to abolish the planet several times over were armed and poised in hidden bunkers? His answer was that our charade of normalcy demanded a vast distortion of inner life. It could be pulled off only by internalizing the cause of such terrifying knowledge, which means stripping the danger from its actual source in external reality and treating it as though it stems from inside oneself. Once people have succeeded in trapping such feelings inside, they can repress them and experience the looming missiles as little more than an abstract idea.[23]

Children who live with cruel and irrationally punitive parents go through a similar process: They internalize the parents' rage and gain an illusion of control over it by turning it against themselves or repressing it. Then they can imagine that there is something vaguely wrong with them but at least they still have good parents. It is essential for children to believe that they have reliable, protective caretakers, even at such tremendous cost to themselves. In accounts of the relations between O. J. Simpson and his ex-wife Nicole Brown

Simpson that have emerged since her murder, one can discern the same sort of process at work. Evidence came out that he had repeatedly beat her up, and she was reported to have confided in friends that if she could only be better or different, the relationship would "work" and presumably the beatings would stop. This, of course, is a common syndrome among battered wives.

Thus we survive, roughly speaking, totally untenable situations at great psychological cost, making ourselves oblivious to our inner feelings and only abstractly aware of external horrors. Since the repression of powerful emotional truths takes constant vigilant effort, lest by nature they burst forth into the daylight, people who have had to resort to repression are compelled to keep themselves in chronic states of great tension. When they get together with others, the relationships that form are often characterized by a hair-trigger irritability, as though bottled-up fear or rage may break out any second.

Now that the cold war is over and the nuclear missiles are no longer, so far as we know, still cocked and aimed at our cities, it may well be that when people come into close contact, their previously disowned feelings are starting to come out more openly—but directed at each other. Perhaps repressed terror and aggression so color our relations at present that many of us are coming to see only the predatory prospects of intimacy.

It is true that the media have not helped alleviate our sense of alarm. Culture communicates, but it also serves as a mirror that heightens or exaggerates what it reflects. Since the advent of television, events are not only covered as they happen, but they are converted with equal speed into rumor, opinion, analysis, and image able to penetrate the consciousness of the entire country in one blow.

Television didn't originate our sensitivity to abuse; however, it has probably expanded and overstimulated it. We may have created a moral bandwagon, jumped on by people with diverse agendas, from passing the buck for the painfulness of life to political gain, from acquiring a book contract to satisfying a desire for revenge. Add to this the Cotton Mathers among mental-health professionals, who strive to persuade patients that virtually every complaint or symptom is proof that they have repressed their awareness of being abused in childhood, and we arrive at all the incoherence of behavior, to borrow Irving Howe's phrase again, that a society could possibly conceive.

All this is evidence of how far the histrionic side of American life can penetrate not just the media, but even the inner workings of our professions. More than once in the history of professional disciplines, especially in the social sciences, an admirable beginning becomes rapidly inflated into an all-purpose program, transforming valuable insights into dubious ideologies. Perhaps this is the underside of our zeal to be scientific—that it can lead us to settle for cause-and-effect theories that create premature certitude. It is also the dark side of our free marketplace for services. Take any important idea developed by careful and committed professionals, and before long you will get a batch of gurus, charlatans, and self-appointed experts pushing it far beyond its useful limits. Its most worrisome consequence in the case of abuse theory is when accusations and denunciations encouraged by experts overly influence both social and legal judgment. Diagnosis blurs too soon nowadays into verdict. Another mode of relieving the anxiety of uncertainty is to pin the blame—burn the witches, blackball the Communists. It is much easier to seek answers by choosing scapegoats than by opening oneself to the complex and ambiguous meanings of events.

My main concern, however, is not to determine what might be true and what ought to be questioned amid the floodtide of abuse tales and dramas, but what all of it, appearance and reality alike, indicates about eros in the contemporary world. Love inseparable from abuse is love enslaved to power. If this is what things are coming to—or we think they are—it suggests that the anxiety of erotic intimacy has become too difficult for many of us to bear. The framework provided by romantic love doubtlessly helped people contain and tolerate the tensions of sex, its volatility, its risks, its setbacks. Without something equivalent to replace romantic postponement or sublimation, the only thing some people seem able to do is discharge the tension in a violent spasm of negative instant gratification, one in which anxiety and desire, relief and satisfaction cannot be told apart. The receptacle for this kind of impulsive discharge is usually the nearest and most helpless person within range.

Rom..ntic love may have been an ideal of sexual intimacy suited to a society in which the adolescent's work of integrating autonomy and intimacy still remains to be done, but at least it extolled the virtues of patience, heroic effort, tolerance of mystery, and the hope of transcendence. The imagery of romance gave us the figure of a lover pursuing a beloved. Consummation was hard-won, if achieved at all. The imagery of abuse gives us only an oppressor obtaining gratification by callously victimizing a dependent or a partner, often in the name of love.

Thus the culture of abuse is filled with harrowing reminders of how broad a spectrum sex traverses in human relations, from the closest imaginable union between two people in love to an ugly exercise of power by people in positions of authority over those who depend on them for protection, inspiration, guidance, even survival. Lovers touch one another in tender places for the sake of closeness and mutual pleasure; abusers do it to those dependent on them for the sake of having their way.

It is hard to conceive that incest, rape, or domestic violence could hold any special interest for adults who can tolerate the freedom of a sexual partner equal to and genuinely distinct from themselves. They wouldn't dream of contaminating their protective concern for the well-being of others less powerful and importantly involved with them. But there are plenty of people who cannot tolerate erotic love with an independent, much less equal, partner, because it puts the self too much at risk. In some cases, they may turn to the sexual perversions, which are radical techniques for experiencing sexual excitement without facing the threatening uncertainties of sexual intimacy. Perversions circumscribe sex through dire strategies of control, such as reducing one's partner (or oneself) to a silhouette to be lorded over, peeped at, overpowered, or hurt. If too much ambiguous and unpredictable humanity still remains, one can drop the actual partner altogether and simply substitute articles of clothing or similar personal objects. Some of these methods are relatively harmless, some obviously are abusive, some can be downright deadly. What they share in common is that sexual excitement can only be allowed to arise and express itself within a relationship based on the primacy of power over love.

Incest is related to the perversions in that it abolishes the risk and uncertainty, the potential for rejection or abandonment, that one takes on in reaching out into the world for sexual fulfillment. Incest yields an immediate and especially vulnerable partner, willing or not, usually not even capable of the choice, who is thus directly under one's control. This is intimacy reduced to utter familiarity; the emotional bonds of love are already hooked in place. The incestuous parent is completely safe, lodged at the opposite pole from the frustrated and anxious romantic lover. He has sexual access to the child he ravishes whenever he wants it, and she can hardly abandon him. He only need worry about hiding his tracks and stifling the voice that might expose him. In this sense, incest is a kind of primal form of sexual abuse. Rape and domestic violence are variations on its themes: The effort in all three is to assume total control over the other person.

There have always been both lovers and abusers, and no doubt there always will be. The history of love is filled with ample evidence to prove that erotic desire can breed violation and humiliation as well as appreciation, pain as well as pleasure. Heaven knows, it's not that sexual mistreatment is a new phenomenon in the history of civilization. But it has certainly never before been so explicit in our common social awareness. What does the prevalence of abusive sexuality, the continual revelations of it, the preoccupation with it suggest about the present direction of the American psyche? Are we passing through a transient dark region as twilight settles over romantic love? Or is abuse a symptom, along with our waning industrial strength and racial distress, of our entrance into a period of decadence, like that of the late Weimar Republic, a hint of our descent into a pre-fascist mood? Or are we perhaps witnessing in our personal relations a bitter finale to American individualism? Is it an indication that we are increasingly unable to muster enough belief in ourselves to pursue sexual love on the basis of equality and mutual free will?

Probably all of these factors are involved in the decline of intimacy. In any case, one thing is certain: Making close connections with others requires a certain faith in the benevolence of their motives, and that is precisely what we have lost. In the present climate for intimacy, the approach of another expressing sexual interest is deemed predatory until proven otherwise; to respond to it might be to offer oneself up as prey. Modern love is as ambiguous as the seduction ritual of a vampire—you don't know whether to expect a passionate kiss on the neck or the sinking of fangs into your jugular.

Mistrust raised to this height leaves people staring across a gulf at each other, on guard and feeling chillingly alone. If you don't believe that the intimate or neighboring portions of the social environment will support your needs and interests, you cannot take the risk of giving up enough control to allow others to come and go as they see fit, the freedom of choice that is essential to have anything approximating a reciprocal human relationship. Underlying this lonely armored stance is a profound sense of powerlessness. Rollo May once remarked that Lord Acton's famous maxim which says that power corrupts is incorrect. The truth, suggests May, is that it's powerlessness that corrupts.[24]

Thus the most basic values and ideas—communal, political, and spiritual—that endow us with basic respect for one another seem to have failed and abandoned us, or we have failed and abandoned them. In other words, we operate less and less from a fundamental sense of civility. I think that both the sense of oneself as powerless and the failure of civility are the outcome of a direction that we have been headed toward for a long time. They flow from a view of the self in its social world that has become disastrous, if not tragic. In America we have traditionally called this view individualism, and we have always celebrated it.

At its extreme, individualism takes half the story of social life, the pole of autonomy, and turns it into a kind of parody of independence. It rips the single person out of the web of community, surrounds him or her in a hard casing, and calls this building a strong character. In Chapter 5, I discussed Michael Balint's notion that this kind of strong character, which has characterized our image of the captain of industry or the workaholic professional, is a reduction, a lessening, a diminishing of loving and being loved. It is deeply connected to our interpretation of individualism. Such a person cannot take the risk of making full contact, cannot take the risk of allowing another person to be at once different and as large as himself.

The increasing feelings of powerlessness and loss of contact in our private relations have had a curious and ambiguous side effect in our popular culture. More and more people are revealing, being playful toward, and even taking pride in indulging those aspects of sex that used to be considered weird, deviant, or shameful and therefore relegated to the dark corners of society. As a cultural phenomenon, erotic abuse is not only an expanding pathology in our behavior, it has also become an *au courant* style, particularly at that juncture where it shades into the abuse-tainted sexual perversions, like sadomasochism, bondage and domination, leather fetishism. Madonna is the priestess of this movement, and Camille Paglia, author of *Sexual Personae,* its main intellectual apologist. The front page of the "Styles" section of the Sunday *New York Times* for November 1, 1992, wondered in large type whether a new line of women's fashions was "Chic or Cruel?" And the header continued, "Gianni Versace's styles take a cue from the world of S & M. Some women say it makes them feel powerful; others find it demeaning." A photograph shows two rather demure models decked out in black-leather outfits full of studs, buckles, and harness straps. The accompanying article quotes Mr. Versace remarking gleefully about his show at the Seventh Regiment Armory on Park Avenue (appropriate setting!), "Last night there were 200 socialites in bondage!" That example comes off as cute and playful; what doesn't feel so playful is the fascination with rape, mutilation, and worse that has proliferated in recent novels and movies.

In its passion for unseemly revelations, the culture of abuse carries on a tendency that has been evolving over the whole second half of the twentieth century—the widespread impulse to reveal everything, to make the self and its relations with others entirely public. We have had a confessional school of poetry, which includes such distinguished writers as Robert Lowell, Anne Sexton, and Sylvia Plath. Dozens of biographies and autobiographies, memoirs, published diaries, and collections of letters have appeared, and continue to appear in abundance, that leave no stone of personality unturned, no quirk of behavior unscrutinized. The more shameful the skeletons in the closet—insanity, drunkenness, drug addiction, personal failings and weaknesses—the more we want them hauled out and paraded before us, especially if they belong to revered or towering figures.

I recall a review of a new book about Freud a couple of years ago, in which the reviewer made much of learning that Freud was so nervous or awestruck by his first sight of America that he peed in his pants. We want smaller-than-life heroes now, not romantic or charismatic ones. We want a Freud who pees in his pants. What we do not seem to want any longer is a Freud who overwhelms us with his brilliance and achievements, his major contributions to Western thought. Our current scholarship turns its sights on bringing celebrated figures down to size. Thus a large amount of the recent commentary on psychoanalysis has been intent on proving that Freud was a coward and a sellout who falsified some of his more controversial discoveries for opportunistic reasons.

In a similar vein, a recent biography of F. Scott Fitzgerald, by Jeffrey Meyers, portrays the novelist as a self-centered, pathetic buffoon, mired in alcoholism, and has little of literary importance to say about his novels. Another recent book seems more interested in a Virginia Woolf who may have been molested by her brother than a Virginia Woolf who wrote some of the most powerfully innovative fiction of the modernist period. There is also a prize-winning biography of the poet Anne Sexton, by Diane Middlebrook, that presents her at her worst—as a cruel, depressed, and impossible human being on her way to suicide (with a childhood, naturally, marred by sexual abuse). All of it is no doubt true; the point is that one can't imagine such a biography being published in an earlier era. Middlebrook even managed to get hold of and include taped transcripts of

Sexton's therapy sessions with a psychiatrist. Perhaps it is a reflection of the same drive toward public humility that President Clinton asked his supporters to contribute toward the legal expenses for defending himself against charges of sexual harassment and financial improprieties.

Maybe the public exposure of shameful facts is the only way we feel we can identify with each other in a time of profound alienation from communal and public life. People want to know and be known by others, and that is not easy to accomplish nowadays. Even psychotherapy, which took place only in the most private, confidential circumstances, like a secret tryst, has been supplemented by the recovery movement, especially its twelve-step wing, where people in various kinds of trouble tell all in front of large groups of fellow sufferers.

These phenomena all fit into the story of our entire culture's movement toward personal revelation. But with the increasing emphasis on abuse, the purpose of confessions and revelations changes. There are no longer just suffering victims; the victimizers are now inextricably in the picture, too. Therapy patients come out from behind the closed doors of clinics or private offices and head for courtrooms, which are now stealing a good deal of thunder from Broadway and Hollywood. We have passed on from the return of the repressed, which psychotherapy strove for, to the retaliation of the oppressed.

If not dealt with, a state of social incoherence can degenerate into something approximating a hallucinatory condition, like madness. We appeared to have reached that point on the evening of June 17, 1994, an hour or so before sundown, Pacific time. Most channels switched over from scheduled programs to present us with a remarkable image: O. J. Simpson—winner of the Heisman Trophy, one of the finest running backs of all time, a Hollywood star, a man who had pulled himself up from a childhood among the broken families and street gangs of a poor San Francisco neighborhood to a status not only of wealth and success but of a role model for both black and white youths and adults alike—was in full flight from the

LAPD on the interstate system that surrounds Los Angeles. A nation that had recently witnessed elevated freeways break apart and underground gas lines explode into infernal geysers during earthquakes in that part of the country, not to mention videotaped episodes of racial violence, had not seen anything quite like this.

One had to blink a few times to make sure that this was not another sequel to *Naked Gun,* the series of hilarious cops-and-robbers films in which Simpson had a starring role. It took a while to realize that this was in fact another landmark event, perhaps the most macabre one yet, in the unfolding cultural saga of abuse. The Simpson episode immediately raised our horror and fascination with domestic violence by several notches. Incredibly, the ex–football player, sports announcer, and actor in movies and TV commercials was a desperado on the lam for real, wanted on an all points bulletin for arraignment on two counts of first-degree murder—of his ex-wife and her male friend.

During the freeway spectacle, an old teammate of Simpson's from the Buffalo Bills came on a CNN news special from where he was watching in Lynchburg, Virginia. "I don't know what's happening to this country," he said, referring to what he called the "carnival atmosphere" surrounding Simpson's attempted escape. And just after Simpson had given himself up, Peter Jennings on ABC spoke in his cultivated melancholy voice of how "excruciatingly sad" this all was, and he added that already "people were trying to find the balance between O.J., the man they admired, and O.J., the man accused of murder."

There was no balance to be found. Barbara Walters also appeared on ABC, pointing out that the cell in Los Angeles County Men's Jail where Simpson would be held awaiting arraignment was right next to the one, currently empty, where Erik Menendez had been incarcerated. The underlying irony, of course, was that Menendez was one of the two brothers who had just figured in another pair of our seemingly contagious rash of spectacular trials bristling with abuse charges. In the case of the Menendez brothers, the abuse charges were posthumous, leveled by the two young men against their parents, whom they had methodically slaughtered with shotguns. Sexual and physical abuse were the key elements in their defenses, and this was persuasive enough that both their trials ended in hung juries.

Walters also took note of the difference between Simpson's gentle "public exterior" and his internal "private torment," as she put it, caused by the "passionate tumultuous relationship" between him and his former wife. Indeed, there was an all-too-typical history of spousal battery behind the current horrors: In 1989 Simpson had pleaded no contest to wife-beating charges, and there were reports that his wife, Nicole Brown Simpson, had since that time made several 911 calls for emergency help while her husband was in the process of assaulting her. There were reports, too, obtained from friends of Nicole Simpson, that he had been stalking her in restaurants and bars, reports that included word from one friend who said that the former Mrs. Simpson had told her that she would never be able to leave O.J. completely because they were in each other's blood. This is the kind of sentiment frequently expressed by women who become trapped in relationships with men who brutalize them, apologize profusely, deny they meant to do it, and declare their love once again. It happens over and over until it is too late. Later, more reports came out to the effect that Nicole Simpson had just begun to make something of an independent life for herself. But now she was dead.

Whatever had happened, it was clear that Simpson was a changed man from the dapper, easygoing, likable figure who had so often appeared on the screen. In the fleeting glimpses the country got from photographs accompanying television and newspaper updates shortly after he was arrested, Simpson's charismatically handsome face had hardened into a pained mask, and his eyes looked bleak, maddened, like those of a man in the midst of a psychotic episode.

It's hard not to keep piling on the evidence—not of guilt but of how our culture is being transformed by the prevalence of abuse in both deed and idea. Among the local correspondents, attorneys, domestic-violence experts, friends of Simpson's, former teammates, and random people polled by the networks for reactions, there appeared on CNN as the chase approached its conclusion a Dr. Alfred

Messer, a psychiatrist, who told us about "separation homicide," which he defined as a kind of extraordinarily explosive abandonment panic. He described O. J. Simpson as the case of a man who grew up in poverty and deprivation, but who through heroic perseverance had reached the pinnacle of success. When he got there, he invested it all in a dependent love for a beautiful woman whom he married. As the marriage fell apart, he slipped into a crazed depression, a state of utter despair.

This was a rather pat piece of analysis, hardly enough to account for the wife-battering syndrome that Simpson shares with so many men, deprived or spoiled, rich and poor alike, whose egos insist on controlling the women in their lives at all costs. Yet it probably contained something of the truth. Whatever Dr. Messer may have intended, his diagnosis points beyond itself to a facet of the Simpson drama that belongs to twentieth-century cultural history as much as to current notions about the psychopathology of abuse. Whether or not he did what he is accused of doing, Simpson's story tells of a man born near the bottom of society, emerging out of a desolate background of hopeless prospects. Through a combination of talent, charismatic charm, hustle, a large spirit, and sheer self-reliant will, he ends up at the top, with wealth, celebrity status, power, and a splendid home in one of the best neighborhoods. Along the way he falls in love with a glamorous figure, a young woman whose beauty comes to stand as a romantic symbol embodying all of these meanings and aspirations. So he must have her as well.

In other words, the magnificent success and tragic finale of O. J. Simpson's career mirror the tragedy of Fitzgerald's Jay Gatsby, brought forward into the 1990s. Like Gatsby, he was a man's man as well as a self-made man—the one a war hero, the other a sports hero. Like Gatsby, he always displayed in public a cool and generous savoir faire amid the high life of the wealthy with their ostentatious, glittering material props. But underneath the outward composure of both the fictional character and the actual one, there burns a tumultuous, impossible faith in romantic love that undermines their pose of self-reliance. The fantasy of self-realization, which stems from early youth for Gatsby and probably for Simpson as well, is a grand fusion of heroic masculine accomplishment, material success, power, and sex. This is a fantasy that never matures beyond adolescence, but it is stubbornly clung to into adulthood nevertheless, so stubbornly that both men nearly bring it off. For both Gatsby and Simpson, the possibility of failure, including failure with the woman they have each chosen to embody ideal love, cannot be tolerated or even conceived.

Of course, there are differences of detail in the two scripts that embed Gatsby in his times and Simpson in ours. The most obvious one would seem to be that Gatsby is a fictional character in a novel, and Simpson part of our actual celebrity life. In our times, though, it gets harder to tell where reality ends and fiction begins. Then there is the fact that Simpson marries the girl and beats her up before he allegedly murders her, whereas Gatsby, equally unwilling to suffer the loss of his romantic ideal, never touches Daisy in any way beyond the first kisses during their brief moment of youthful infatuation. This is a significant difference. *The Great Gatsby* begins with romantic idealism, blends it with power and status, and ends in a tragedy based on disillusionment and mistaken identity. There can be no marriage between Gatsby and Daisy, for in the old romantic world, marriage is a culmination, the traditional happy ending. In the case of Simpson, it is after marriage and children that the real tragedy begins, a tragedy born of an invasive and possessive love willing to use any force or means necessary to possess its object. The delicacy, the touch of chivalry still inherent in Gatsby's love has vanished; contemporary romance has sunk so far that no partitions any longer separate love from power, and any means, at least for men, justify the elimination of anxiety. The story of O. J. Simpson is a new version of *The Great Gatsby*, rewritten for television in the era of intimate terrorism, domestic violence, and the exercise of power through desperate acts of assault that can lead even to murder. Simpson's terrible deterioration reflects the general deterioration of intimacy and marriage in our times.

The carelessness of the people surrounding Jay Gatsby, a carelessness that repelled Nick Carraway in the wake of Gatsby's useless murder, has reached an apocalyptic extreme in our day. It is probably only too fitting that the symptoms of carelessness have headed west from the Long Island and Manhattan of Fitzgerald's novel, so that the apocalypse takes place today in southern California.

Comparing these two forlorn fables—the one a great novel, the other a sordid blow-by-blow instantaneous documentary; the one already prophesizing the end of romance amid the affluence and glitter of the Jazz Age, the other exemplifying a lethal extreme in a decadent culture of abuse—is enough to leave us out of breath at the edge of modern history, wondering where we can possibly go from here. How much longer will our sunsets remain suffused with poignancy, now that what is left of the old dreams, the bittersweet hesitations, and even the disappointments of what we thought love promised seems to be guttering out? Of what use will be moonlight, already becoming eclipsed by our darkening cynicism in the age of abuse?

8

Epilogue: "Re-statement of Romance"

"Those lips that Love's own hand did make /
Breath'd forth the sound that said 'I hate.'"
—*Shakespeare, Sonnet CXLV*

"After such knowledge, what forgiveness?" asks the poet T. S. Eliot. Admittedly, I have thus far delivered a rather gloomy sequence of sermons about our current crisis of love, sex, and marriage. I cannot imagine, though, that they would strike anyone as unnecessarily pessimistic, and I will argue that they by no means add up to hopelessness about the future of love. It is true, however, that holding on to romantic hopes about intimacy, given the surrounding weather, puts one in the position of a hiker who has been negotiating an extremely steep trail when a ledge gives way, tossing him over the side of a ravine. On the way down, our romantic adventurer has managed to grab hold of a scruffy piece of perpendicular vegetation, but his weight, the weight of the human condition in our times, is causing the bush gradually to tear loose by the roots. When this sort of thing happens in the movies, somebody arrives with a rope and struggles to pull the fallen climber back up before it is too late. For those of us still clinging to the last twigs and shoots of romance, where is the rescue party?

There is certainly nothing much by way of rescue yet in sight, neither from the popular media nor literature nor the fine arts, not from the schools of psychology or philosophy, not from the churches or the politics of family values. Our expectations from love and marriage have, if anything, diminished further, especially if one gauges the national mood from the evening news, which carries us so swiftly from east to west and event to event, creating instant history, almost instant myth. Everything changes so fast that one barely has time to reflect on its implications. Reading the papers or watching TV at times is like viewing a pornographic slasher movie under a strobe light. We get endless information about sexual crimes and scandals; we hear about accusations and indictments; now and then, there is word of sentences or acquittals. Almost always what remains are unresolved loose ends. They often leave us with the nagging feeling that love and sex no longer have anything to do with passionate moments of agreement, only with victims and perpetrators vying with one another.

At its worst, our social behavior has come to resemble the film director Roger Corman's view that movies are in a state of decline: He told an interviewer on CNN that current films are substituting gore for creativity. Even apart from all the violence, we live in an age dense with events and inventions but almost stripped of values and myths that stay in place. This situation, if it has not yet succeeded in turning us into nihilists, tends at best to make us view things too pragmatically, a bleak prospect when it comes to love because the erotic is neither reasonable nor just: It generates too much heat; it is forever capable of confronting us with its darkly anxious, impulsive side. Whereas pragmatism, which depends on people's rational perception that accommodation to society's best interests is in their own best interests, does not hold up well when it is faced with the demonic aspects of human nature.

On all these grounds, I hope that we can find our way back to some kind of romanticism. It seems to me that sex without a touch of poetry or idealism leaves us overly vulnerable to the animal on the prowl in quest of self-gratification. The old romanticism, however, as I have tried to demonstrate from several different perspectives, is clearly inadequate. When circumstances overwhelm established ideals, as is now the case, the tradition they represent tends to become sentimental and maudlin. Then its poetry, in the broad sense of that word—for there is always inherent poetry in a vital tradition—turns merely "poetic"; it rings not with conviction but with a glorified false note. That is one distortion of reality that occurs during difficult, changing times. Another is the rise of violent deeds, ideologies, and repressions of the sort that exemplify our spreading culture of abuse. Precisely at times like this the humanistic critical spirit, though often denounced as hopelessly old-fashioned these days, performs its most important work. I believe that we need it badly—that, in fact, it is necessary to our future welfare.

Critics, to be sure, are more prone to take things apart than to help with reconstruction. In these final pages I want to resist that tendency long enough to offer at least a sketch of a few themes that might further the creation of a new, more viable romanticism, a more ironical version of romantic love, tailored to the complications of our times. The therapeutic ethos we have inherited from Freud is helpful at this point. It tells us that a full look at the worst is not a counsel of despair but the first step in a process of change for the better. "In a dark time the eye begins to see," the poet Theodore Roethke once wrote.

When something is not working, one needs to begin with a diagnosis of the problem, in order to convert what seems to be compulsion into choice. It is also useful to have an interpretation of the options. This, to my thinking at least, is what psychotherapy ought to be all about. Of course, the therapeutic focus has been directed mainly toward individual pathology, but a large part of my concern has been to extend it to social and cultural malaise as well.

With regard to love and sex, the painful experiences of the modern era, from intimate terrorism to abuse, have corroded our innocence, probably once and for all. Perhaps it is time to realize that we never were all that innocent anyway. Explanations that appeal to a lost innocence lead mainly to an unproductive nostalgia or mere wringing of hands. As lovers and spouses, we have always been fallen creatures; human sexual history began with exile from a paradise of unmitigated conjugal bliss and other happinesses. But this may not be such bad news. The medieval view that I discussed in Chapter 6, the idea that the Fall was a "Fortunate Sin," an introduction of challenge and the possibility of change into human experience, more or less resembles the stringently qualified optimism that I have in mind: It begins with the assumption that an intimate relationship is fraught with difficulties, but these obstacles themselves can be transformed into occasions whereby two people might continue to grow up.

Hegel claimed that the owl of Minerva spreads its wings only at dusk, by which he meant that wisdom comes, if at all, late in the game. If we have to wait until dusk to gain some wisdom about intimacy, we have certainly arrived at the right time—the sun is sinking fast. A piece of wisdom one can retrieve from some of the harder experiences in life says that we learn mainly from our mistakes, not from what we already know how to do perfectly well. That kind of thinking is a basis of psychotherapy: Few people consult a psychotherapist and shell out a hundred or more dollars an hour merely to chat about experiences that they have already thoroughly mastered, unless they don't believe themselves. To apply this premise to love requires a permissive attitude toward one's mistakes, one that supports the idea that failing at a relationship can be as fertile a ground for getting ahead as success, and that disappointment, even if not immediately eradicated (which usually means repressed), does not leave a permanent scar on one's identity.

In a society that bases so much of its self-esteem on technological progress, the glory of individual achievement, and winning all its wars with God's help, the person who suffers disappointment, who fails at love or work, feels shabby and unwanted. This is the case because our society makes it difficult to tell love, power, and anxiety apart. But the outcome of our recent wars, our declining rank in industrial competition and general standard of urban living, along with criticism from the less hostile sectors of the women's movement are among the factors that might move us to rethink our addiction to success (the hostile attacks, though, simply stiffen one's resistance). An ironical attitude becomes particularly valuable in such periods of unease, because it tolerates rather well imperfect, disappointing outcomes, sees even these as potentially useful, and thus prevents the hopelessness or fanaticism that generally accompanies submission to despair.

Since I'm a psychotherapist not a social engineer, I can best show how such rethinking might play out in the idiosyncratic circumstances of individual behavior. To be addicted to success usually means that one is obsessed with failure. A person trapped in the imperatives of our success ethic constantly anticipates failing, knots himself or herself up with the effort to avoid it, and therefore has little resilience available to deal with it when it hits.

For example, a young man, a playwright as it turned out, comes to see me for an initial consultation because he is up to his neck in marital hot water and nearly blocked from writing. He and his wife, he informs me without delay, are on the verge of divorce. When they got married barely two and a half years ago, they were head over heels in love. But now they seem to hate each other most of the time, and their evenings are consumed by bitter quarrels. From other background information he volunteers, I get the sense that this marriage began as a mutual rescue mission, rather like that of Deborah and Seth whose troubles launched Chapter 4.

I listen, but I also watch him closely, trying to take in his presence as well as his presentation, the music along with the words. A wiry, athletic-looking man, he nearly groans under the weight of his depression. No doubt this burden is partly due to his marital crisis. But it is not hard to tell that he has always been pretty much like this. His dead voice and slumped shoulders, his victimized look and self-deprecating talk come from years of inward sadness and preoccupation.

He says that the battles with his wife leave him paralyzed with guilt and frustration so that he is unable to work for days afterward. Amidst a blow-by-blow description of one of these fights, I also learn that he fears becoming like his father, whom he portrays as a stiff, withdrawn man, one whose primary form of contact with his family apparently consisted of issuing complaints. Though an outwardly successful executive, the father became increasingly persuaded that he had wasted his life since he himself had once had artistic aspirations. (Is my playwright carrying out his father's frustrated wishes by becoming an artist and then rebelling by sabotaging the rest of his life? This is a question I tuck in the back of my mind for future reference.)

The father's eventual collapse into depression was severe enough to keep his family in a perpetual state of tension and worry. And now the son lives in terror that his own fate will be similar: His marriage will fail and it will have been his fault; he will be unable to write; life will become meaningless.

Self-pity, obsessive guilt, and a sense of doom are the grand motifs my client brings in. This is the stuff of tragedy, or at least melodrama, so I am prompted to ask him about his plays. To my surprise, it turns out that he writes satirical comedies. When I hear the note of pride with which he tells me this, I wonder if he has acted in any of his own plays and find out that he never has. I suggest that he present me again with his latest marital blowup, but this time I will be the audience, and he is to stage it as though it were one of his most cynical satires. Moreover, he is to play both leading roles—husband and wife—taking first one part, then the other. At first he objects to this silliness, so I urge him on. After stumbling around for a few minutes, he begins to get into it and enjoy himself. He turns into a very funny man, full of antic gestures, as he discovers the predictability of their argument—how he knows perfectly well that a certain comment will set her off, and indeed it does, right on schedule; how rapidly both of them resort to delivering pompous ultimatums.

At this point, their battle begins to seem to him inflated and contrived. He feels a momentary burst of contempt directed mainly at himself, but then a sadder amusement at the spectacle overtakes him. And from this new distance, he is more responsive to their mutual plight. His sorrow now extends to her as well as to himself. For the moment at least, his depression has changed into something more generous that might be useful to both of them.

When my playwright-patient becomes a ham, he begins to free himself from the endless cycles of self-pity that keep him soaked in chronic mournfulness. He cannot avoid seeing what thin partitions sometimes divide the tragic from the absurd. Depression is an instance where absurdity helps restore some flexibility, some breathing room. If people who cling to the miseries of their childhoods can discover something ridiculous about how they have imported that pain into their present relationships, they may have taken a crucial step toward freeing themselves to become adults—and to feeling better. Indeed, if the playwright can hold on to the thread of absurdity that he contacted in my office, his marriage (and his writing) has a chance for renewal. Not that domesticity ought to be, as if it could, a slapstick stand-up routine—but bringing the comic to bear when one's take on life has become overly heavy and tragic is a large part of what I mean by ironical. Another part is opening oneself to the negative aspects of a situation without losing contact with the positive ones. And of all institutions, marriage, heaven knows, can use a large dose of irony.

Several widely applicable ideas can be extrapolated from situations like that of the playwright and his wife. Obviously, cultivating an ironical romantic attitude, which means accepting uncertainty, a measure of tension, and multiple meanings in one's love life, requires a good deal of discipline and maturity. It also takes a playful sense of humor, which is exactly what I fortuitously discovered lurking in the playwright. He just hadn't thought to try it on for size in his life as well as in his art. But on the whole, tolerating tension and accommodating uncertainty are not widespread natural talents among intimate partners. So most of us need a good deal of help from the surrounding culture. Ours, however, with its swings from extolling romantic unity between intimates to deploring their abusive raids on one another, doesn't afford much support for irony or playfulness.

Good psychotherapy, the kind I think is worthwhile at any rate, is by definition ironical. Like art (though art is not made with this intention), its interpretative and exploratory ironies can help people accept limitation, imperfection, complexity, and the points of view of others. In irony begins empathy after a fall—especially a fall into troubled relations with others. Perhaps for the playwright and his wife, importing a comic note into their desperation will mellow things between them a bit. They may even get to a wistful, empathetic alliance based on more mutual understanding of how they manage to keep hurting each other.

The psychoanalytic tradition focuses on helping people accept limitations, but it tends toward a tragic view of the individual buffeted between eros and death. With couples, I think what is especially needed is comedy, which provides the sense that errors, misunderstandings, pride, and stubbornness, once brought into the light, can culminate in resolution and integration. This outlook follows from a belief that people largely create their circumstances. Tragedy implies that character is fate, comedy that character is will.

Actually we need both perspectives. Maintaining the tragic and comic sides of life in some balance with each other, which could almost be a definition of the ironical, is not a half-bad program for making relationships work. If two people keep in mind that there is more than one reality open to them, they always have options. And once they see things in an ironical light, it becomes more difficult to carry on as though their unhappiness is destiny.

Thus an ironical outlook helps construct a vision of romance that incorporates hardship and disappointment as essential ingredients without regarding them as lethal. It enables two people to grow rueful with each other, which is a pretty decent way to be together: They may come to recognize the pain they can cause each other with more sorrow and less blame. An ironical view of love also needs to be historical, because real life unfolds in time, involves declining powers, and does not promise things will always stay the same. Of course, all this adds up to a bittersweet vision, not a promise of eternal bliss. But I think that it is essential that we develop a language in which to speak about the pleasures of sexual love and lasting companionship, especially in teaching them to our children, without representing them as unalloyed joy or evil. They may be a gateway to a possible good life or an anxious one but not inevitably to paradise or hell.

Our culture also needs to teach that intimacy requires a measure of discipline and craft—that there is an *art* to love in a literal sense—because constructing a mature, flourishing relationship is at least as hard a labor as learning to play the flute or carve a work of sculpture. In fact, one could argue that the raw materials of intimacy are even more recalcitrant and the anxiety of a failed performance or exhibition even more debilitating. This is a perspective that traditional romantic love virtually ignored, because it was so absorbed in extraordinary experiences. It went straight from "Some enchanted evening / You will meet a stranger" to "And they lived happily ever after." In collapsing the intervening steps between these two, it skipped over ordinary life, which is where most of us live most of the time. If you don't practice the scales or the techniques of using a chisel, which are painstakingly ordinary tasks, you wind up with bleats or fragments of rock.

Certainly by this time enough evidence is in to persuade us that if people don't take some care with the ordinary day-by-day routine and friction involved in living together, "Some enchanted evening" ends in the divorce courts or even in domestic violence. One can also find in great novels plenty of lessons about the consequences of turning one's back on the common details in order to pursue extraordinary excitements. Compare Kitty and Levin, who work hard at ordinary domesticity, to Anna and Vronski, who are in love with the extraordinary in *Anna Karenina*. Look what happens to Gerald and Gudrun, who are so thunderstruck with each other's beauty that they never bother to learn much about one another's character in *Women in Love*. Their impulsive, demanding passion culminates in a fatal power struggle. Whatever one thinks of Lawrence's idiosyncratic philosophy of intimate relations, expressed through his other couple, Rupert and Ursula, at least they take time to spell out who they are and what they believe to each other.

Emma Bovary's romantic yearnings lead her to abandon a decent ordinary domestic existence in pursuit of passionate fulfillment. One can readily sympathize with her search for something vital, for a hint of transcendent adventure, which she is not likely to derive from her husband. But her subsequent romantic attachments are careless and misguided, and her quest turns increasingly desperate and tawdry. At the beginning of *Middlemarch*, Dorothea Brooke dismisses, almost without paying attention, a suitor who genuinely cares about her and appears to have much to give her. Longing to participate in some important intellectual venture, she marries the selfish and obsessive Edward Casaubon, who seduces her not sexually, but with his cosmic scholarly aspirations. In their subsequent life together these aspirations turn out to be completely hollow. Similarly, Isabel Archer in Henry James's *Portrait of a Lady* bypasses her steadfast, sensitive, and truly appreciative admirer, Ralph Tovchett, who deeply if quietly loves her. Instead, she falls for the glittering mask presented by Gilbert Osmond, a shallow, mean-spirited aesthete, and finds herself in a cruelly empty marriage to him.

This last group of novels uses female protagonists to demonstrate the dangers of a romantic lust for the extraordinary. In my experience, however, it's more often men in our culture who take a fall through treating everyday events as relatively meaningless, especially in their relationships. American men tend to be overly enamored of extraordinary feelings, happenings, and accomplishments, which I take to be another corollary of our individualistic outlook.

For instance, among my male patients, there have been several who have achieved high professional standing yet find themselves bored with their work, their family lives, and themselves. In asking them about their experiences growing up, I found that all they recalled with any sharp particularity were the big moments when the reward was bestowed, the achievement consummated. They remembered the accolades—catching the touchdown pass that won the game; walking up to the podium to receive the diploma; making love for the first time, as if in a dream, to the girl who had seemed unreachable. But life in between such moments—on the way to them or afterward—was mostly a blur in their memories because it had not seemed worth giving serious attention to. It was just time passing. Now they still live in a state of waiting for the great event. Here again, *Gatsby* is one of our key fables for understanding American lives. In at least some cases I have encountered, the philosophy of the great event rendered such men partially impotent in their marriages. Neither they nor their wives could possibly live up to a steady diet of extraordinary performances.

On numerous occasions, couples who spend their day-to-day existence in misery or intolerable tension have come to a therapy session after taking a vacation together and announced that they had a marvelous time, hardly quarreled, made love again like when they were first married, and so on. Vacations can be great for marriages. So can moving, having a baby, any number of events outside the swim of ordinary life—but only temporarily as a rule. Couples who come to depend on extraordinary measures, such as buying a dream house to preserve a faltering marriage, soon learn that it doesn't work. "We get along just fine when there are no differences," one woman told me at a time when she and her husband were settling into a new house that they had coveted and finally managed to buy. Yes, and so did Adam and Eve in Eden where there were no limits to ease and pleasure. The friction that arises from constantly having to deal with one another over frustrating everyday matters vanishes in the sheen of wonderful times. You could say that no moment was an ordinary moment in the Garden, yet apparently even that wasn't enough. And therein lies the rub: If marriage could be a perpetual vacation or a perpetual orgasm, as some people seem to expect it will be when they fall in love, it could still turn out to be a painful bore because the extraordinary prolonged becomes bland and familiar.

So in addition to ironical romance, we need a romance of the ordinary. In a sense, though, these amount to the same thing. The playfulness of irony that enables it to be detached without being disconnected, and its openness to uncertainty and differences, helps ordinary experience remain alive. To accept the ordinariness of marriage, for example, is not to consign oneself to monotony and resignation, even if it goes against the traditional romantic expectation. When you look at the careers of great artists, the flamboyance of their early work usually thins out into much more simplicity, a kind of ordinariness, in their very late work. From this, one learns that the ordinary has its own aesthetic merits; these include economy, gracefulness, and even a sense of surprise that come from being more deeply in touch with reality. The problem for couples isn't with ordinary life, which changes from moment to moment and therefore is unpredictable. The problem is the dreadful feeling of sameness and fixation that follows from two people imagining that they know each other because they are always together.

This in itself could be construed as an ironical remark. Whom do you know better, after all, than your lover or spouse? But in fact, thinking that you know the other person only too well is one of the occupational hazards of marriage. It stems from the various anxieties that intimacy rouses and the effort to control them by creating an illusion of certitude. The danger in two people assuming that they know each other through familiarity is like staring. When you stare at something for long enough, you may see it more intensely or sharply at first, but after a while your eye muscles grow weary, your forehead and temples register the tension, and the unrelieved monotony makes the life go out of the scene. By then you are no longer really seeing it, even if it is a beautiful sunset. The stage is thus set for stereotyping, which is accomplished by fixing experience in place. It's time to blink or look away. Then you can go back for a fresh look.

Another way in which husbands and wives come to "know" one another without either of them really knowing what's going on with the other person is through taking each other too personally. Two people living together, with both their identities on the line, tend to respond to every flicker of each other's eyebrows, every frown or momentary bad mood, as a message that they are doing something wrong. But this is to treat another individual as a mirror, and you can't see anything on the other side of a mirror.

On both these counts, I often try, in therapy with couples, to teach people to take each other less personally, to disengage themselves from the lump of togetherness that they have become stuck in. They don't have to divorce to do this; they just have to blink or look away for a moment. Then they can go back and see the other person or the situation in a different light, like my playwright. If a marriage is in trouble, the husband and wife almost always need to disengage—at least a little, and sometimes from a marital death grip on one another—in order to navigate between the twin perils of demanding perfect union and blaming each other for every failing in the relationship. They also need the breathing space between them to look at their differences with a measure of good humor if their intimacy is to grow. If there isn't any such room, they will surely go to battle to make some.

These last thoughts are mostly notes from the therapist's chair. However, cultures also tackle the same kinds of issues. The way in which many cultures handle the need to detach or disengage, for example (our direct ancestor, courtly love, is a good example), is by treating love explicitly as a ritual or game. Thus they create a degree of independence from the ups and downs of individual personality. No doubt it only works in part—probably no one's self-esteem gets completely off the hook from being subject to the other person when sex is involved. But it helps expand people's ability to tolerate tension, delay, and imperfection, in contrast to our insistence on immediate, total fulfillment, which is like a return to infancy.

An important task for any society is to help people get beyond their demands for instant gratification of needs and immediate surcease of anxiety. These are perfectly healthy demands—in an infant. Erik Erikson has pointed out that a society "must take care of the unavoidable remnants of infantility in its adults."[1] For instance, every Western society has recognized that erotic love arouses anxiety. Perhaps none before our own, however, has left the individual so alone to deal with it. The ancient Greeks blamed it on the gods and gave Cupid a bow and arrow to remind people that desire is a kind of wound. Medieval Europe elevated the anxiety of loving into an ethical ideal and transformed its energies into art and playfulness, a chance for heroic deeds, and a spiritual path. In the communal households closer to our own times, anxious-making libidinal intensities were muted, in principle at least, through being channeled into shared socially essential labors. There was a price to be paid, no doubt, in sublimation or repression. Nevertheless, a portion of love served to bind the community as its members went about their work.

These are instances where culture supported intimacy and cushioned anxiety through religion, ritual and ceremony, art, moral codes, and social responsibilities. We have in their place psychotherapy, recovery groups, Prozac, divorce, and abuse trials—all moppings up after it is, in effect, too late. We need a culture that affords us more preventive medicine.

In other words, at the risk of repeating myself, we need a new myth of love. One of the important threads running through this book is the premise that every society, every period of cultural change, evolves its own myths of intimacy. There is no question that we need such myths to live by, including ones to guide us through the disquiet into which erotic feelings often lead us. You could say that myths are the poetic constructs that mediate between cultural values and individual conduct, helping connect us to each other and the community in a network of mutual responsibilities to one another. If these myths lose the pluralism of poetry, which allows room for diverse individual styles and preferences, if they harden into dogma, so much the worse for the quality of life. When the primary social myths of an era become obsolete because they no longer fit enough people's needs—and this has already happened to romantic love as we knew it for so long—they have to be refurbished.

Sexual love traverses wildly various terrain, ranging from serene woodland paths to treacherous swamps where one can end up lost and terrified. Our traditional popular myth of romantic love provided one map to guide us through the territory, but its idealizations by now seem abstract and out of date. When it doesn't indulge in naive celebrations of erotic experience, seemingly blind to pitfalls and dangers, it goes in for pessimistic overkill, turning them into scenes of tragedy and death.

In replacing romance with a myth of abuse, we treat the sexual landscape as though it were little more than an urban jungle strewn with refuse. At first this may appear to be a new realism that demystifies. To be sure, it has brought to light shocking realities concerning the cruel exercise of power, the structure of male domination, the deployment of sex in the service of everything except love. It is crucially important to haul domestic violence and incest out from under their hidden suburban canopies, to incriminate the denying rapist and sweet-talking batterer. But we are also struggling with the swing to the opposite pole—the abuse of abuse, as I have called it—which shows us that the "truths" of abuse can become no less extreme and abstract than those of romantic love just because they are negative.

Such violent polarizations between good and evil, as I suggested in the preceding chapter, occur with regularity in our social, cultural, and political debates. They remind us that American culture, perhaps all Western culture, has always labored under a dialectical conflict between repression and freedom. Repression, broadly understood, goes in for taboos, for a phobic insistence on controlling everyone's behavior and thoughts as well, if possible, and for stifling the body as an instrument of pleasure. Freedom, unfortunately, has been too much applied to seeking hedonistic self-gratification, usually at the expense of others. Observing the sinking of romance into abuse, one needs to recall that this country was founded on individual liberty combined with gloom-ridden Puritan constraints. The Puritan emphasis says give people a sexual inch, and they will take a mile. And indeed it appears to be the case: We passed through the unprecedented sexual liberation of the 1960s and 1970s, and now we tend to think of ourselves as casualties of abuse, collapsed marriages, and shamefully blighted families.

It wouldn't be the first time that loosening the shackles on conduct widens our perception to include some bad news. Human nature is such that when things head in one direction, the opposite is never far behind. Freud lifted the lid on Victorian sexual repression and discovered sexual abuse of children at the same moment, though in the spirit of a genteel liberalism that backed off from attacking too much of the established order at once, he later recanted on the abuse issue. We are hardly so shy about abuse. Is it because we overdosed on freedom and pleasure? In the era of AIDS, "safe sex," broken homes, domestic violence, and orgasm by modem or dialing 1-900, we seem well on the way to a new puritanism, an attitude that shrinks from any intimate touching of one another. "Puritanism," I once wrote in another context, "is part of the weather pattern in America, a cold wind that blows through our culture to lower the temperature of our political, sexual, even our metaphysical impulses. Kierkegaard defined anxiety as the dizziness of freedom. One could think of puritanism as the anxiety of democracy.''2

So our erotic history in the twentieth century goes something like this: We tried romantic idealism, then sexual hedonism, and now we are trying a return to puritanism. None of it has worked very well. However we might now try to redraw the boundaries of intimacy, it seems to me we have to do a better job of including the most primal polarity of all, one that plagues the playwright and his wife along with most of the other couples I have described—and, in fact, our society as a whole: This polarity is the alternation between our two most elemental passions, love and hate.

Where intimate relations are concerned, there is no passionate love without a tinge of hate, or hate without a thread of love. That fact has less to do with so grand a conception as Freud's instinctual myths of Eros and Thanatos, through which he represented the fundamental forces of life and death, or with anything inherently neurotic, than with our movements toward and away from one another and the anxieties that accompany them. Love, in bringing us close to one another, tends to blur the differences between two people and create an emotional experience of two selves merging into one, a kind of steaming romantic stew. It also gives rise to an inevitable anxiety—fear of loss of oneself. Hate, at least in the context of intimate relations, is a desperate attempt to become separate again, to recover the self, though at the expense of the other person.

To be sure, there are also cold, annihilating hatreds, murderous hatreds that want to regain separateness and power by simply destroying the other person. But more typically, hatred itself is hot and passionate, and in the very effort to regain separateness, it nevertheless remains attached to its object, often to a degree that can be as obsessive as falling in love. Hate individualizes and divides, it accumulates and hoards power, but it is also another way to not be alone.

An ironical romanticism, like that which I was hoping to steer the playwright toward, rejects the all-or-nothing perception of our intimate struggles. Irony holds multiple, even apparently contradictory states in its embrace at the same time. It can thus continue to love despite a quotient of hostility, live with tension and uncertainty, retrieve what is positive even in contacting the negative. Jealousy, for example, contains a mixture of love and hate. So do sadistic feelings of vindictiveness toward an intimate partner. Even boredom might be considered a combination of love and hate: If it kills off vitality in both oneself and the other, it still keeps two people attached to one another through fixation, like uninterested high-school students obeying an imperative and staring at the blackboard, although this is a deadened, immobilizing attachment. Then there are the carefully, if unconsciously, regulated proportions of love and hate that preserve a constant distance, but not too much distance, between two people, protecting them from more intimacy than they can handle.

All of these states end up in psychological culs-de-sacs. They don't lead anywhere, but they also all contain, however distorted in form, attempts to balance the competing claims of the need to be separate and the need to be together, to alleviate abandonment and engulfment anxieties, and to maintain a sense of control when faced with the threat of loss of control at the hands of another person.

When love and hate are treated as though they are mutually exclusive, the tendency is to idealize the one and demonize the other. I believe that this is at the root of the oppositions we find throughout the problematic, anguished history of modern love. Our passage from a culture of romantic love to a culture of abuse is rather like the fate of an individual relationship writ large—it travels a path from enchantment to despair, from joyfulness to depression. For that matter, one frequently sees the same cycle occur when a nation idealizes a new leader as its savior. As soon as he proves unable to live up to the promise, the populace becomes disillusioned and is ready to drag him through the streets.

I have argued that our fading romantic ideal has ultimately betrayed us because it has left us beached on the shoals of adolescence, with the essential task of adolescent development—reconciling the claims of both autonomy and intimacy—still incomplete. When two people fall in love, the intense experience of fusion, of being utterly tuned in to each other, the mutual satisfaction that comes from idealizing another person and, in turn, being idealized oneself, brings with it the illusion that any difficulty in one's ability to be oneself and, at the same time, be with another has been instantly resolved.

An idealizing passion is a strange and wonderful state: It melts all obstructions in its path—at least temporarily. Ultimately it cannot last much longer than did those psychedelic highs in the 1960s which gave many people an experience of existence at concert pitch, living fully in the present moment, feeling at one with the world. Afterward, there was usually a depressing return to ordinary life. These peak experiences—being in love or being high—might give one a sharper taste for fulfillment and point toward goals worth working for, but they say nothing about the disciplined, prolonged labor that is required, or that such states can never be achieved for more than a brief spell anyway. The hazard of peak experiences is that they can leave one merely addicted to love or drugs.

Traditional romantic love, when it is offered as the basis for serious intimacy, such as marriage, in effect promises resolution through intensity as a permanent condition. But in reality this is a premature resolution that glosses over what has been left unfinished in the lovers' personalities. It sets them up for a profound fall into disillusionment when they enter the everyday world of making a life together.

Disappointment, however, is another of those emotions that blends both love and hate, and it can be a particularly fruitful one. It has the potential to create a new mood between people if they can find an ironical stance toward it, which prevents it from curdling into disillusionment. Disappointment combines sorrow and anger, and it reaches with a kind of yearning toward the other person. At the same time, it keeps the other at bay by treating him or her as a diminished figure, one that failed to live up to expectations. In therapy, when you talk openly with a fighting couple about each antagonist's disappointment, it helps soften the rigid idealizations each of them continues to cling to through holding on to feelings of betrayal. Unlike jealousy, cruelty, or boredom, disappointment contains secret hints of mutuality. It can interrupt what *New Yorker* drama critic John Lahr, reviewing an Arthur Miller play about a tortured marriage, called "the cycle of blame that has infected and seems to have stalemated modern life . . . with an irrational, often righteous fury that is at once a mask and an admission of fear."[3] It is not such a long stretch from disappointment to empathy.

An ironical view of romance would include such themes and thus help us learn how to be intimate in a fallen world. Remembering that there is no love without hate makes one more cautious about the idealizations that spring up instantly when people fall in love. That there is no hate between intimates without love, even if the love is buried under the debris of their history together, is what provides the hope of restoring, whether through therapy or some other means, an affectionate relationship between two people who have succumbed to the horrors of intimate terrorism.

The playwright's shift from tragedy to rueful comedy illustrates something else that I regard as a very important point: Love, whatever else it might be, is a willed performance. Of course, such an idea goes against the grain of some of our favorite traditional assumptions about love. We tend to treat intimacy as though it were merely a feeling, a state one falls into, rather than a relationship that one actively makes. But then, too, making things entails learning the requisite skills. The common attitude toward love in our society mistakes the spontaneous arousal of an emotion for an achievement. Love, according to such a view, is supposed to be both impulsive and sincere.

This outlook fits with our sense that what happens spontaneously is the most real. I am not against spontaneity in love—or life, or art; it can be a creative force in all these areas. But the kind of spontaneity that contributes to the creation of something worthwhile is considerably more than the expression of strong impulses paired with convincing intentions. The latter two qualities are perfectly well exemplified in an adolescent crush. They can also be thoroughly self-aggrandizing, leading, say, to episodes of sexual harassment or what we nowadays call "date rape," because neither impulses nor sincere feelings in themselves necessarily take into account the other person. What appears to be spontaneous behavior is often just the path of least resistance. It's easy to imagine that habit is nature and immediacy or intensity the sign of authenticity. The ancient Chinese, who, judging from their paintings, liked a panoramic perspective that chastens the ego, had a proverb that says to be sincere in love is to be grotesque. That may be an extreme formulation for our taste, but presumably it means that when emotional involvement gets too heavy and serious, it narrows one's horizons and leads to a loss of balance in relationships.

The kind of spontaneity that best serves intimacy is not simply freewheeling self-expression. It is freedom that proceeds from a foundation of attention to the other's needs as well as one's own. You could consider this one way of defining trust: When two intimates are most free with one another in a positive sense, each has faith that the other's freedom is not exacted at the sacrifice of one's own. This is a freedom tempered by the discipline and form of affection. One might think of it also as improvisation, because it is rather analogous to jazz, another activity in which freedom flourishes on the basis of mutual agreement about a carefully established foundation. In bad jazz, like a bad marriage, the musicians keep drowning each other out.

Great jazz, by contrast, offers one of the best vehicles for loosening up one's sense of life's ironies. It is one of our culture's most sophisticated forms of conversation. Musicians like Dizzy Gillespie, John Coltrane, Miles Davis, Betty Carter, and Herbie Hancock, to take a few of my own favorite examples, talk through their music about loneliness and loss, abandonment, jealousy, betrayal, victimization, and oppression. Even as they take on such dire topics, though, they continually play with the beat—falling behind it, like someone pausing for another look back; leaping ahead of it a few steps into the unknown. When they add a blue note, one of the most wistful, ironical devices ever invented, they get across a touch of depression, a lament for the past, but bend it coyly around its own mournfulness and add a little antic pelvic thrust toward the future.

This, I suspect, is one reason that jazz musicians like to launch their improvisations with tunes from Broadway and Hollywood musicals, which tend to be about pure ideal love and its loss—in other words, the music of American adolescence. That is only a starting point for jazz; the irony is in the unexpected things that happen next. When the music is good, it almost always surprises us, surprises even the players themselves. Dizzy Gillespie could doodle on his horn with a sad "standard" tune and then suddenly switch gears into astonishing flights of sardonic enthusiasm. When Betty Carter, the superb jazz vocalist, sings "Everything I Have Is Yours," an old popular standard, you know that she is not just handing herself over to depend on some guy, though the words may imply this. Her voice can ruminate darkly about the idea, then tease it by surrendering and holding back at the same time. It's a voice in love with its capacity to reach out and touch the world in both playful and poignant ways. One could do far worse than develop a jazzy marriage.

A good marriage is an improvised performance, an ironical mix of love and hate, better described with verbs than nouns. What would such a marriage look like in practice? Given a culture that seems to stall at adolescence, we have taken too many of our cues for marriage from young love. Perhaps it's time to look for new directions in later romance—a stage of second thoughts, so to speak, after the initial bloom has already begun to wilt under the pressure of disappointments, conflicts, and other assorted difficulties. For example, I imagine that almost everyone knows, somewhere among their relatives or friends, a marriage that seems to work because both husband and wife are each aware of their own and the other's shortcomings and treat these with a kind of affectionate amusement. They play off of them in a spirit of improvisation that carries them forward in life. But where among the scattered resources of our culture are we to find models that we can draw on in a general way to fashion our new, somewhat humbler myth of ironical romantic love?

Interestingly enough, our classic serious literature turns out not to be very helpful at this point. It is filled with brilliant diagnostic insights into the dangers of overly idealized intimacy. However, our writers tend to be incredibly pessimistic about marriage. Either they oppose domesticity altogether and send their male heroes scampering off with the other boys to wander through the woods, hit the road, or set sail for diverse adventures and moral tests of manhood (Cooper, Melville, Twain, Hemingway, Kerouac)—a point of view which, I take it, is still about adolescence—or they criticize adolescent romantic idealism with telling effectiveness by demonstrating the havoc its demands produce upon people trying to make lives with one another; then they leave them stuck there with little hope as tragedy or gothic gloom settles over their love affairs and marriages (James, Wharton, Fitzgerald, Cather). Both of these themes indicate how much trouble we have leaving adolescence behind or getting beyond it in America.

Thus ill-equipped for the limitations and complications of adult life, one's first marriage may amount to little more than a kind of dress rehearsal for the real thing. As we all know, things have been tending in this direction, as increasing numbers of people move on to their second or third marriages. Of course, such serial monogamy leaves open the question of just how much anyone learns from the first failed marriage and divorce before embarking on what is apt to be the second. The emotional extremes of adolescence—idealization or despair—won't do as responses to the inevitable oscillations of day-to-day intimate relations. It's not that we marry too young, necessarily; the difficulty has more to do with the connections between emotional development and communal support than with chronological age. Many societies have married off their young much earlier than we do, and things seem to go along pretty well. Our distinctive problem is that we have so little usable structure or instruction to take up the slack between individual experience and the achieved wisdom of the community.

I have been making a plea for more comic ingredients in our recipe for marriage. With domestic tragedy an everyday occurrence, however, where can people turn for a little wise levity about so daunting an institution? Classical comedy won't do, because it is a comedy of errors based on failures to communicate. Traditional comedy takes off from (and therefore depends on) a context of widely accepted social values. It creates frustrating and incongruous situations out of deviations from such values—therein lies its humor—and then it resoundingly shows that everything can be re-solved by unraveling the underlying confusions and misunderstand-ings. Once the facts are straightened out in traditional comedy, the return to social harmony is almost always expressed by a reconcilia-tion between a young hero and heroine, who wind up getting mar-ried, surrounded by festivity and mirth, as the curtain drops. But if that once seemed an end point, it is just the beginning of the trouble for us.

Just as psychoanalysis has a dash of the tragic, old-fashioned mari-tal counseling, the kind provided by social agencies and pastoral counselors before abuse came into the foreground, has something in common with this genre of comedy. It, too, was forever dealing with failures to communicate. Although that can be helpful in cor-recting misperceptions, on the whole, individuals do not change very profoundly in either comedies or counseling.

If the first marriage is likely to be only a disorderly rehearsal, wouldn't it be fitting if the second could take place between the *same* two people, choosing each other anew because they have deeply learned something along the way? The surprising thing is that there are in fact some wonderful examples of this possibility availa-ble in our culture. And they contain more than a glimmer of the mythic. You have to go back a good many decades, though—to Hollywood's "golden years"—to dig them up.

During the 1930s and 1940s, movie directors such as Frank Capra, George Cukor, and Leo McCarey made a sequence of ur-bane comedies that contain probing, if hilarious, explorations of modern marriage. They starred Cary Grant, Irene Dunne, Clark Gable, Claudette Colbert, Katharine Hepburn, Spencer Tracy, and other such terrific screen presences. Film historians often refer to them as "screwball comedies" and fondly describe their main char-acters, especially the female leads, as "madcap." Those labels, how-ever, simply don't capture the amount of useful instruction about intimacy that takes place in this group of films.

In an idiosyncratic and fascinating study of such films, the philos-opher Stanley Cavell points out that they comprise a distinctly new comic genre all their own, one that portrays a valuable philosophy of married life. He calls them "comedies of remarriage," because their plots spring from the attempt "not to get the central pair together, but to get them *back* together, together *again*. Hence the fact of marriage . . . is subjected to the fact or the threat of divorce."[4] As far as I'm concerned, they represent an epitome of ironical romance. In virtually all of them, marital conflict with potential for tragedy—loss of faith, threats of infidelity, actual divorce—turns into sophisticated humor, thanks to the lead couple's underlying goodwill and steady, if temporarily submerged, caring about each other.

In Leo McCarey's *The Awful Truth* (1937), Lucy and Jerry War-riner (Irene Dunne and Cary Grant), a cultivated, affluent, and gorgeous married couple, return separately to their apartment, after a brief spell apart on business or vacation, to ambiguous intimations that each has been unfaithful to the other. After a series of pointed, humorous exchanges, they get to the heart of the matter. Soon they are at each other's throats, suspecting the worst, both feeling disappointed, betrayed, and unloved. Amid the charges and counter-charges, Lucy tells Jerry, "There can't be any doubt in marriage. The whole thing is built on faith. If you've lost that, well, you've lost everything." Jerry replies, "I haven't any faith left in anyone." And she mutters, "I know how you feel." With mounting anger and hopelessness, they decide to divorce.

Of course, Lucy is right. Her speech is a key one, for the question of faith is the central motif of the film, but in this opening scene it doesn't yet amount to much. It is premature trust, the kind that is supposed to be automatically built into romantic love. Until it is put to the test, it has very little real substance. In this respect, the insistence on instant trust in love is like the poet Milton's "cloister'd virtue," which he felt was a meaningless ideal of virginity because it had never been subjected to temptation. When one depends on such ideals, at once brittle and shallow, the slightest hint of inconstancy usually results in an immediate slide into disillusionment.

The Warriners' burden is that their faith is tested up one side and down the other through a long and complicated series of painfully slapstick situations. They live separately yet still keep finding themselves involved in fantastic misadventures with each other. They have even become engaged to others with whom they are thoroughly incompatible. As the film ends in a marvelously tentative and charming bedroom scene, minutes before their divorce becomes final, they both realize that they have changed. They rediscover faith in each other based on a deep caring about one another that has been evident and yet unseen by either of them all along. It is testimony to the film's maturity that the ambiguous behavior that broke them up in the first place is never fully resolved. It's as if the Warriners have learned that married faith requires a note of skepticism, a space of unknowability for the private self. Yet they come to accept how they are with each other as love.

In *The Awful Truth* and other films like it, such as *The Philadelphia Story* and *Adam's Rib,* the central marriage itself usually breaks apart or comes close to it over mistrust and differences. After numerous ordeals, ranging from the sublime to the ridiculous, the alienated spouses end up choosing each other again. Neither of them escapes with their personalities unscathed, however. Both husband and wife are forced to undergo an education by painful hard knocks that prepares them to live together in a civilized intimacy. If I were commissioned to design a marital therapy to supply our culture with a seasoned ideal for adult intimacy, I would just about base it on these comedies of remarriage.

These older films, like *The Awful Truth* and *Adam's Rib,* were something of a high point in American popular culture. They remind us of a possibility that we have now tended to lose sight of—that intimacy, precisely because of the kind of problems it creates, provides one of our most vivid and immediate opportunities for growing up. Taking part in an important intimate relationship is always a risky proposition: It can steer people, or, rather, they can steer it, toward tragedy; but the comic perspective suggests that difficult stretches can also culminate in happier consummations. In an age when warring ideologies and pervasive litigiousness, contending claims for victimhood and confusion about both sex and sex roles have all but obliterated the sense that individuals are responsible for much of anything, it is tempting to cling to passive or deterministic views of love as well. Love is biology, according to a current line of thinking, a mysterious ripple in the molecules; or it sprouts from rubbing two temperaments together (as in the notion that opposites attract or that similarities, like laughing at the same things, make for soulmates); or it's just plain inexplicable, as in "what could she possibly see in *him!*" All true; all just about equally uninteresting.

In fact, I think that most causal explanations of love are relatively uninteresting. What is of real significance is what two people make of an opportunity. When marriages used to be arranged by families—an approach that we would regard as fantasically oppressive and high-handed—it is doubtful that anyone assumed that the bride and groom were madly in love with each other. I can hardly recommend a return to such a procedure, but nevertheless it is intriguing to contemplate the idea that such a couple, rather forcibly shoved under the same roof, might *learn* to love one another.

Could we perhaps get some similar mileage from conceiving love not just as what is given at the beginning (which is then supposed to take care of itself for several decades), but as an outcome of a sometimes pleasurable, sometimes arduous process of being together? This would resemble an ancient point of view, called teleology, quite different in emphasis from our modern science of cause and effect. Teleology claims that a desirable end comes about from the proper realization of a potential. For instance, you wouldn't say that the acorn caused an oak tree; but the potential for a tree is in the acorn, and with a little support from the soil and weather, a tree will indeed come to be. The path from infatuation to a lasting intimate relationship, it seems to me, is something like that.

Many of us lament the passing of frontiers while congestion, monotony, and random violence accumulate to diminish the quality of American life. There's not much room left to head for the hills or light out for the territory. If you try it, you are likely to wind up in bumper-to-bumper traffic and find that it costs you a bundle when you get there. The conquest of space, which stirred our imaginations some twenty-five years ago, no longer appears to excite us very much. But maybe the bright side of a loss that we still struggle with—the loss of romantic love as a gateway to paradise—could be that it provides us with a new frontier, one right under everybody's noses. Now that marriage has become so terrifying an enterprise, a dark, obstacle-strewn expedition through two psyches, we could consider treating it as one of our most important adventures. After all, don't husbands and wives have to go to heroic lengths to make a marriage work these days? Perhaps marriage in the modern world, with all its restless energy, its labyrinths of complex meanings to negotiate, its ordeals and setbacks to overcome, could be our next arena for heroic deeds: our domestic Fortunate Fall.

Notes

Introduction

1. Anatole Broyard, *Kafka Was the Rage: A Greenwich Village Memoir* (New York: Carol Southern Books [an imprint of Crown Publishers], 1993), p. 63.

1 The Politics of Anxiety

1. Willard Waller, *The Family: A Dynamic Interpretation* (New York: Dryden Press, 1938; 2nd rev. ed., 1951), pp. 191–192.

2. John Cheever, "Journals," *The New Yorker,* 1/21/91, pp. 34–35.

3. Donald Barthelme, "Critique de la Vie Quotidienne," in *Sadness* (New York: Bantam Books, 1974), p. 3.

4. Jean-Paul Sartre, *The Philosophy of Jean-Paul Sartre,* edited by Robert D. Cumming (New York: Modern Library, 1966), p. 475.

5. Ibid., p. 476.

6. Soren Kierkegaard, *Either/Or* (New York: Doubleday Anchor Books, 1959), Vol I, p. 152.

7. Elaine Walster, "Passionate Love," in *Intimacy, Family, and Society,* edited by Arlene and Jerome Skolnick (Boston: Little, Brown, 1974), pp. 277–89.

8. Ernest G. Schachtel, *Metamorphosis: On the Development of Affect, Perception, Attention, and Memory* (New York: Basic Books, 1959), p. 6.

9. Erving Goffman, *Relations in Public: Microstudies of the Public Order* (New York: Harper Colophon Books, 1972), p. 279.

10. This is a pattern known as the double bind. The classic paper on the double bind and how it can drive people crazy is "Toward a Theory of Schizophrenia" by Gregory Bateson, Don D. Jackson, and John Weakland (1956). It is reprinted in Bateson's *Steps to an Ecology of Mind* (New York: Ballantine Books, 1972).

11. Georg Simmel, *The Sociology of Georg Simmel,* translated and edited by Kurt H. Wolff (New York: Free Press, 1964), p. 329.

12. Ibid., p. 328.

13. Ralph Waldo Emerson, *Selections from Ralph Waldo Emerson,* edited by Stephen E. Whicher (Boston: Riverside Press, 1950), p. 120.

2: The Postmodern Battle of the Sexes

1. *New York Times,* 8/17/94.

2. Leonard Kriegel, "Gender and Its Discontents," *Partisan Review* (Summer 1993), p. 453.

3. H. W. Fowler, *A Dictionary of Modern English Usage,* 2nd edition, revised by Sir Ernest Gowers (New York: Oxford University Press, 1965 [orig. 1926]), p. 221.

4. Annette Lawson, *Adultery: An Analysis of Love and Betrayal* (New York: Basic Books, 1988), p. 36.

5. Willa Cather, *Not Under Forty* (Lincoln: University of Nebraska Press, Bison Books, 1988 [orig. 1922]), p. 136.

6. D. H. Lawrence, "We Need One Another," in *Phoenix: The Posthumous Papers of D. H. Lawrence, 1936,* edited by Edward D. McDonald (New York: Penguin Books, 1980), p. 188.

7. Otto Rank, *Will Therapy and Truth and Reality* (New York: Alfred A. Knopf, 1972), p. 132.

3: "I Concentrate on You": A Brief History of Romantic Love

1. Philip E. Slater, *The Pursuit of Loneliness: American Culture at the Breaking Point* (Boston: Beacon Press, 1970), pp. 54–55.

2. E. P. Thompson, *Customs in Common: Studies in Traditional Popular Culture* (New York: The New Press, 1993), pp. 45ff.

3. See, for example, Denis de Rougemont, *Love in the Western World* (New York: Doubleday Anchor Books, 1957), pp. 105–27.

4. John Demos, *A Little Commonwealth: Family Life in Plymouth Colony* (New York: Oxford University Press, 1970), pp. 183–84.

5. Ibid., pp. 93–97.

6. Christopher Lasch, *Haven in a Heartless World: The Family Besieged* (New York: Basic Books, 1977), is good on the evolution of the modern family.

7. Richard Sennett, *Families Against the City: Middle Class Homes of Industrial Chicago, 1872–1890* (New York: Vintage Books, 1974), p. 195.

8. Thom Gunn, "Jamesian," in *The Man with Night Sweats* (New York: Farrar, Straus & Giroux, 1992), p. 46.

9. Paul Goodman, *Nature Heals: Psychological Essays,* edited by Taylor Stoehr, with an introduction by Michael Vincent Miller (Highland, New York: Gestalt Journal Publications, 1991), p. 96.

4: Darwinian Love

1. Edith Wharton, *The Age of Innocence* (New York: Signet Classics, 1962), p. 275.

2. Sylvia Plath, "The Munich Mannequins," in *Ariel* (London: Faber and Faber, 1965), p. 74.

3. Harry Stack Sullivan, *The Interpersonal Theory of Psychiatry* (New York: W. W. Norton, 1953), p. 8.

4. David T. Bazelon, *Power in America: The Politics of the New Class* (New York: New American Library, 1967), p. 52.

5: The Fixed Diameter of Eros

1. Edith Wharton, "Souls Belated," in *Roman Fever and Other Stories* (New York: Collier Books, 1993), p. 120.

2. Michael Balint, *Primary Love and Psycho-analytic Technique* (New York: Liveright, 1965), p. 160.

3. For example, R. A. Spitz, "Hospitalism," in *The Psychoanalytic Study of the Child,* Vol. I (New York: International Universities Press, 1945), pp. 53–74. This was one of the key early papers on this phenomenon.

4. Erik H. Erikson, *Childhood and Society* (Harmondsworth, England: Penguin Books, 1965), p. 130.

5. Ibid., p. 131.

6. D. W. Winnicott, *The Child, the Family, and the Outside World* (New York: Penguin Books, 1969), p. 144.

7. Johan Huizinga, *Homo Ludens: A Study of the Play Element in Culture* (Boston: Beacon Press, 1955), p. 47.

8. Ibid., p. 45.

9. Anne Carson, *Eros the Bittersweet: An Essay* (Princeton, New Jersey: Princeton University Press, 1988), pp. 20–21.

10. Harold Bloom, *Agon: Towards a Theory of Revisionism* (New York: Oxford University Press, 1982), p. 110.

11. John Updike, *Too Far to Go: The Maple Stories* (New York: Fawcett Crest Books, 1979), p. 33.

12. Ibid., p. 40.

13. Ibid., p. 61.

14. Ibid., pp. 59–60.

15. Ibid., p. 113.

16. Ibid., p. 232.

17. Ibid., pp. 252–53.

18. Ibid., pp. 117–18.

6: Failure and Disappointment in America

1. Evelyn Waugh, *Brideshead Revisited* (Boston: Little, Brown, 1945), p. 6.

2. Ford Madox Ford, *The Good Soldier: A Tale of Passion* (New York: Vintage Books, n.d.), p. 123.

3. Van Wyck Brooks, *America's Coming of Age* (New York: Doubleday Anchor Books, 1958), p. 92.

4. There have been some recent attempts to do this. For instance, Barry Dym and Michael Glenn, *Couples: Exploring and Understanding the Cycles of Intimate Relationships* (New York: HarperCollins, 1993).

5. John Cheever, "The Swimmer," in *The Brigadier and the Golf Widow* (New York: Bantam Books, 1965), pp. 54–55.

6. Ibid., p. 55.

7. Ibid., p. 60.

8. Ambrose Bierce, "An Occurrence at Owl Creek Bridge," in *In the Midst of Life* (New York: Signet Classics, 1961).

9. F. Scott Fitzgerald, *The Great Gatsby* (New York: Charles Scribner's Sons, n.d. [orig. 1925]), p. 2.

10. Ibid., p. 39.

11. Ibid., p. 111.

12. Ibid., p. 133.

7: The Age of Abuse

1. *New York Times*, 7/5/93, p. 3.

2. *New York Times*, 5/28/94, p. 19.

3. Katherine Dunn, "Truth Abuse," *The New Republic*, 8/1/94, pp. 16–18.

4. See R. F. Fortune, *Sorcerers of Dobu: The Social Anthropology of the Dobu Islanders of the Western Pacific* (New York: E. P. Dutton, 1963 [orig. 1932]). Fortune points out (p. 245) that one of the Dobuans' verbs for sexual intercourse, used as an adjective, means "diseased, evil, or bad." Sound familiar?

5. C. S. Lewis, *The Allegory of Love: A Study in Medieval Tradition* (London: Oxford University Press, 1959), p. 4.

6. Wilhelm Stekel, *The Beloved Ego*, translated by Rosalie Gabler (London: Moffat, 1921), p. 15.

7. Edward Sapir, *Culture, Language and Personality: Selected Essays*, edited by David G. Mandelbaum (Berkeley: University of California Press, 1966), p. 72.

8. Irving Howe, "What's the Trouble?," in *The Critical Point: On Literature and Culture* (New York: Horizon Press, 1973), p. 14.

9. *New York Times*, 4/4/93.

10. Ibid.

11. *New York Times*, 3/31/93.

12. *New York Times*, 4/4/93.

13. Leon Botstein, "German Terrorism from Afar," *Partisan Review*, April 1979, p. 192.

14. Judith Lewis Herman, *Trauma and Recovery* (New York: Basic Books, 1992).

15. Robert Hughes, *Culture of Complaint: The Fraying of America* (New York: Oxford University Press, 1993), p. 146.

16. *Boston Globe*, 9/25/93.

17. Duncan Kennedy, *Sexy Dressing Etc.: Essays on the Power and Politics of Cultural Identity* (Cambridge: Harvard University Press, 1993), Chapter 4.

18. Mary Midgley, *Wickedness: A Philosophical Essay* (London: Ark Paperbacks, 1986), p. 49.

19. *New York Times*, 3/31/93.

20. Midgley, p. 75.

21. Niccolo Machiavelli, *The Prince and the Discourses* (New York: Modern Library, 1950), p. 56.

22. *New York Times*, 5/12/94.

23. Personal communication, 1991.

24. Rollo May, *Power and Innocence: A Search for the Sources of Violence* (New York: W. W. Norton, 1972), p. 24.

8: Epilogue: "Re-statement of Romance"

1. Erik H. Erikson, *Childhood and Society* (New York: W. W. Norton, 1963), p. 405.

2. Michael Vincent Miller, "Fiction Has Never Been Just Fiction," *The Responsive Community* (Spring 1992), p. 61.

3. John Lahr, review of Arthur Miller's "Broken Glass," *The New Yorker,* 5/9/94, p. 94.

4. Stanley Cavell, *Pursuits of Happiness: The Hollywood Comedy of Remarriage* (Cambridge: Harvard University Press, 1981), p. 2. I am indebted to Cavell's book for making me aware of the originality and depth of these films.

Index